THE RELIGIOUS MAN

The Religious Man

A psychological study of religious attitudes

ANTOINE VERGOTE

Translated by

SISTER MARIE-BERNARD SAID, O.S.B.

PFLAUM PRESS  DAYTON, OHIO 1969

First published in 1969 by
Gill and Macmillan Ltd.
2 Belvedere Place
Dublin I.

Originally published as
Psychologie Religieuse
by Drukkerij — Uitgeverij Lannoo
Tielt, Belgium

Nihil obstat: Michael Bertramus Crowe
Censor Deputatus

Imprimi potest: ✠ Ioannes Carolus
Archiep. Dublinen:
Hiberniae Primas
Dublini, die 5a Februarii, 1969

Library of Congress Catalog Card No. 70-93006

PRINTED IN THE UNITED STATES OF AMERICA

CONTENTS

CONTENTS

PREFACE

In the vast current of human sciences which hold such an important place in contemporary culture, numerous works have been devoted to the study of religious phenomena; and the psychological sciences, among others, have made a special contribution in this field. The aim of this book is to bring together the contributions of these many works on religious psychology, to interpret them and to complete them on some essential points.

However imperfect and even impossible this attempt at interpretation and synthesis may appear, it will be justified if it succeeds in emphasizing the importance of some points which may have escaped even the most conscientious research. This book will also be justified if it stimulates new research into truth and if it helps the reader, whatever may be his leanings, to reconsider some of his opinions concerning religious phenomena.

We have tried to present the facts of religious psychology in a way that will be easily accessible to the intelligent reader. For this reason we have carefully avoided using terms which are too specialized. Nevertheless, for reasons of scientific honesty, we have sometimes been obliged to clarify and justify our point of view in rather technical language. The reader for whom these scientific developments hold no particular interest can omit the introductory chapter and the first sections of both Chapter 2 and Chapter 4 without any inconvenience.

We should like to express our gratitude to the colleagues, friends and collaborators who have helped in the writing of this book. In particular we wish to thank our collaborators and students at the University of Louvain to whom we are pleased to dedicate this book.

THE RELIGIOUS MAN

INTRODUCTION

The Psychologist and Religious Phenomena

The relationship between psychology and religion has not yet been firmly established. The general idea which people have of religion is somewhat variable. Furthermore, one sometimes has the impression that the different psychological disciplines which grapple with religion have not very much in common, but whatever may be the variety of questions and methods involved, psychologists of religion are only concerned with psychology and do not pretend to deal with either theology or philosophy. They are inspired by a single aim which, through many trials and changes, has gradually evolved in such a way as to constitute the history of the psychology of religion. We do not intend to trace this history here. We shall merely point out one or two principles which have emerged from the gradual unfolding of religious psychology, because they define our point of view and mark off the field of our research. Since we propose making psychological investigations into religion, we shall also have to say what we mean by the term, religious psychology. This does not in any way imply that we want to give an explanation of religious phenomena, but until we have made the definition we shall not see exactly the extent of our objective. Without this definition we shall have no criterion for distinguishing the religious from the ethical, or normal from pathological religious phenomena.

Psychology as a Positive Science

Psychology in its probings into personality, culture and religion has gradually come to set itself up as an independent science distinct from both philosophy and physiology. Psychology is a specific science; the positive science of man. This means that there is no such thing as a branch of psychology which is religious by nature. It can only be called religious in view of its object. When we use the term 'religious psychology', we must realize that the adjective stands instead of a genitive.

Religious psychology is first and foremost an investigation into the experiences, attitudes and expressions of religion. It observes and analyses data by means of the various techniques used by every other branch of psychology: coded analysis of personal documents, questionnaires, attitude scales, projective techniques, systematic observation of behaviour, interviews, semantic analysis scales and even depth analysis by clinical methods. As is the case for every other science, the working out of techniques has led to an increasingly fine differentiation of the various factors and the different registers which go to make up the object of this discipline. We are now able to distinguish more clearly the varying dimensions and focuses of religious phenomena as they are expressed in human beliefs, values, experiences, attitudes, behaviour and rites, and it is the work of the psychologist to try to understand their correlation and interaction. Rather than draw up a tiresome list of definitions at this point, we prefer to wait until we use them systematically. Similarly, in this introduction we shall not stop to give an outline of the history of religious psychology and of its different systems and researches. We shall give a short historical introduction to each of the main problems as they occur. Science is the fruit of exchange between research workers, and historical references are often useful in helping to pin-point questions and methods and to show up their contingency.

Benevolent Neutrality

As a positive science, religious psychology does not pronounce on the truth of religion. It observes, describes and analyses religious phenomena as objects in themselves and as the contents of consciousness and behaviour. But, to borrow an expression from phenomenology, it neglects any significant value they may have as regards reality. It sets aside the fact of the effective existence of the God to whom religious rites and attitudes refer.

We might query the lawfulness of ignoring the focus of religion. If religion concerns the whole man in his relation to God then how can it be described without taking God into consideration? The history of religious psychology shows that this does indeed present a real problem. Psychologists have often been tempted to pose as strict observers and, from this viewpoint, to reduce the religious intention to a purely human phenomenon. This is a typically 'psychologistic' attitude which aims at being able to give a complete explanation to every religious fact in the light of psychology. Instead of showing up a supra-natural dimension in man it tries to bring religion down to a mere epiphenomenon of purely natural dynamisms.

Surely the aim of religious psychology is to make us grasp the human factors and substructures upon which the religious attitude is built. Normally the religious man forgets his human status. We have only to read through the Bible and mythologies to see that they attribute to God very human thoughts nurtured by the cultural setting in which beliefs are rooted. It is difficult to make a scientific study of myths and to credit them with the reality of truth. The simple fact of mentioning them seems to be enough to disperse these mirages in the same way as we only have to call evil spirits by name in order to exorcize them. Nevertheless, does not scientific investigation of religion necessarily imply an attempt to give a human explanation to supra-human facts in such a way that the God of metaphysics penetrates and mingles with human experiences?

The distrust with which certain theologians look upon religious psychology gives added weight to this preliminary question. We may quote, for example, the radical opposition of a Calvinist like Karl Barth who is known to be one of the greatest theologians of our times: ' "God in us"—then why not also I in you and you in me? . . . Experience becomes its own enjoyment, its own sufficiency, its own end. Motion becomes emotion . . . Suffice it to say that the history of religion got started somehow, or rather, the history of the untrue in religion, in contrast to what religion really is. For at the moment when religion becomes conscious of religion, when it becomes a psychologically and historically conceivable magnitude in the world, it falls away from its inner character, from its truth, to idols.'[1] Karl Barth's theological judgement of religion sentences religious psychology to being nothing more than the science of idolatries.

Catholic theologians are not quite so severe, but they have

often shown distrust of religious psychology. They fear the risk which underlies its working hypothesis. There is the danger that all religious objectives might be reduced to specifically human factors. These misgivings correspond to a renewed ambition among psychologists who would like to reconsider every theological fact in the light of psychology. In this way the study of divine things would be replaced by a science dealing solely with human things. We shall cite a few telling examples of this when we come to consider the chapter on religious experiences.

Exclusion of the Transcendent

The principle of the method of exclusion of the transcendent is one that can only be clarified as our research progresses. But a few explanations must be made here and they will serve as an introduction. It seems that we can identify both a religious mode of behaviour and a religious attitude without necessarily taking into account the actual and essential value of the underlying religious intention. Psychological investigation deals with the strictly human manner of making contact with what is believed to be the absolute. The psychologist has only to observe beliefs as they are expressed in words, symbols and behaviour and to set up the data thus obtained in a system. We may say, then, that to neglect the existence of God signifies that it is not considered, *a priori*, as being at the centre of religion. It is acknowledged only by a certain sympathy rooted in the affections and in reason; and that only in so far as it cannot be ignored as something humanly possible. In this way, both believers and unbelievers are in a position, by the simple fact of their connaturality, to make an intelligent observation of theism and atheism.

In view of his position the psychologist must reconcile, at least to start with, two exacting demands which have sometimes been considered radically opposed. In religious psychology we must be willing from the outset to conform to the principle stated by T. Flournoy.[2] This implies adopting a method which excludes the transcendent. The psychologist must be on his guard against regarding God as an observable fact. By definition God is excluded from the sphere of the psychologist. No empirical method can be employed to observe God. He only means something to the psychologist in so far as man refers to him in specifically human acts, but the religious and the psychological must not be treated as coinciding. Conscience and the religious act have a referential and intentional nature which the psychologist must maintain. In studying the psychic he must respect the specific character of the human conscience which is to be open to the world, to others and to God. To restrict religion to human beings closed in on themselves would be to deform the object of religious psychology. This means that we must examine the observable facts of religion expressed in language and gesture and yet refrain from giving a religious assent which accepts these outward expressions as actually referring to a transhuman reality.

There are many who expect psychology to point the way to the heart of religion; to reveal its intimate meaning. The first psychologists of religion, Starbuck and James, had such hopes too. Urged on by strictly philosophical aims, they tried to discover the distinctive essence of religion by means of psychological investigation.[3] But we must admit that the hope of discovering the intrinsic nature and final significance of religion is an illusion. These are questions beyond the scope of psychology and are the concern of either metaphysics or theology. Philosophy alone has the right to speculate on the being of a phenomenon in order to discover its essential structures. Psychology as a positive science is only concerned with phenomena: religion as manifested and built up in man.

Purely Scientific Respect for the Object

The investigation of phenomena does not, however, imply a restriction to appearances. Psychology endeavours to come to some understanding of its object within the limits of the means employed. Every psychology is inspired by the desire to probe man's behaviour, but schools of psychological thought have widely differing conceptions of this aim. The history of religious psychology, in common with the history of other psychological disciplines, has been marked from the beginning by periods of crisis through which it has passed in its strivings after scientific standing. We cannot do more here than mention the contradictions and revisions besetting a discipline which has to be an objective science and a science of man; a discipline which seeks to formulate laws and at the same time to understand the significance of behaviour. For various reasons psychologists have rejected introspection. In an excess of objectivity the behaviourists have even gone so far as to eliminate from psychology even the idea of significance. Their lack of rigorous method has led them to confuse the search for significance with introspection. Other psychologists have erred in the opposite direction and considered psychoanalysis, reflective psychology and even phenomenology, as introspection. So it is that we find ourselves in the paradoxical situation of having psychologists who, in their anxiety to be objective, have forgotten what it is they are dealing with when they talk about thought, feeling, the relationship with others, or for that matter, about any psychological phenomenon at all.

In conclusion we reaffirm our conviction that the objective nature of psychology lies in its capacity for defining its object. We are also convinced that scientific honesty is nothing else than the rigorous use of the methods relevant to a particular field. To imagine that psychology can be studied by the use of the same methods as are used in physics is the worst of biased opinions because it means sacrificing the object of psychology to a purely formal notion of objective science.

Psychology Passes Judgement on Truth

The purpose of this book is to take stock of the varieties of religious behaviour, to examine their significant differences and to try to understand them in relation to other human phenomena. This means that we shall look for the inner structure of religious experiences and behaviour. We propose making a systematic examination of religious facts in their human setting and expect in this way to discover something of their content and significance. But psychology can only examine the human meaning and relative truth of these facts in so far as they are part of the many structural levels of man. We cannot hope to arrive at the ultimate meaning or the final truth of the facts so observed.

We can say that psychology passes judgement on the truth of religious facts. By objective observation of the religious man it can do nothing more than follow up an attempt to discern an expressed religious attitude and humanly sincere religion. For the psychologist religion may finally be nothing more than an illusion, a vain dream. Nevertheless, beyond this final judgement, a distinction must be made between false and true religion. We shall see that the study of motivation inevitably leads us to make a statement about human truth. This means that once we have asked the question 'how?' in connection with a mode of behaviour we must necessarily query its truth. Furthermore, we may well wonder whether, in setting up religion in a relationship of motivation with other factors, we are not explaining it by something other than itself, either wholly or in part, according to the author. Face to face with psychology, religion ceases to be pure contact with the absolute. It gives us a picture of man in his natural world, placed with his anxieties and desires in a setting of material things and his fellow men. It shows us religion caught up in the network of mutual relationships with the world from which it in some way emerges; a religion able to subsist in varying degrees at the level of worldly relations. To track down the motivation of religious behaviour is not necessarily the same thing as setting up an absolute system of universal explanation. But at least it shows up the different sources of religion and emphasizes types of relative truths. To point out religious facts is to uncover their significance and to determine their relative truth with regard to the religious subject's environment and interests.

Psychology Excludes God as Cause

As a result of the scientific principle which leads him to adopt a method of exclusion of the transcendent, the psychologist is no longer in a position to explain observed facts by the intervention of the transcendent. In the first place, the transcendent as such cannot be scientifically observed. None of man's actions or experiences can be taken as objective evidence of a supernatural power whose intervention is only possible by incarnation in human behaviour. The supernatural only yields itself to a person capable of interpreting the signs written in the human. This implies calling upon principles of interpretation which do not belong to the field of psychology. Only strictly theological and metaphysical references will reveal the unseen supernatural elements in the visibly human.

Religious psychology, then, does not provide a supernatural explanation for the relation of cause to effect. It is restricted to purely psychological situations and merely considers religion in so far as it affects personality and society. Such a restriction, which is founded on psychological understanding, has the disadvantage of being incomplete. Psychology is not a closed system. It opens out to physiology and to metaphysics, and perhaps also to other disciplines. Often, in attempting to give explanations, psychology has erred by closing in on itself. But on heuristic principles, psychology aims at giving a total explanation, at leaving no stone unturned. It wants to give a definite answer to the question, 'Why is man a religious being?'

Psychology holds an important place in the history of modern atheism. It aims at restoring man to himself, and in this way has helped to free him from myth and other elements foreign to his religious nature. We have no right to oppose a principle of non-acceptance to this attempt though we may have reservations as to the method. For religious psychology to be recognized as a science, it is not necessary for it to arrive at the conclusion of the non-existence of God, nor to state his existence as a matter of principle. There is, indeed, no reason why religious psychology should not be founded on the basic hypothesis of a purely human explanation of religion. This is at the origin of many Freudian attempts to apply psychoanalytical methods to religion. Freud's disciples hope to make progressive evaluations of religious facts and thus reduce them to their human elements. This heuristic principle has made their research fruitful. Nevertheless the scientific method used in psychology does not allow us to erect as a thesis this hypothesis of the exhaustive explanation of human phenomena. We must also add that the assumption of an exclusively atheistic heuristic position restricts the objective openness of observation. It has often been noticed that psychologists who are avowed atheists treat religious facts as though they were stripped of their obvious meaning. Their basic hypothesis blinds them to many sides of the problem which they propose to examine. It is obvious that the religious factor must be perceived before an attempt can be made to clarify its specific contents. Whatever may be his private opinions, the psychologist must take into account the religious intention directing religious facts.

We may say that as a matter of principle, religious psychology neglects the existence of God and divine intervention. In this sense it is a neutral discipline or, to use a paradoxical expression, it is a-theistic; which does not mean that it is anti-theist. For psychology, religion is founded on neither God nor the purely human; and should it seek direct recourse to the supernatural, or count exclusively on the sub-religious element, it will fail to see its own capacity for explaining religion. Religious psychology runs the same risk as does any other psychology. Carried away by the desire to give a final explanation, it easily oversteps the mark, and, going beyond the bounds of its own territory, encroaches on either metaphysics or physiology. Psychology gains nothing from this; on the contrary, it loses its own identity.

What is Religion?

Religious psychology, a-theistic in principle, must keep in constant touch with religion. To fulfil its role it must follow the direction pointed out by religion's objective indices: beliefs and inalienable modes of behaviour.

Since religious psychology proposes to study religion we shall have to define what we mean by religion. When we speak of definition, we do not mean a mere nominal construction elaborated as a result of pure thought. Our intention is to establish the field of investigation in accordance with objective experience. Etymologically, to define means to settle the limits of, to mark off the limits of the phenomenon under consideration. In religious geography, just as in every other human area, there is always a centre and a periphery. In this case, the centre is religion as it is most adequately and sincerely expressed. The periphery is made up of the phenomena which orbit round this centre. They may move inwards or outwards, but are only considered as having a religious nature in so far as they are related to the centre.

Strictly speaking, this definition is much more the concern of a phenomenologist or a theologian than of a psychologist, though he cannot do without it. We shall adopt the rather narrow but not exclusive definition given by Thouless who wrote that religion is a felt practical relationship with what is believed in as a superhuman being or beings. Consequently, according to this author, religion is a mode of behaviour and a system of beliefs and feelings.[4] We regard religious feelings, religious experiences, rites and beliefs, as partial phenomena. We do not deny that an individual religious attitude can exist independently of an outward expression in social rites; and we can easily see that it is possible for an individual to perform religious rites without interior commitment to their devotional significance. But considering religion both subjectively and objectively, that is to say from the point of view of existing religions, we believe that the religious act is a complex reality made up of beliefs, praxis and orientated feeling. It is this entity which fulfils the religious intention. The various theories as to the essence of religion which have been proposed by the different schools of thought offer us the alternatives of external or interior religion. Schleiermacher, William James and Rudolph Otto thought of religion as based on feelings, whereas Durkheim identified it with the beliefs, rites and institutions which build up societies into self-recognizable units. He gave this definition to the lower forms of religion, but it is possible that he considered it to be true of the higher forms as well.

This choice of an essentially interior or an essentially socialized religion is not the only possibility offered by the many definitions. J. Leuba collected forty-eight and added two of his own. But as he was unable to justify them by objective criteria he finally gave up the attempt to define religion. In more recent times, the American psychologist of religion, W. H. Clark, questioned sixty-three social scientists. He received such varied replies that the definitions seem irreconcilable. They are based sometimes on the supernatural, sometimes on the notion of the group, or on institutionalized beliefs. Such contradictions will astonish only those who insist on clear-cut definitions. But to define is to interpret, and in the shifting sands of contingent phenomena a definition sets a boundary and points out the underlying issues. A definition always gives shape to an amorphous mass.

The definition which we have adopted excludes the alternatives of a completely interior or a completely socialized religion. The history of religion and the picture of man sketched by anthropology, psychology and philosophy, show that religion is both interior and external; it is neither a mere concept nor a system of ritual practices. It consists of an encounter between man and the sacred, or divine, and of man's response to this by praxis. The encounter may be the result of intuition, of symbolic interpretation of the world, of hearing the sacred word in a moment of initiation or of ecstasy, or of a vision or illumination. It is an encounter involving the whole man; an affective and intelligent being. Flesh and spirit open up to the sacred in a movement of the heart. Religion is a controlled and structural entity of feelings and thoughts through which man and society become vitally conscious of the ultimate nature of their being and through which the immanence of the sacred powers makes itself felt. The encounter and the effectual reply may be simultaneous or successive. Jacob (*Gen.* 28) saw in a dream the angels of the Lord, and heard the Lord himself say, 'I am the Lord God, the God of Abraham your father and the God of Isaac . . . and I will keep you.' Jacob awoke. He was afraid and said, 'How awesome is this place!' He took the stone which he had laid under his head and set it up as a pillar, pouring oil on it. And he named the place Bethel. The encounter with God in both dream and words revealed a God both awe-inspiring and benevolent. Jacob responded with an act of worship and a vow of fidelity, 'The Lord shall be my God.' In other types of religion the act of worship precedes and prepares the encounter. A rite may be performed to integrate man with the sacred power which animates the life and death cycle and assures the succession of generations. It may be the means by which individuals and communities, actors and spectators enter the sacred order. In moments of ecstasy they may even strive to rise to the same heights as the Other.

It is probable that the relationship between interior religion on the one hand, and ritual and institutional religion on the other, is dependent on the cultural setting; even in societies the relationship may be linked with the individual's psychological development. In primitive societies, for instance, where religion is a function of the group, either clan or nation, the religious life of the individual is founded on and moulded by the social expressions of religion. In our western societies, religions are both more universal and more individual. Religion is first learnt in the coded system of language, moral laws and ritual observances. But since it is both universal and at the same time more closely tied to the individual in his quest for personal salvation, it tends to give more weight to the existential orientation of the subject. Personal consent and ethical disposition play a major role, and this to such an extent that it is possible for an individual to live his religion without giving it any expression in formal rites of worship. But even though ethical practice and prayer expressing religious convictions may be less symbolic and less institutional, they are just as much forms of praxis, and thus more or less social and evident modes of behaviour.

When writers express contradictory conceptions of religion it is probably because their methods lead them to narrow religion down to the phenomena which come within their grasp. This explains why the sociologist Durkheim considered religion as something social; and James, who set out to make an ideographic analysis of personal documents, thought of it as a special entity made up of affective relationships. For his part, the present-day psychologist who has a dynamic conception of the whole person, sees religion as a comprehensive system of human activity. This was Freud's vision and he was one of the pioneers in the study of the whole man. For Freud religion articulates the whole personality: feelings, beliefs and modes of behaviour, and assumes man's entire psychic life: his suffering and desire, his relationship with society and the world, his confrontation with death and guilt. This means that religion is rooted in the individual's most hidden past. It is concerned with man's most intimate and lasting bonds, and it is the greatest test which reason has to meet.

If we were to attempt a reconciliation of the various definitions given by psychologists and sociologists, we would run the risk of falling back on the old-fashioned divisions of faculty psychology which aimed at housing the essential elements of the human make-up in one or other prevailing faculty: reason, will or emotions. Or, again, we would risk giving support to the unfortunate opposition set up by sociologists and behaviourists between the interior man and the social man. It has been a great achievement of anthropology to draw attention to the fact that though man is a product of society and of structures which pre-exist him and extend beyond him, he also comes to self-knowledge within the institutional forms by the ferment of creative intention which he pours into them. Furthermore, within the subject, emotions, reason and practical will interpenetrate and are in a state of permanent dynamic interaction. One of the major purposes of our enquiry will be to investigate the dialectic relationship existing between the component parts of religion, religion which is always the act and the total expression of a human—that is, of a being at the same time 'pathic' and rational, an individual and a member of society.

Humanitarian Mysticism and Religion

In defining religion we still have to state clearly the object of what we have called religious beliefs, feelings and behaviour. We have said that religion is a relationship with what is believed in as superhuman. In explaining this definition we have used the word 'sacred'. 'Superhuman' indicates a state of more than philosophical awareness. 'Divine' and 'sacred' refer more directly to the specific object of the religious act with its affective and ritual significance. These words are certainly adequate expressions of the mystery referred to by the religious act. But since, by an ambiguous refinement of exaltation or of spirituality, the term 'sacred' has sometimes been used of purely earthly ties, it must be specified by narrowing the boundaries of the object of religious beliefs.

We define religion as the individual's position in presence of the reality and activity of the divine, which is recognized by its otherness in relation to the world of men. In spite of the fact that in certain religious quests there is a dominant tendency to absorptive union, we can only conceive of religion when the sacred pole appears as superhuman or, to use the metaphysical word, transcendent. And we consider that there is only transcendence when the sacred is thought of as a being in some way personal: a centre of consciousness and will. The importance of salvation presented by the sacred or the divine lies in a lived relationship with a transcendent centre of salvific will; though, as in human love, many other, impersonal, factors also play their part in the religious quest. And perhaps this is the very reason why religious psychology is so important. All man's vital forces of emotion and of intelligence are drawn upwards by desires and fears into a relationship with the divine. However, our discussion of religion will only be concerned with those psychic forces which are drawn towards a divine that transcends the human and acts as a more or less autonomous centre of attraction. The definition which we have adopted may be criticized for its dependence on a philosophy that is tributary to Christian theology. There are thinkers who hold that if a religious man follows his experience through to the end he will finally go beyond every conception of God and arrive at a point devoid of consciousness. Others hold that religion is the bond felt with primal life forces or even with the dark forces of evil. In reply to this we must state again that we are only investigating the religion of those who believe in a more or less personal God. Any other religious attitudes or experiences will be placed in relation to this centre, and we shall try to discover their reference to it and interaction with it in so far as this can be observed in both atheists and theists. We do not, for example, regard as religious the fervent emotions which Péguy, and others after him, have called mystical. These feelings, which we prefer to call pseudo-mystical, inspire the great humanitarian movements of our times: socialism, Marxism, nationalism and even scientism. It does not seem right, either, to classify atheistic humanisms as 'religions'. Humanism seems to be an adequate word for describing their enthusiastic and ethical quest for human values. It would embarrass us to classify convinced atheists with the religious. Such a classification would mean ignoring their deliberate choice and dishonouring them by suggesting that they have a bad, or at least a deformed, conscience.

The Christian Fact

It is self-evident that in the western world most religious people are adepts of Christianity at different levels, and there is no problem there from the psychological point of view. Nevertheless, as we have already pointed out, certain theological views raise objections to religious psychology, and this calls for a justification of the idea we have of the relationship existing between psychology and Christianity. The psychologist, and the Christian psychologist no less than any other, regards Christianity as a particular form of religious belief. Though he ignores the historical and theological truth of Christian dogmas and takes no account of the influence of grace on a subject's behaviour, he respects the genuineness of the living relationship with the realities expressed by Christian dogmas. The chief failing of many studies in religious psychology is that they make every religious attitude fit into *a priori* theories of a non-differentiated religiosity and ignore the specific features of each particular form of belief. This is what we can call psychologism, the shadow of psychology. However, the significance of an attitude depends as much on the assent given to the realities of faith, as on the subjective conditions, both individual and social, of such faith. It is very necessary then, to make a strict analysis of the effective content of beliefs and to discover a subject's position with regard to it: the way in which he allows himself to be questioned, the way he reacts or defends himself, surrenders or holds himself back.

If the psychologist rarely pays attention to dogmatic beliefs and the transformations which they can bring about, it may simply be because he regards them as fictitious—mere emanations of religious subjectivity. And the psychologist who takes such beliefs seriously easily passes for a reluctant theologian.

In querying dogmatic faith we touch upon the greatest difficulty with which any psychology of the person has to deal. The problem is to decide whether the individual reflects the cultural society, or whether it is the society which expresses the individual. Here again we come up against the conflict between subjectivist and sociological theories of religion. Dynamic psychology, we have already pointed out, overcomes this contradiction and recognizes in man himself the site for the interaction of the two poles. No language psychologist would think of basing his investigation upon either of these poles to the exclusion of the other. Recent trends in linguistics strongly postulate the autonomous nature of language in itself. It is a world of symbols and cannot be reduced to either genetic interiority or social codes. The individual fits into this world of symbols. He lets himself be moulded by it, but he also gives it a creative centre. In the same way, real religion also consists in the multiple relationships set up between the religious subject, the religious society to which he belongs, and the world of beliefs and rites adhered to by both the individual and society. The psychologist, then, though he ignores the effective reality of religious dogmas, must respect the primordial bonds between an individual, a society and ritual.

Certain theologians, though from fundamentally differing positions, agree in denying the right which psychology claims, that of examining Christian phenomena. Karl Barth, faithful to Luther's thesis, sees religion and Christianity as absolutely opposed. According to him, revelation and divine grace annul religion. What is more, in comparison with God's gift, religion is simply unbelief (*Unglaube*);[5] and revelation has shown that religion is the greatest qualitative distance separating man and God. It is no more than a human work. The true religion can be recognized only when the gaze is turned away from man and his psychic and mental structures and fixed on God and his work.

We cannot accept Karl Barth's censure of religious psychology for two reasons: the first is based on our standpoint as a psychologist, and the second on a deliberate theological choice. We have already said that we cannot agree that the whole of religion is found in the sphere of natural man as observed by psychology. Also, we firmly believe that the Christian supernatural does not do away with the religious element in man but enters into it and espouses its tendencies, purifying them and raising them to a higher level. The object of religious psychology does not lie solely in man's obscure gropings after the divine; it is also to be found in every one of the ways and means by which man enters into a living relationship with the God who reveals himself in the perceptible, in the ethical, or in his word. Even the Christian, when he realizes he is called by the original Word, uttered in a moment of history, cannot escape the conclusion that he must move towards it with his entire humanity; and his assent will be continually weighed down by the human matter which is essential to the personal character of his act of faith. Man is not just an empty place where the spoken word of God echoes and where grace is poured in. Much more than that: by man's subjective working he who is God in himself becomes God for man. From the standpoint of faith the close alliance set up between God's word and man gives the human sciences an inalienable right to study, each in its own way, the religious attitude of Christians.

Towards a Dynamic Psychology

The debate between theology and psychology sums up the problem posed in this introduction and inspires the plan of the book. Religious psychology is a science dealing with religious facts; a science concerning the real man who responds to what he believes to be the manifestation of the divine. It does not take the place of either philosophy of religion or theology. It is not a universal system of thought which sets out to clarify the necessary conditions of a religious act; neither is it theology, judging religious acts in the light of God's own words on religion. Psychology examines the religious response of man as he is in his natural and cultural environment: empirical man subject to all kinds of drives, and echoing the sacred in his emotions: man who conjures up a necessarily human idea of the divine in order to be able to acknowledge it by an act of faith: man who expresses his experiences and beliefs in acts and modes of behaviour, and who adheres both to those religious institutions which existed before him and to those which he has created.

This conception of man accounts for the plan of the present

work, which corresponds with our dynamic theory of psychology and religion. Man *is* no more religious that he *is* a moral or political being. He *becomes* such. True religious psychology, then, must be genetic. The axis of this genetic religious psychology will not be time, as if the adult could only be understood in relation to the child, for the contrary is equally true: the child can only be understood in relation to the adult. Genetics is structural. Man is a complex being and he *becomes* as all his elements structure themselves—his experiences, drives, feelings, thoughts, decisions, the impact on him of reality and the presence of the Other.

In Part One of this book we shall, then, examine the elaboration of this synthesis which we call the religious attitude. We shall be guided by the natural dimensions of a developing personality as it passes from the involuntary to the voluntary, from the immediate to the assumed conviction. The order of chapters in Part One will correspond to the phases of religious becoming.

Part Two will group the data of genetic religious psychology in the technical sense of the term. It will sketch the history of man's religious—or atheistic—becoming as we see it in the major stages of his life: childhood, adolescence, adulthood. This general genetic view will not repeat what is said in Part One because the child is, in his own way, a complete personality, and at each stage of his life all the psychological factors are at work within him. The successive importance of the different elements and their gradual build-up, will nevertheless help us to understand the adult better. Adult religious life has a psychological history; it can only be clearly understood in the light of a genetic study, which will illuminate its true nature. On the other hand, a comparison of the adult with the child will provide us with the necessary elements for defining the child's natural religion and assessing its truth.

1 K. Barth, *Word of God and Word of Man*, (E. tr.), New York 1957, 68.
2 T. Flournoy, 'Les principes de la psychologie religieuse', *Archives de psychologie*, Paris 1902.
3 E. Starbuck, *The Psychology of Religion*, London 1899, 16–17; W. James, *The Varieties of Religious Experience*, London 1902.
4 See R.H. Thouless, *An Introduction to the Psychology of Religion*, London 1961.
5 *Kirchliche Dogmatik*, VI, 3.

Part One

FROM RELIGIOUS EXPERIENCE TO RELIGIOUS ATTITUDE

Before modern times, religion was as evident to men and cultures as, today, is the world we see around us. Modern philosophy and the sciences of man have made a problem of it. In the past, religion was the natural foundation of the visible. But present-day thought has brought about such a rupture that anthropologists often ask themselves whether it is not so much God as the religious spirit that is one of the most impenetrable enigmas of human existence.

From this contrast between natural religious faith and a militant questioning we can see that religion used to be very much an *a priori* faith; vital, a naïvely accepted tissue of faith, spun from the thread which linked man with his own life, society, and the world, a world which was the natural gate-way to the beyond.

This immediacy of a sacred presence is adequately expressed by the word 'experience'. Furthermore, we know that the word 'religion' denotes the vital bond between man and society on the one hand and the source of their being on the other. Between the two determining poles of man's and society's becoming, between the vital bond with the world and man's coming into possession of both himself and the world, spreads a whole labyrinth made up of the different forms of religion and the questions which they provoke.

Religion is a dynamic reality in constant evolution embracing both the person and culture. It is the business of concrete psychology to examine religion in this historical setting. We shall only be able to grasp the living roots of contemporary religious attitudes, doubts, or atheism, by comparing the information resulting from present-day practical research with historical religious evidence.

There are many psychological roots of religion: fear, hope of a future life, wonder in face of the mystery of the world and existence, the immediate meaning of participation in the universe, guilt, and still other factors. Similarly, the content of lived religion is made up of very diverse elements: feelings of dependence and respect, confidence, the search for the meaning of existence, a feeling of security, and fear in face of the strangeness of the world. We could make a study of these and classify the various types of religions. But, unfortunately, practical studies of this subject are too rare to allow us to elaborate a religious typology. Whatever might be the interest of any such study, it will not be our major concern in the first part of this book. The religious attitude is the final term of a long process of becoming, and our first aim will be to discover the inner tensions structuring the attitude of the religious man and those of the atheist. We shall try to understand how a religious attitude is formed and it is this investigation which will be the central theme of our book.

It is not our intention, however, to identify the process of becoming with development in time. Therefore the reader must not expect to find a genetic study of religion detailing its characteristics from childhood, through adulthood, to old age. The child is too polymorphous and too different to warrant his religion being taken as the basis of adult religion. We have in mind a quite different type of becoming. It consists in the dynamic inter-relationships set up between the components of the religious attitude. It is clear that the first element of this structuring is the perception of the world as a sign of a beyond which is transcendent and yet present in the world we perceive. Religion is the emergence of a belief which, though rooted in the perception of the world, is something more than perception because it rebounds on the Other. The first stage of the religious structure we shall call experience. By this we mean awareness of the world as a cypher of God or the divine. The happenings of life bring about many close relationships between God and man. Man's intercourse with the things of this world is punctuated by moments of crisis and moments of joy. These lead him to keener, more interested awareness of something which he perceives as outside and beyond his immediate ken. Anguish, distress, guilt, the imminence of death, are crisis situations which normally intensify the religious movement. Here we are not dealing with perception of the world as a sign of God, but the first stirrings of prayer caused by well-defined and directed psychological emotions.

Man calls upon God to save or maintain him in existence. In this case the religious attitude is ordered by clearly defined motives which we shall discuss in Chapter 2 under the heading 'Motives underlying religious behaviour'. Since these motives are often used to give a psychological explanation of religion, we shall have to reply in the same chapter to a question of principle: do motives really explain religious behaviour?

The perceived world awakens man to the religious dimension, but it is the parental images which mediate the divine person. These images and the perceived world are symbols of God and are, therefore, factors in the formation of the religious structure. Furthermore their symbolism is dynamic. Not only do they represent God, but they introduce certain dynamic factors into the human psyche; factors which direct religion along two main lines. In Chapter 3 we shall try to make an impartial study of the evolution of religion.

Chapter 4 will recapitulate the process of religious becoming as it appears at the close of the three phases which we have just outlined. We shall also consider how this process is actually brought about in man. We can say that the whole of religion is present from the beginning of the religious experience; but it must also be said that in spite of this fact, religion continues to be a task to be accomplished, a truth to be discovered. Religion is a self-regulating movement. This means that we are able to examine its different dynamic phases: conflicts, resistances, conversion, identification with models, ritual unification of the person, reinterpretation of the world in the light of personally assumed faith. The resulting differentiated personal organization is summed up in the concept of attitude. This explains the title of Chapter 4: 'The religious attitude'.

The last chapter of Part One will show the negative aspect of religious becoming: atheism. This will bring us back to the elements of resistance aroused by the religious appeal and we shall thus be able to point out the seeds of atheism that underlie a religious attitude as it struggles into existence.

CHAPTER I

RELIGIOUS EXPERIENCE

For most unbelievers a religious man is one who has had a religious experience: one who feels that he has been in contact with the divine from whom he receives a direct message. Speaking of himself, the unbeliever says that he does not believe because he has not had this experience of God. There are, of course, believers for whom God is a reality because they have had such an experience. In some way, perhaps in a moment of inward peace, or else in a sudden flash which has heightened existence by shedding light from above on the world, or even by some incident which is interpreted as being miraculous help, in some way God's presence has come to impose itself as irresistible.

For the majority of believers, however, experience is a short-lived deception. They fight shy of it and think that the unbeliever has a strange idea of religion in referring it to a religious experience which, for them, is not a sufficient foundation for religious belief.

This divergence of opinion is significant: it bears witness to the ambiguity inseparable from the double aspect of the fact of religious experience. On the one hand we see that in the absence of any such experience, no rational view can justify the religious attitude. And yet those who do have such an experience go beyond it in accomplishing the religious act itself. This implies that the religious experience is both indispensable and insufficient;

testimony to truth and bearer of illusion; possession and estrangement. Moreover, we shall see that enquiries made among adult believers indicate that the very people who question the religious experience admit their incapacity to accept facts of faith which do not lie within their experience.

Religious experience has something of the ambiguity which is to be found in the core of the irrational. It is not for nothing that in the climate of contemporary culture, the emotions should be the most disputed and yet the most studied of human dimensions. Nor is it by mere chance that modern theology is torn between a current of religious thought founded solely on the revealing potential of human experience, and another which leans wholly upon the revelation of the divine word.

In this chapter we shall be chiefly concerned with pointing out the ambiguities of religious experience. We might wonder whether all the phenomena which we have been able to group under this heading have a common origin. Are we dealing with the same phenomenon in different mental worlds? It would be useless to seek for an *a priori* definition. We shall therefore start by analysing the different types of religious experiences and then ask ourselves whether they do have some focal point.

We shall first consider how the question of religious experience has come to be raised, and the place it occupies in the history of thought. The expression has come down to us from certain theologians and philosophers who mark the beginnings of the contemporary era. While we recognize these thinkers as our precursors in the problems we are dealing with, we must both draw inspiration from their teaching and learn from their failures.

The following section will examine the facts of the ethnology and phenomenology of religion in order to learn something about religious experience in primitive civilizations. This excursion into a domain on the outskirts of psychology is justified by the fact that on the one hand the phenomenology of religion has left us a prototype and model of analysis of religious experience; and on the other hand, the history of religions has shown us that the earliest religious experiences were lived in a social setting which no longer exists. These are facts which will be useful in helping us to define the religious experience. Contemporary man has a better understanding of himself when he is able to see his profile outlined against the horizon of his past.

The third section will survey some research work which has been done on present-day religious experience but we shall refrain from making a pre-judgement as to the exact meaning which it confers on this term. Through critical reflection we shall consider whether the diverse forms of past and present religions are not finally dependent on the same fundamental intuition. This is not a matter of words. It means recognizing the mental and emotional schema which direct man in the movement leading him from the world to God.

A few preliminary brief definitions will serve as guide lines for the analysis we intend to make in the following pages.

Experience

In English, as in French, the word 'experience' is generally taken to mean a certain knowledge acquired by the mind in the exercising of its faculties (e.g. to have experience of a profession or a country). It designates, then, the knowledge gathered by practical dealings with objects or men. This is the fundamental meaning underlying the word 'experience' even when used in its most technical sense. Thus, in the philosophies of knowledge, experience, exterior or interior, has to do with the contribution of real knowledge made by the world perceived as something exterior to the mind. Here again the concept expresses the empirical element of knowledge. In philosophy, as in psychology, experience expresses 'the fact of feeling something inasmuch as this fact is considered not only as a passing phenomenon, but also as broadening and pervading thought'.[1] Even in the strict definition given by Kant, experience still expresses contact with reality, structured indeed, by *a priori* categories of reason, but filled as to the content by the perception of present objects.

The German word *Erfahrung* and the Dutch *ervaring* correspond to 'experience' in expressing the immediate and empirical element of knowledge. The etymology of the word is, moreover, significant: originally the word *Erfahrung* means to go through (a country, for example) to find out for oneself and to retain the knowledge thus acquired.

In psychology, experience means the manner of knowing through an intuitive and affective grasping of meanings and values perceived in a world which puts out qualitatively differentiated signs and signals. It is the spontaneous involuntary[2] movement by which man knows that he is solicited by the world, by an object, by another.

I. The Theme of Experience in Recent Religious Literature

Discovery of the Non-rational

It has been the privilege of western thought that for long centuries it has tended to express truth in the transparency of concepts. This striving after rigorous command of both self and the world began with Greek philosophy and science. Greek culture, fed as it was on the non-rational that was present in the world in a thousand different ways, struggled from the sixth century B.C. onwards to wrest from it the light of reason.[3] Religious thought, which was also to be found everywhere in ancient times, was haunted by the mystery of the divine as manifested in the Dionysian trance, Pythian ecstasies or in dreams. The religious impulses and their magical and mystical incantations were rationalized by Plato. Christian thought and western philosophy continued this effort of rationalization. Modern thought, however, has reverted to forgotten non-rational origins. Hegel, Nietzsche, the philosophy of life, existentialism and psychoanalysis all represent so many attempts to explore the non-rational, which criss-crosses and moulds existence. The aim of all these thinkers has been, of course, to shed light on the powers of darkness out of which human existence arose, and to align them with reason. But in so doing they have stretched the bounds of reason and arranged it according to its dialectic relations with the non-rational.

The interest which modern thinkers show in religious experience shares in the emergence of this broadened scope of reason; it shares not only in the discoveries of reason, but also in its attendant ambiguities and confusions. In modern times there has arisen in philosophy and theology a new tradition which underlines the receptive, the pathic aspect of religion and minimizes the constructive role of reason. It has taken the place of the rationalist criticism of religion which Kant had already established. Kant's criticism, it will be remembered, undermined the rational basis of religion and it also emptied it of all sacred significance. According to Kant 'religion within the limits of reason' boils down to human ethics pursued in a religious hope of eschatological justice. We find this ethical outlook among many Christian intellectuals too, and it is in this vacuum of religious thought that modern philosophers have discovered religious sentiments. In 1799 F. Schleiermacher, who inaugurated the tradition of a philosophy of religious experience, wrote of religion in the following terms: 'In its essence it is neither thought nor action, but intuitive contemplation and sentiment.'[4] Again, 'Religiosity, considered in itself, is neither a knowing nor an action, but a determination of feeling or of self-awareness.'[5] It is 'the sense and the taste for the Infinite',[6] the feeling of absolute dependence. Religion is a truth: it is the consciousness of our unity with the infinite reflected in nature. This consciousness is an immediate self-awareness brought about in that innermost sanctuary which is untouched by either reason or will. Hence the sole truth of 'dogmas', as religious and rational representations, consists in the states of soul which they express. Schleiermacher reduces religion to sentiment. This subjectivism will be criticized later on: to our way of thinking, sentiment is no longer the normative form of experience. We cannot deny, however, that Schleiermacher discovered, even if inadequately, the subjective and pre-reflective ground in which the beginnings of religion can be traced. In so doing he has pointed out a particular field for research: religion, not as objective and universal thought, but as lived experience and human reality, an affective and fleshly substance. This particular orientation of religious thought has not been without some unfortunate results. It has meant that, at first, religious psychology was too closely confined to introspective exploring of interior states. It prepared the way for atheistic criticisms starting with the humanism of Feuerbach and leading to Freud's study of motivation. Nevertheless we must admit that this religious psychology has asked a fundamental question: what is God for man? It has drawn attention to the fact that a living religion not only is a matter of concepts and ethical practice but also implies personal interiority.

Phenomenology of Religion

The phenomenology of religion, whether inspired by history or by philosophy, has often recognized religion as a non-rational relationship with the divine, an encounter with the numinous. Rudolph Otto,[7] taking for his authority the philosophy of Kant, established an *a priori* category of the non-rational type that he called the sense of the sacred. God and the soul, regarded by Kant as empty ideas, were given specific content by Otto who connected them with the data perceived by the senses as a result of contact between our affective patterns and the world which man perceives according to *a priori* patterns of his affectivity. So, for example, the inborn sense of the sacred throws light on the divine qualities of the perceived world and gives content to the idea of God. Thus, in the symbolic forms of the earthly, man has an intuitive and affective perception of the mystery of God just as he has an intuitive and affective perception of their beauty.

This primary experience of the sacred or the numinous has been described and explored more deeply by a series of thinkers such as, to quote but a few names, F. Heiler, J. Geyser, E. Durkheim, N. Söderblom, W. Schmidt, M. Scheler, J. Hessen, M. Eliade; all of whom have endeavoured to point out the specific nature of living religion which is to be reduced to neither rational interpretation of the world, nor a will for perfection (the 'holy will' of Kant). These thinkers are of considerable importance for religious psychology both on account of their method, which attempts the analysis of religious testimony, and also because of their definition of the proper domain of religious psychology: consciousness and religious behaviour. Some of these thinkers have applied themselves to a more directly phenomenological analysis of a few religious facts. Others have devoted themselves to the discipline of historical religious evidence. M. Scheler, a phenomenologist trained by E. Husserl, in his work *Vom Ewigen im Menschen* (*On the Eternal in Man*) states that religious consciousness has its own power, its own evidence. It has a specific object inaccessible to any other branches of knowledge, even metaphysics. This object can only be grasped by religious acts which cannot be reduced to any other expression of the human spirit. In this sense it can be said that the ultimate source of religion is not a historical revelation but a natural one present in the permanent facts of the outer and inner world and thus accessible to all. Nothing is more immediate or primal in the person than the religious act.[8] Every other actualization of the human spirit is preceded by and founded upon it, in the order of both psycho-genesis and essence.[9] We shall see that Scheler's phenomenological analysis links up with the experimental data furnished by studies in sociology and religious psychology. Man, by the immediate experience he has of his own dependence and the mystery which enfolds him, is a primarily religious being. At this point one may well ask whether cultural evolution does not lie precisely in transcending this immediate religious consciousness. Modern civilization sometimes appears to assert itself by shaking off primeval religious dependence. This leads us to ask what has become in our days of the fundamental religious experience analysed by Scheler.

Mircea Eliade and G. van der Leeuw, by their studies on the historical evidence of religion, have also greatly helped to bring to light the genuineness of the experience of the sacred. Mircea Eliade has studied religious phenomena in their symbols, modalities and structures. He gives less attention to the subjective side, but he considers that the subjective awareness of hierophanies is a genuine experience to which he has given the now classical name of 'religious experience'.[10] In the same way van der Leeuw suggests that a genuine experience is the basis of all religion. He thinks that this experience is astonishment at the power of the 'Other' and the immediate feeling of being bound to him: 'In company with Söderblom we should find wonder at the beginning not only of philosophy but also of religion. It is by no means a matter yet of the supernatural or the transcendent for we should be able to speak of "God" only with impropriety. But there is a profound experience bound up with the "other" who astonishes us . . . We are content with the empirical observation: this is something out of the ordinary. It results from the power which it develops.' 'Every dogma, every ritual act can only be understood as reflecting a lived experience . . .'[11] 'The lived religious experience is the one whose significance is tied up with the whole . . . It sets man a final term, a limit. This could not be if it were not also a first term, a beginning. Its meaning is experienced and felt as being "quite other"; its essence is a revelation. Thus there exists something beyond our usual terms of reference, incomprehensible in principle, yet something in which religion sees the condition of all comprehension.'[12]

Theology of Experience

The discovery of religious subjectivity has had a profound effect on theology, especially Protestant theology,[13] and has given rise to a line of thought which may be defined as theology of experience, in which experience is taken as the source and the norm of all theological thought.[14] Thus Harnack was fond of repeating: 'God and the soul, the soul and God, are the entire content of the Gospel.'[15] It is within himself, free of the temporal, that man meets God. And just as certain phenomenologists of religion, such as Heiler, van der Leeuw or Mensching, regard religious myths as the creations of dawning religious consciousness, there are liberal theologians who try to relate religious truths, Christian dogmas, to the different states of soul which make of them the content of truth. An example of this is to be seen in G. Wobbermin's psychological interpretation[16] of the doctrine of the blessed Trinity. The paternity of God and the concepts of Son and holy Spirit would seem to express respectively our feeling of dependence with regard to the absolute Lord, our feeling of being protected, sheltered in a universe governed by the divine power and, finally, our personal union with God. This kind of theology is really nothing else than a rather easy-going religious philosophy. By the method of 'productive introspection' (*produktive Einfühlung*) it aims at defining the essence of religion as found in the immediate grasp, in the primary impression of the man who feels himself to be receptive before God. Religious conviction, the second phase, is followed in its turn by conceptualization, which branches out into images and particular concepts. Wobbermin's ideas give a good picture of the empiricism and the psychologism which characterized the first religious psychology as set out by James and Starbuck. We do not subscribe to this psychologism for it is a constant danger to religious psychology, as indeed it is to every other branch of psychology. It rests on ignorance of the dynamic build-up of the person. It will be remembered that our research is centred on the exchange between the person on the one hand, and the objects and other persons of his environment on the other. Through his experiences, desires, conflicts and self-transformations, man becomes a religious being. He has to find his own true identity. In this dynamic conception of the religious man we differ also from many of the more recent psychologists whom we criticize for still having a much too psychologistic view of man and his religion, as is evident, for example, in the studies of C. G. Jung and even those of G. Allport[17] and W. H. Clark.[18]

Religious Experience and Christian Experience

A number of Catholic theologians have emphasized the fact that at the very heart of orthodox belief there is a certitude of experience. Being reticent about religious emotions which are subjective and arbitrary, they use the word 'experience' to designate that profound disposition which enables the believer to grasp the superior religious values of Christian truths and mysteries[19] in a direct God-man relationship. These theologians were as anxious as the authors we have just mentioned to save faith from an excessive externalism which would empty adhesion to mere dogmatic concepts of its religious qualities. What they have in fact done is to elaborate the element of intuition which is presupposed in Thomist teaching and according to which the object of faith is not mere concepts but God himself in his saving acts.

Certain theologians, of whom R. Guardini is the most authoritative representative, have clearly distinguished between specifically Christian religious experience and another type of religious experience which occurs at the beginning of the religious life and can develop and be changed into Christian faith. This natural religious experience is not necessarily first, chronologically speaking, but it is so in the structural order. It is the first religious situation in which revelation can get a foothold. And, indeed, if man did not contemplate God in his works, how could he interpret the word of God which speaks of a new relationship with the human world as he knows it? We may ask whether in order for man to hear the timeless word it is not necessary that the temporal word should manifest God, and that his immanent word, apparent at least in the dim light of intuition and affectivity, should contain a natural revelation. A theologian, without neglecting the discontinuity which separates the order of revelation from that of natural religion, must recognize that God can only speak to the man who is capable of himself of hearing this word. We can look for God in the historical word only if we have already had a presentiment of him somewhere.

We must not, then, confuse religious experience and Christian experience.[20] Besides the strictly Christian assent of faith, the proposed truths find an echo in the depths of affectivity and, by means of his concepts of them, the believer enters upon a relationship with those truths themselves. The concomitance of these two elements confers an intuitive nature on the Christian faith.

A religious truth for which a subject is groping in the darkness may suddenly become present and real in a flash of understanding that penetrates the soul. Converts witness to the truth of this. It happened with Claudel,[21] a distinguished unbeliever to whom revelation came suddenly as he heard the Magnificat being sung at Christmas. He said to himself, 'How happy are those who believe! But supposing it were true? It *is* true! God exists, he is there, he is someone, he is a being just as personal as I: he loves me, he is calling me.' He suddenly had 'the rending sentiment of the innocence, the eternal childhood of God, an unspeakable revelation'. It was the same with Miss Baker who, at the end of

a long search for God and on the occasion of an event insigni-
ficant in itself, was suddenly enlightened by the existential
meaning of this God for whom she was looking: 'The sermon,
as far as I know, taught me nothing new; only, these truths
already known came to me with a new meaning and I understood,
as I had never done, that Catholicism is not a theory of creation,
a mere logical deduction, a problem to be solved by the intellect
alone, but devotion to a Person and union with a living God.'[22]

In these cases we have every right to speak of religious experience, because we are dealing with the affective break-through
which fills already known concepts with their existential density.
This experience however, comes about through the mediation of
historical signs of a distinctly personal God. It is of another
order than that of natural sensitivity to the divine mystery present
in the world and in life. The intuitive grasping of the personal
God is not restricted, however, to the sudden illumination which
sparks off religious belief. Even if the inner adherence is not
always conscious of being experience, it may be presumed that
a moment of experience underlies and subtends it, giving it a
kind of assurance for a commitment in which, by definition,
every intellectual guarantee is wanting. The Christian existentialist philosophers have made a theme of this type of religious
experience in which man finds access to God in the very depths of
his existence, in the tangled paradox of subjectivity. Kierkegaard,
as is known, was the first to introduce this term 'existence' in its
present sense. In his opinion the man who seeks to know the
truth at its deepest level must lay himself open to invasion. His
knowledge must become interiority, subjectivity. This is only
achieved by the inner action and accompaniment of the soul.[23]

Gabriel Marcel has also frequently analysed the experiential
character of religious faith where what is recognized corresponds
with the interior intuition. God only makes himself known to
faith wedded with love: 'When faith ceases to love, it gets into a
rut of objective belief in a power more or less physically conceived. And, on the other hand, love which is not faith (and
which does not propound the transcendence of the loved God)
is only a kind of abstract play.'[24]

The studies which have been devoted to the mystics have shown that in its perfection, reasoned and considered faith ends in still higher experience, less emotional, but not less deeply affective. On the level of purified affectivity, we speak once more of intuition rather than experience.

We can thus say that the word 'experience' is analogical. It follows the evolution of lived religion and signifies, at every point, the intuitive, immediate and deeply affective element of man's presence before God. However, in its primary and obvious sense, it signifies a grasp of the world as a sign of the divine. Imbued with the invisible, torn from his own self, man gropes in the darkness towards a reality which is other, a reality which has burst in upon his existence. That is why in the text which follows we shall not deal with religious experience in the sense of higher religious experience for it no longer has the same character of immediacy which we attribute to experience. Religious faith supposes a transformation of the person. When the effort which the intellect makes to grasp the divine is followed by considered adherence there follows a transmutation of the religious person. We call this resulting religious faith the religious attitude.

The psychological problem for us is to know whether there does exist some religious experience which is part of human existence. If so, what exactly is it? Is it really universal and lasting? How is it connected with a cultural world in evolution? What is its position in relation to an act of dogmatic faith? These are the important questions which we are bound to endeavour to answer.

II. Nature and Structure of Religious Experience in Primitive Religions

Our definition of religious experience might seem to imply the thesis of a naturally religious man. The phenomenologists of religion, moreover, tend to reduce the differences and distances which abound in religious history. The eidetic phenomenologies aim at liberating the essences in the resemblances of individual facts. Truth to say, if there exists an essence of the religious act, and of the object (*noema*) which responds to it, the religious experience, since it is by nature the subjective advent of the religious sense, cannot be treated as a stable essence in contact with the world. Like every other first experience, it is both natural and cultural. It expresses the inner echo which the world sets up in an affective and pathic being. But it is also set in a cultural tradition, since affectivity is subject to the changing styles of language and relationship with the world. Thus, rather than presupposing a natural religious experience, inherent in man, we ought to ask whether it is a permanent and universal fact. This question leads us to compare phenomenological analyses based on historical documents, with psychological enquiries made in various contemporary environments.

The phenomenological studies of religion have given us a picture of an extraordinarily religious man. Before modern times man saw the cosmos as a hierophany, a manifestation of the sacred. Through cosmic symbols man entered into a relationship with the fundamental reality of existence. Sun and earth, water, mountain, forest, rock . . . were all so many things which manifested the divine. Before modern times man moved in a world open to the Other. The Other appeared, became present in the signs found in the human world. He pervaded things so that they ceased to be merely cultural or natural objects.

M. Eliade[25] emphasizes the fact that religion always assumes that there is an opposition between the sacred and the profane, and that each thing is susceptible of becoming a sacred fact. 'This contradiction is only apparent because . . . it remains . . . true that there is no known religion or race which has accumulated, in the course of its history, all these hierophanies . . .' 'A hierophany supposes a *choice*, a distinct detachment of the hierophanic object in relation to the other things surrounding it.' The religious rite also embodies the sacred. It repeats 'an archetypal gesture accomplished *in illo tempore* (at the beginning of "history") by our ancestors or the gods . . . The rite *coincides*, by repetition, with its archetype (in the sense of its original model); profane time is abolished. We assist so to speak *at the same act* accomplished *in illo tempore* at the moment of cosmogonical dawning. Consequently, in transforming all physiological acts into ceremonies, early man endeavoured to "pass over", to project himself beyond time (becoming) into eternity.'[26]

Religious life is made up of theory-elements, cosmogonical and genealogical myths, ideograms and so on, which also make the sacred present. They express, in symbols and concepts, the sacred presence of man's origins and last ends. It is through them that man integrates himself with the Other who gives salvation.

This sacralization not only affects the temporal succession of the universe, but also its spatial structure.[27] The presence of the sacred introduces a centre of reference into uniform earthly space; a fixed point from which space is suspended; a place where it is founded. This is not only, or principally, a question of cosmic theory. Nor must it be thought that the sacred is restricted to any one place. What is important is the fact that the thing or place pervaded by the sacred becomes symbolically the point at which the universe is moored to the Other. Religious experience organizes space, not according to reason, but according to its meaning and basis.

The variety of religious forms is infinite, so that certain contemporary specialists of the sciences of religion consider any attempt at synthesis and definition as nothing more than an arbitrary opinion.[28] Such exacting demands for accuracy are certainly more to the honour of the specialists than was the naïve credulity with which the first theorists of the nineteenth century set out their brief syntheses. We must admit however that phenomenology as expounded by Eliade does succeed in bringing into relief the main features of natural religions; and it cannot be denied that their essential characteristic is precisely the symbolic presence of the sacred. The forms which this presence takes are varied and symbolism can differ greatly from one religion to another. But man always finds himself set in a milieu which is meaningful and well-grounded because, through its centre, he comes into contact with the sacred in which he participates and he is, in his turn, pervaded by it.

If we consider the Psalms of the Bible we shall see that they are in great part a religious reading of the world. But this does not mean that the Israelites were religious in the sense which we have just been dealing with. If the universe spoke to them of God, it was because they found in it the historical word spoken by the God of Abraham. Their religious symbolism had quite a different origin; it reflected in the relationship with the universe, belief in the one true living God who had revealed himself by prophetic signs.

Having made this brief survey of the natural religions of early civilizations which should help our psychological understanding of the religious man, we must now consider two dialectic tensions which cut across it; experience and rationalization on the one hand, and on the other, theism and cosmo-vitalist participation. It is also instructive to note the influence of the economic and cultural setting on these religions.

In the case of primitive religions, religious experience is essentially characterized by the fact that it is an immediate existential experience. The sacred is the omnipresent horizon of the human world, in the same sense that for Gestalt psychologists, or for the present-day phenomenologists of perception, the world is the horizon against which every human being is profiled. This all-embracing presence of the sacred can be actualized in symbols, rites and various myths, but any specific actualization does nothing more than formulate and make available an immediate virtual presence. A great student of the history of religion says, 'The primitive mentality is distinguished by the fact that even where there is an idea of the world, it is not that which counts for the primitive, but his being-in-the-world. He does not want to conceive of the world as being set totally outside his ego, nor his ego as outside the world.'[29] Man becomes conscious of his situation in the world and immediately knows that he participates in a form of existence which is infinitely beyond him. He sees his position as bound up with universal destiny.

In the nineteenth century several theories were advanced with a view to explaining religion. Tylor thought that the primitives were originally animists and that the gods were the avatar of the spirits. Marret and Preuss suggested an even more primitive stage: pre-animism, in which the experience of an impersonal power (*mana*) dominated the perception of the universe. In Durkheim's first works we see that he regarded totemism as the origin of religion whereas Lévy-Bruhl thought that it was to be found in a pre-logical mentality. Freud combined these different elements and gave a genetic explanation of religion. Others, such as Lang and Schmidt, basing themselves on their historical studies of religion, opted for an original monotheism. Since then, more thorough historical research has proved the existence of different types of religion from the earliest times. These researches have shown that true religion existed side by side with animism and magic. They have also shown that forms of religion depend upon economic and social situations. Thus every attempt to give a genetic explanation of religion which starts from too simple an idea of the elements of religion must be rejected. The religion of primitives is undoubtedly something more than the simple out-come of other beliefs such as the belief in spirits. It should not be thought of as bound, in spite of a desire for rationality, to remain below the level of logical reason. The history of religions shows that the religious position is a genuine fact, an immediate symbolic experience and perception.

Mythology shows that the evolution remarked in myths is not merely the development of obscure thought towards the affirma-tion of God or gods as though this marked a final attempt at rationalization. The development is inverse. It starts from an immediate participation in the divine, expressed in symbols, rites, symbolic histories (in primitive myths), and unfolds in attempts at rational explanation, by a gnostic elaboration of myths.[30] Religion is reasoned. Myths become less religious and develop as systems of cosmological or cultural explanations. From an original religious experience reason picks out whatever can be queried by the intellect. In attacking the mystery of religious origins, the sciences of religion, anxious to have objective, causal explanations, have unconsciously allowed themselves to be guided by a rational bias. According to this bias, the religious attitude, considered in its totality as a relationship with the world and existence, ought to develop from the partial elements which normally precede and compose it, that is to say, from reason in

4

its pre-logical forms and from that technique which in the pre-scientific state is called magic. New theories of anthropology have made it possible to provide a better interpretation of religious facts. Moreover, progress in historical knowledge has done much to restore these facts to their true original setting.

The second dialectic of primitive religion, we have said, lies in the tension of between theism and cosmo-vitalism; a cleavage in keeping with the laws proper to the dynamism of religion as well as with certain socio-cultural influences. We draw attention to this tension because it sheds considerable light on some analogous phenomena which can be observed, as we shall see, in the believers of our own times.

According to recent researches, it appears that monotheism is not only a late cultural phenomonon, resulting from the contraction of multiple divinities which represent different functions and powers into a single all-powerful and really transcendent being. Even at the dawn of history men were conscious of depending on a divine and heavenly being, conceived as the sole Lord and master of life and the world; a God-Father, admired, invoked and respected in the innocence of a culture still very close to its infancy. It is astonishing to note that this very simple and very pure religious attitude is to be found among the economically poorest of peoples, the most undeveloped: the food-gatherers and the pygmies.[31] It is also interesting to note that with socio-cultural evolution this religious attitude became more complex, mingled with elements of lesser religious character, or became deism. The shepherds developed a uranian symbolism which branched out into mythological speculation on cosmic origins. At the same time their God, grasped in uranian symbols, became distant, more transcendent, more formally all-powerful, but also more absent, separated from the life bond with mankind. The tillers, on the other hand, turned to the earth and the powers of fertility. They favoured mystery myths and rites. They celebrated the life-giving power, endeavouring to participate by words and acts in its immanent presence in all living things. This kind of consciousness of the universe, and this mode of integration with it, were characteristic of what has been called the cosmo-vitalist system, although it was more a matter of a global and active outlook than of a systematic theory. This universe did not exclude theist belief; there are religious texts which prove a certain co-existence of the two attitudes. Here, however, the pole of attraction was to be found in adherence to the immanent forces of the earth; these were still transcendent in relation to the individual and the clan, but not in relation to fruit-bearing nature. Again, in this spiritual world, the God adhered to withdrew from the vital relationship which normally leads to religious worship and prayer. And this to such an extent that such a God earned the title *deus otiosus*, an inactive and absent God. The absence of all religious worship has even led certain ethnologists to come to the conclusion that there was practical, if not explicit, atheism. It has however been noticed that in times of crisis these people rediscovered the significance of an appeal made to a God usually forgotten. In a moment of catastrophe, they rediscovered a forgotten God and reactualized an original theist experience veiled by the network of the bonds linking man with life.

We must restrict ourselves to these few facts of the history of religions, but they serve to bring out both the nature of the religious experience and the dynamism by which it may be fashioned.

In the first instance man was religious through an immediate grasp of his situation in the world. He felt himself to be surrounded by and dependent upon some sacred mystery whose presence he detected powerfully at work in the phenomena of life. 'We cannot legitimately reduce the primitive mentality or the religion of primitive peoples to any single one of the themes dealt with by religious ethnology: animism, magic, or even an idea of God. All known cases offer these three types of tendencies and experiences. But the degree of development of one or other varies with the environment. Nevertheless, there is a basic unity from which these different attitudes take their direction and which they simply approach and express in varying ways. The hub of all religious experience is the mystery of life!'[32]

The symbolical and mythological speculations which are grafted on to the religious attitude make of God a distant being in the infinity of the stellar world. But .there is also a still more important phenomenon. A cleavage is introduced between the relationship with God, author of life, and the integration into the cosmic forces which the cosmo-vitalist mentality celebrates and fosters. In this case the rift between participation and adoration, between immanence and transcendence is evident. In ancient cultures immanence, without excluding transcendence, tended to obliterate it. The modern mentality sets out for a deliberate conquest of natural forces and this gives rise to an atheism which is no longer a practical deism, but a systematic anti-theism. But even here the discovery of new cosmic dimensions contains, as we shall see, the germs of a new religious symbolism in which modern man opens up to the transcendent from an immanence recognized as such.

The Structure of the Religious Experience

We have said that the religious experience is a grasp, in all that is human and terrestrial, of the impact of the Other. This Other is the prop of existence, the horizon of the true reality to which the passing phenomena of life should be referred, the absolute owner of all human existence. Present and distant, pervading significant objects without coinciding with them; that is what is meant by the antithesis of the sacred and the profane which is the only way religion can be characterized.

In several languages (Hebrew, Latin, Greek), the very word 'sacred' expresses in a spatial symbolism the idea of separation and cultural demarcation. The Polynesian word 'taboo' which ethnologists and psychologists have borrowed and consecrated, also denotes that an object, place or person is marked by a particular intensity, is then sanctified, and thus is set apart and dangerous because of the power it holds. 'Profane', on the other hand, signified *pro fanum*, that is, 'outside the sacred place'.

This distinction between profane and sacred is fundamentally the same as that between the ordinary and the transcendent, the natural and the super-natural. The sacred is the super-powerful, true strength and reality.[33] It may be found in a superior divine person. It tends to be omnipresent, in a vague sort of way, as in cosmo-vitalism. It may be the object of veneration, or the celebrated power with which man integrates himself in ritual performance, or which he captures by magic technique. The different forms, we have seen, can co-exist to some extent; this may lead us to wonder to which particular form of cult is reserved the name of religion. Such discussions are to no purpose. It is more profitable to reset every form of the sacred, whatever it may be, in the total religious dynamic, as we have just outlined it.

R. Otto has brought out the essential elements of the numinous in his well-known and still relevant work, *The Idea of the Holy*. We summarize this work here because it is an authentic phenomenology of religious sentiments and their structure.

Otto sets out to define those sentiments which apprehend the numinous as such. The religious sentiments—gratitude, confidence, love, security, humble submission—do not make up the whole of the specifically religious experience.[34] The feeling of dependence, emphasized by Schleiermacher, is a subjective reflection of an experience which bears directly on the sacred subject but Otto, a meticulous phenomonologist, tries to define the sentiments which have intentional bearing on the sacred object. He sums them up in the response to the numinous defined as the experience of a mystery which is at one and the same time *tremendum* and *fascinosum*, awe-inspiring and fascinating. In this Otto echoes the extraordinary intuition of St Augustine who confesses to God: 'Who shall understand this? Who shall relate it? What is that light which shines upon me but not continuously, and strikes upon my heart with no wounding? I draw back in terror: I am on fire with longing: terror in so far as I am different from it, longing in the degree of my likeness to it.'[35]

The *tremendum* itself is made up of a group of feelings, corresponding to different qualities of the numinous. By the fact of its absolute inaccessibility, its radical remoteness, it is something which inspires fear. Fear, awe, terror, even horror, or trembling stupor, are all so many words abounding in religious writings, and which correspond to the terrible aspect of the divine, his wrath, his jealousy, his zeal.

The recognition of the divine majesty and glory is a second

phase in the experience of the Other, and the feeling of creature-liness is the accompanying subjective reflection. These elements imply a third: the power of the numinous which is force, move-ment, will. Certain powerful biblical symbols, such as in the vision which Ezechiel describes where we see the dazzling apparition of Yahweh on his chariot drawn by the fiery cherubim, provide a good representation of this overpowering divinity manifesting himself in all the splendour of his glory. Finally the *tremendum* is mystery, not as problem, but as that strange, astonishing otherness before which man is struck dumb, stupefied. But the sacred is also that which fascinates, captivates, attracts; it is the marvellous. He to whom the sacred reveals itself becomes aware of it according to a whole series of particular sentiments which all express joy, ranging from Dionysian exaltation to blessed felicity. The divine is comforting mystery and blessed benevolence.

Remote and close, strange but fascinating, the sacred is a harmony of contrasts. In this polarity of sentiments we can surely detect the inner repercussion of the twin attributes of the divine: absolute transcendence and immanence. Even where cosmo-vitalism bursts the bounds of immanence and transcendence, we still find the polarity of the sacred in the celebration of the forces of nature. It is this polarity which is the specific characteristic of the religious experience, whatever form it may assume. The experience may be calm or violent, blessed or demonic, but it is always an immediate and simultaneous grasp of two poles contrasted and inseparable in their irreducible tension. This harmony of contrasts is found even in the most subtle of theo-logical concepts. Proof may be found in the double idea which the Bible gives of divine justice: justice which judges and yet justifies.[36] In the gospels, as in the rest of the Bible, God is always the God of judgement and the God of grace; and grace is both kindness, and tenderness which forgives and creates anew. Heaven and hell are the two corresponding realizations of the divine polarity. In the psychological analyses which we shall make later, we shall have to guard against minimizing the element of religious awe as do those psychologists who regard every kind of anguish as pathological and every religious fear as a base and inferior sentiment.

The Ambiguities of the Religious Experience

We have discovered a profound unity in the varied phenomena which make up religion: it is the immediate presence of the sacred, and that whether we are dealing with theism, cosmo-vitalism or deism. This implies that religion can be mixed with foreign elements. Arising as it does on the border of man's existential experience of the world, emerging from his sense of time, space and living nature, the religious experience can, as it were, remain bogged down to the point of losing its transcendent nature. These feelings which throw open the divine world to man remain very human feelings, and religion has often been party to their ambiguities. Therefore we think it best to give a brief sketch of these ambiguities which have often disfigured religion in the course of history. They indicate certain ever-present tendencies to which the religious experience may lend itself. A number of our atheist contemporaries are tempted to identify religion with these mixed forms, finding in them serious reasons for rejecting it.

The Blending of Sacred and Cosmic

On the level of affective experience, the signs of the divine are themselves pervaded by the divine. Certainly, in primitive religious history, there are very pure experiences, where man refers himself to God who is Father, Author of life and to whom the universe belongs. But once man begins cultivating the earth, the earth itself takes on the aspect of sacred powers. The dynamic of his affectivity urges man to unite himself with the natural forces which haunt the cosmos. To become affectively integrated with the cosmos is to become fused with it. The whole universe becomes sacred power. When every physiological act becomes direct sacral participation, the sacred and the cosmic become one. The cosmic ceases to be symbol and becomes sacral substance. Some authors speak of pantheism. We can accept this term on condition that it is transposed to the level of affective participation and that its speculative implications—which, however, we regard as essential—are removed. In this spiritual universe, the sacred is part of the cosmos, and though the idea of a god remains present on the border of religious consciousness, religious practice becomes idolatrous and magical. The degeneration of symbols into idols constitutes a permanent threat to any religiosity lived on the plane of affective participation. The reference to the transcendent overlaps the sphere of what belongs to earth. This is often called paganism in Christian language. The prophets of Israel brandished their anathemas against it and proclaimed the wrath and jealousy of the Other.

The Blending of Sacred and Erotic

Sexuality is first of all access to the forces of nature and to the extraordinary. It links man with the powerful fertility of nature. The whole cosmos responds to him and offers him symbolic signs: earth, moon, tree, fire, cave . . . The earth is perceived as being adorned with sexual emblems. What experience could better link man with sacralized nature than sexuality? Furthermore, the erotic experience contains certain elements which may be termed 'mystic': much more than merely skin-deep pleasure, this experience is a return to primal unity, to blessed obscurity, to immediate innocence. In works which still inspire western culture, this last aspect, that of subjective plenitude, has been celebrated by the Greeks. In primitive religions, it is not so much subjective experience of plenitude and original integrity which gives significance to erotic exaltation, as participation, both pathic and active, in fertile life and in the cosmic cycle of life, death and rebirth. The sexual deeply penetrates the sacred for the cosmo-vitalists. Studies in ethnology have shown the extraordinary power of this current of Dionysian participation; initiation rites, phallic statuettes, mystery celebrations, worship of the divinities of fertility, all these abound in the religions which we call pagan. The prophets of Israel stood in horror of them. With a deeper knowledge of man and of his religious roots in dreams and emotions, we are inclined to be more tolerant in modern times. In the blend of the sacred and the erotic we recognize the ambiguity inherent in every religious experience. Lived on a level of profound affectivity and mediated by cosmic and biological signs it shifts spontaneously towards the celebration of an immanent absolute life. The people of modern times, isolated as they are from nature, have elaborated another perspective of the erotico-mystic quest: desire which stretches out to the infinite and seeks to satisfy itself by breaking down every barrier of separation. We shall speak of this in the chapter devoted to mysticism. Thus ambiguity can be discovered in the present-day trend. The erotic may serve as a symbol for mystic perfection, but it can also close in on itself and nurture, even under cover of religious images, its own undefined immanence.

The Blending of Sacred and Demonic

Religious inconography has familiarized us with a world of weird divinities with monstrous heads and terrifying gestures; and myths depict the metamorphosis of gods into demons. The power of terror which R. Otto has recognized as one of the component factors of the *tremendum*, is the seed ground of both demons and gods. And we are only too well aware of the almost mystical exaltation which forces of destruction and hate can set loose in man. In the dark powers of death, man can experience some sort of absolute. Life itself, indeed, is only one of the two faces of the double mystery of life and death. There exists, then, a diabolic sacred which can overlay the divine sacred and even evict it. Even in forms of worship, the two faces of the terrestrial sacred give rise to rituals of life and celebrations of death. There is often a sacred element in war by reason of the almost mystical exaltation which it arouses. According to A. Malraux, 'the demonic domain is everything in man which seeks to destroy him. The basic themes are blood, sex and death.'[37]

It is not surprising that, since R. Smith, historians of religion should have constantly emphasized the kinship between the divine and the demonic. Durkheim puts it very neatly though the present state of our historical knowledge no longer permits the generalization of his thesis that every religious life turns on two poles between which there is the same opposition as between the

pure and the impure, the holy and the sacrilegious, the divine and
the diabolic. The pure and the impure, he says, are not two
different types, but two varieties of the same type which contains
all things sacred.

That the experience of evil is among the resources of a quasi-
religious exaltation is shown by a whole current of western
literature; J. K. Huysmans, E. Jünger and H. Bataille have made
a name for themselves in their attempt to regenerate this experience. However strange this dark mysticism may appear, it is
deeply rooted in the ambiguity of religious experience. K.
Girgensohn's work[38] witnesses to the permanence of this blending
of the divine and the diabolic as realized at the level of affective
experience. When a hymn by Nietzsche to an unknown god was
read to one of the subjects of Girgensohn's enquiry, the following
association was set up: '. . . it is also feeling. You know that
somewhere there is something terrifying, for example in a picture
book. You want to look somewhere else and turn the pages but
that attracts you specially and fascinates you. When I was a
child I felt this so strongly that with a book before me in which
there were pictures of snakes, I felt quite anguished, and yet I
could not turn the page. I felt this terror over again each time.'
It was possibly the same mixed phenomenon of sacred and
diabolic which urged the Christians of Corinth to cry 'anathema
to Jesus' as St Paul tells us (I *Cor.* 12 :3). If we made further
enquiries among Christians about their images of God and the
devil we should probably learn much about the darker side of
their religious experience.

The Ambivalences of Taboo

The objects, persons, places, gestures, which incorporate the
sacred, are set apart from the profane realm. Being repositories
of the Other, they are under interdiction. Like any other sacred
sign, they are symbolic localizations which can become stereotyped, nothing more than mere objects pervaded by the sacred.
They are thus reduced to idols and, according to the degree of
the degradation, from taboo they become superstitious objects
and gestures. The simple fact of using them is thought to be

sufficient. The handling of them is thought to produce some automatic good effect, some direct and sure exorcism of danger. This is a move in the direction of pure magic: magic which has become materialized in its techniques, retaining nothing of its religious content but the forgotten traces of a symbolic experience. Doubtless, as we have seen, magic and theism can coexist. But magic is essentially a mixture of religion and imaginary techniques, and there is constant risk of its deteriorating into a seeking after useful power and nothing more. We are obliged to ask ourselves whether, among Christians, religious practices do not often degenerate into superstition. Too often there remains— in the gestures performed in a moment of anguish, in many weird ex-votos—nothing more of the vital relationship with the God of Jesus Christ than a vague link with a powerful God. When such gestures are made by people who, in the ordinary run of life, are unbelievers and who only make use of Christian signs when in dire distress, there is no doubt that we are in the presence of a superstitious offshoot of a symbolism which has lost any reference to the sacred. It is obvious that the Christian sacraments, by the fact of their being efficacious signs in themselves, are subject to the superstitious uses of taboo. How many practising Christians realize that the sign is efficacious only if it is acknowledged in that theological faith by which the Christian is linked up with the saving action of Christ the God-Man?

Taboo often gives place, in primitive religions, to another ambiguity, that of sacral transgression.[39] Because the taboo is the sacred, present and separated, within grasp and yet forbidden, man uses it to affirm his human condition and at the same time to transcend it. In daily life the taboo is held in respect because it represents a power of 'another ontological level'[40] and as such is a menace to the specific condition of all that is human. But on religious feast days which are the peaks of existence, man enters the forbidden area; he assimilates the higher power and raises himself to the level of the divine. Man's mystical infringement of the taboo and his ritual participation in the Other, normally forbidden because destructive of the human order, are expressed in orgies. It is useless to insist here on the a-religious nature of such practices. Their naturalist tendency, indeed, can be clearly seen in modern times when transgression of taboos and laws give such dizzy exaltation to its adepts that it leads them beyond the pale of good and evil, and assimilates them to the gods. Such orgies mark the radical hostility between a mysticism of *trans-descendence* and the religion of a Transcendent. With primitive peoples the opposition was not felt so long as this mysticism of transgression was part of the movement of cosmo-vitalist participation.

Before leaving the subject of the ambivalence of taboo, there is still another composite type which must be mentioned: the notion of pure and impure. The taboo can just as easily be a consecrated object as a sordid, polluted one: a corpse, a criminal, a menstruous woman, are often considered as taboos because impure. The impure, in common with the diabolic, has a 'dangerous' power and for this reason is cut off from commerce with man. The strange ambiguity of the words *sacer* and *hagios* has been pointed out elsewhere. *Sacer* in Latin means both 'cursed' and 'holy'; and *hagios* in Greek, 'pure' and 'polluted'. These two terms, in a single ambiguous reference to the sacred, sum up everything which, no longer part of a strictly human sphere, conceals a dangerous and fascinating force. Psycho-analysts have tried to discover just how the impure is dangerous. They have shown that man, in the depths of his psyche, is attracted by everything that is inhuman: blood, death, suffering. Terror only appears as a second movement, a defence against an attraction which threatens to destroy the human order. The psychoanalytical explanation helps us to understand, at the level of the human psyche, the ambivalence of the taboo, both pure and impure. But whatever may be the unconscious dynamism which sustains it, the taboo of the impure, by the fact that it is characteristically fascinating and awe-inspiring, assumes a sacral value and merges with religion. This overlay helps us to understand certain obsessional phenomena particularly frequent among children and adolescents where the divine is implicated with the bodily impure; such, for example, as the thought of Christ's defecation.

Religious experience, such as we have defined it, is impregnated with the naïvety and the ambiguity of affectivity. According to different modes of life, and following the patterns of the rhythms of experience, it branches out in different directions; it develops in a complex manner; it is composed of the most diverse feelings all knotted together and merged into one. This explains why religion, which has its origin in the experience of life and existence, is always very fragile; easily becoming an accomplice to the unbridling of every passion, to every form of perversion. It may be frittered away in cosmo-vitalist participation, it may be distracted by stargazing, or set itself up in techniques of power, or become involved in destructive passions. This fragility and overlapping can be noticed especially in children and adolescents and should not be mistaken for pathological forms of religion; when the emotions are uppermost anything is possible. Dubious and lewd experiences are the uncertain paths along which the religious personality wanders as it gropes after its mature self; there is self-criticism as it goes along and finally it flowers in a clear-sighted, deliberate attitude. Pathological forms, on the contrary, find their origin at a more structured level of the personality. They are, as we shall see, caused by a secondary repression which relegates gestures and ideas to forgetfulness, shutting them out of the personal dynamic and in this way unconsciously making them centres of autonomous activity.

All that is impure and fragile in religious experience must be returned to the dynamic which will carry it towards conscious understanding and reasoned discrimination.

The progressive rationalization of culture has destroyed the attitude of participation, the specific attitude in which religious experience, the first moment of religion, finds its origin. This attitude conditions the religious dimension of early cultures and the fact that it has been done away with in modern culture favours the growth of atheism or the progressive destruction of religion. The term 'participation' was introduced into ethnology by L. Lévy-Bruhl who used it in opposition to 'logical reason'. He himself has acknowledged the mistake of this exclusive antithesis. Primitive peoples are just as capable of logical thought as are present-day scientists. But his analysis nevertheless retains an essential value: in relation to the world, primitive peoples live in a state of participation.[41] To describe this attitude and have an adequate idea of its power of impact on all registers of existence, we should have to rally all the resources of contemporary anthropology, phenomenology, psychology of perception and affectivity, ethnology and psychoanalysis: but we shall have to be content with merely mentioning it here.

In his posthumous notes Lévy-Bruhl no longer uses the evolutionist concept of 'pre-logical' to define the primitive attitude; he defines it as an undifferentiated state, both pre-religious and pre-magic, in which participation has predominance over the rational. It is the womb of magic as much as it is of animism or theism. Participation is a 'mystical community of essence among beings'. 'Recognized as a sensible fact, *sui generis*, of life, of smell, etc., without our being able to speak of knowledge, the affective category of the supernatural does reveal something, but only about itself in the presence of a supernatural force and in its action; in other words, it is not accompanied by a concept. Each participation is specific, but the general element is of the affective order.'[42]

Elements which reason regards as contradictory can coexist because there is no formulated law to separate them. As long as the subject is not consciously individualized, death is only a change of place and not complete absence.[43] Through a common fund of communication between beings, and man's affective awareness of the universe, the experience of the sacred springs up spontaneously and takes form as God or as gods, or even as powers which man tries to capture and to direct. In this sphere of vital exchange between man and the world, rational culture introduces factors of dissociation between man and the universe, the subject and the object, the individual and the group. Separation and individualization are the ransom which the spirit must pay for the rational articulation of being and for technical domination of the world. Religion is profoundly affected by this, as we shall be able to observe from the enquiries which we shall be considering in a later chapter.

III. Religious Experience Today

Under this heading we shall deal with some facts collected during relatively diverse and scattered psychological investigations. From some points of view this is a bold undertaking which cannot be attempted without some hesitation. We may ask whether it is possible to elaborate a synthesis of actual religious experience based on sampling. It would certainly be very rash to pretend to sum up in a few pages the immense movement of religious life with its mass of contradictions and every sort of ambiguity. We do believe, however, that even these few chosen witnesses have something to show, and that the specific characteristics they throw into relief teach us something about the meaning and orientation of contemporary religious life. If we study only the very narrow question of religious experience, as being the first awareness of the divine or of God, we shall surely be able to erect milestones along the road which modern man takes in his search for God.

What is more, we have no other choice, for practical enquiries are still very few. We are convinced, however, that even in the absence of sure sociological foundations and perfectly representative statistical assessments of the population, our investigations are sufficient to provide us with certain sign-posts and indices which characterize a religious climate; especially as they offer a contrast with earlier religious eras.

EMPIRICAL STUDIES ON THE NATURE OF THE RELIGIOUS EXPERIENCE

In this section we shall make a brief survey of the enquiries undertaken by German psychologists into religious experience as it was envisaged along the lines traced by Schleiermacher, and according to philosophies and theologies of experience.

The problem, it will be remembered, was that of the specific nature of the religious act. These enquiries, even though they are outstripped by present-day knowledge, still have a certain relevance to a justified empirical definition of the religious experience. Furthermore, it is useful to compare the earlier point of view with current main trends. This will help us to place our problem in perspective.

As an example of the first point of view we shall consider Girgensohn's work in particular. He devoted twenty years to studying the religious act. The title of his book, *Der Seelische Aufbau des religiösen Erlebnis*,[44] tells us what it is about. The author tries to delineate the actual structure of psychic states, having regard for its more subtle points. It is these states which give true significance to the ambiguous indications of the auto-biographical records. Faithful to the direction taken by his master, Külpe, Girgensohn tries to use experimental methods to go further than introspection and thus to shed full light on those dispositions, states and marginal processes which are not fully known to the subjects. To this end, Girgensohn presented fourteen educated subjects with a series of unfamiliar religious texts calculated to arouse strong and fairly lasting impressions. He then asked the subjects to give free rein to their associations. During the interviews which followed, the rockbottom foundations of faith were laid bare and the motives of religious confidence revealed. In this way, lasting records were made of a brief moment in life and the enlargement, so to speak, which was then made, allowed them to be clarified by analysis. At the end of twenty years of considerable labour, Girgensohn felt that he could justly assert on the basis of the facts he had assembled, that religion is neither knowing nor doing, but feeling; a way of being present to self without image. This feeling, however, is something more than pleasure or displeasure. It is in fact characterized by a very strong personal bond (an 'ego-bond') which is connected with the idea of God. Nevertheless, the 'religious sentiment' has nothing to do with either the will or images. This leads Girgensohn to say that it is an undifferentiated affective state,[45] and he quotes Goethe's *Faust*: 'Gefühl ist alles; Name: Schall und Rauch' (Feeling is all; the name is merely sound and smoke). In conclusion he states his complete agreement with Schleiermacher.

It may appear to us that he has set the psychological problem of religion within the framework of faculty psychology, heir to a tradition dating from the seventeenth century. This may be but, even so, Girgensohn, like Michotte and Prümm who were also Külpe's disciples, has the merit of having pointed out, on the basis of experimental analyses, that the psychological centre of the subject is to be found neither in ideas, nor in decisive will, but in what may be called, more or less correctly, feeling, that is to say, an affective state which, because it fundamentally commits the ego to the 'idea of God', is a dynamic relationship.

What is to be learnt from Girgensohn's study is, in the first place, that religion is rooted in the 'heart' of the person, in the vital 'knot' of the ego; any distinction between the faculties is a later stage and it is in this sense that religion is said to be 'sentiment'. A second point to be remembered is that religion is not merely a subjective state for it is a relationship between the ego and 'the idea of God'.

The new psychology and phenomenology will help us to understand Girgensohn's meaning more clearly. Sentiment is both 'state', because it is interiorized appropriation of the object, and 'relationship', because it is vitally linked with the object.

The new psychology helps us to see the limitations of this experimental religious psychology which, while it paves the way for a dynamic psychology, nevertheless remains enslaved to static associationism. In the voluminous documentation of his records, Girgensohn has not picked out the content and motivations which are at work in the formation of the religious 'bond'. He regards religious experience as a state, although in fact it represents the dynamic relationship established between the ego and God who is mediated by the 'idea'. In this relationship the ego may well be interiorized equilibrium, but it is also evolutive and is under the constant impulse of the dynamic drives which underlie experience. Girgensohn, we see, is victim to the epistemological representations of his age and therefore he talks of a 'bond' with the 'idea of God'. But actually, the religious subject goes beyond the idea in order to reach the 'Other'.

The Sacred: Harmony of Contrasts

A. Bolley,[46] using Girgensohn's method, carried out research on the different degrees of union (*Versenkung*) and the experience

5

of God in contemplation. He shows that when man recollects himself and concentrates all his attention on God really present, there is always the polarity which has been described by Otto. Subjects speak of their feelings in such terms as solemn, serious, terrible, or blessedly trusting. They feel that they are face to face with divine royalty, the awful majesty of God. They are conscious of their nothingness. God for them is light and fire. He is awesomely real. Their experience is torn between two opposite poles: God's absolute sublimity (*Erhabenheit*) and closest intimacy. More often than not, a reverential fear constrains those who pray, preventing them from giving way to a too human familiarity. In the moments when they give themselves up to concentrated contemplation, the subjects who are already sensitive to religious experience come up against the ambivalence of the sacred (which is characteristic of every other religion) in their encounter with the personal God of Christianity. It must be noticed, however, that in this interior relationship with a personal God, the sacred polarity acquires a more moral aspect in the measure that it is interiorized and personalized. Awe tends to become sense of sin; attraction leads to abandonment to divine goodness.

THE WORLD AND EXISTENCE AS SIGNS OF GOD

Girgensohn and his disciples attempted to analyse the structure of the psychic act by which man addresses God. For them experience meant a subject's approach to interior communion with God; the sentiment felt by the ego in relation to God. In our days this point of view has been modified. We know that the regions of subjectivity are something more than reason and will, taken as distinct faculties. Furthermore, it is known that man is not pure interiority but that he is first of all aware of the world. Psychology is interested in man's relations with the situations he meets. This brings us back again to our problem: is the world still a place of religious experience?

Our problem is not exactly the same as the one that so many modern writers are grappling with. They in general seek rather to know *why* man is religious; they are interested in the motivations underlying his religious development.

The study undertaken by G. Allport[47] is a good illustration of this problem. His aim is to discover the movements by which man comes spontaneously to a living relationship with God. He lists several: the experience of power considered as the root of the idea of divine almightiness; the need for peace which suggests the idea of God as one who consoles; the need for guidance, manifested in belief in the holy Spirit. In this case the theme of religious experience has become that of the psychogenesis of religion and its motivation. In the next chapter we shall see that this kind of religious psychology may suffer from a deep-rooted ambiguity. There is a danger of compromising religion by seeing it as no more than the subjective expression of the affective life in more or less imaginary concepts. In our opinion the question of experience cannot be reduced to a matter of motives for religious behaviour. The study of primitive religion shows clearly that any explicitly motivated act is preceded by a certain awareness of the divine as it reveals itself in symbols. Religious perception precedes the religious movement motivated by human desires. For this reason we prefer to distinguish two phases: experience of divine presence, and experience of divine response to human appeal. We must then first try to discover the experiences, the perceptions, which open man up to the religious world.

In our investigation into this problem we shall make use of a series of samplings with particular reference to four enquiries carried out by our centre of religious psychology. These enquiries were made among different populations and made use of various methods. The first study, which we shall quote at some length, was based on prolonged interviews (two or three hours) of thirteen adults, seven men and six women aged between twenty-five and forty-three years. All the subjects were university graduates, instructed and practising Catholics.[48] A contents analysis was made with the help of a rigorously established scale. We shall confine our attention to the information which this study provides that is relevant to our problem, as we advance with the discussion of it.

A second enquiry was undertaken in order to establish a scale which, with its nine sub-scales, covers nine categories that, taken together, define the religious attitude. Preliminary investigation and interviews were followed by the application of the scale to 1,800 subjects of both sexes. The majority of the subjects were adolescents and care was taken to tap groups statistically representative of different milieux (classical and modern humanities and various kinds of technical studies).[49]

More specific information was obtained by an enquiry made into the religious repercussions of Teilhard de Chardin and by a projective study of the religious experiences of adolescents. We shall deal with these more fully later.

The problem that concerns us here is how man, aware of the world, discovers in it a religious appeal. We propose to approach this problem in four stages. First we shall examine the ideas evoked for our contemporaries by the expression 'religious experience' so often used by the specialists. This will help us to see how man opens up to God. In other words—which are not necessarily those the subject would use—what are the religious experiences which man undergoes? The second stage of our approach to the problem will be followed by an examination of the influence of Teilhard de Chardin and the results of this will allow us to see if we may legitimately speak of a new sacred, a new religious perception arising from a scientific vision of the universe. Lastly, a 'projective' study will complete the preceding enquiries by supplying some relevant detail.

Religious Experience: Suspect and Desired

In present times adult Christians have a tendency to refuse any 'experience of God'. This is due, in the first place, to the fact that they identify experience with emotion, and in matters of religion they see sentiment as something to be rejected. Some people acknowledge having had some 'experience of God' in adolescence, but looking back on it, they regard it as empty fancies with no guarantee of truth. The word 'mystic' conjures up the same idea of an intense emotional relationship which, because of its immediacy, is evident to the sensitive heart but is nonetheless void of any truth. 'Experience' has come to be analogous with a subjective state where man finds himself in a *tête-à-tête* with himself, with the blissful feeling of being open to the Other.

Looking at things more closely we can recognize four characteristic traits in this refusal of religious experience which is typical of adults. In the first place, modern man has discovered sentiment as such. This clear-sightedness results from a broader outlook, reflective and self-critical, which is one of the universal characteristics of our times. Secondly, in Christian circles, God is clearly perceived as a person even though subjects may speak of the immense difficulty which they have in integrating belief in the mystery of a personal God with their own lived religion. Now, a personal God does not easily lend himself to experience because human experience bears on the palpable. A third element to be taken into consideration is the fact that the subjects who have been brought up in a Christian spirit give special value to 'faith' and this, for many, is opposed to experience. For them the true relationship to God, that of faith, takes root in man at quite another level than that of affectivity. Finally, for the greater number of these subjects, the world has ceased to be a direct sign of God. It has very largely lost any religious referential value as we shall shortly see. One might almost say that God has withdrawn from the cosmos. Many even think that the profane world hides God: it is no longer God who hides himself, as we read in the prophet Isaias (45:15), but the world which closes in upon him.

But this refusal of experience does not occur without some regret. All the adult subjects interviewed state, in effect, that the divergence between faith and experience, between knowing and experiencing, is by far the greatest religious difficulty. To their way of thinking, Christian truths largely remain a scaffolding of concepts beyond the scope of their personal experience. They are conversant with the new theological trends of thought concerning the Christian value of work and earthly goods, but they have no personal experience of the truth of these teachings which remain, for the most part, ideas quite distinct from life. Certain subjects reproach themselves for not reflecting sufficiently about their faith and say that possibly the discrepancy between theory and practice is due to their own inertia and indifference. And yet these same subjects admit that they fear that through systematic reflection they may lose themselves in manufactured theories. Thus their religious life is dominated by a double apprehension: fear of experience of God, and fear of a scaffolding of concepts erected by theology, even the most earth-bound. In the chapter devoted to the religious attitude we shall go more deeply into the problem of this discrepancy between knowledge and experience. It leads to the possibility of a dynamic structuring which is foreign to the psychologistic theories of religions.

Mystery Pointing to God

For the subjects of the enquiry the term 'religious experience' evokes a personal, and therefore affective, presence. They reject it because they know that it is open to the delusions of affectivity. On the other hand they accord a major significance to the all-encompassing mystery inherent in existence and in the world. We can adduce witnesses in support of this statement. A married woman, for instance, says, 'When we fulfil ourselves along the lines we have chosen we have the experience that a great deal is beyond us. We feel that the best way to make sense of life is to try and live as well as we can. We learn that from experience: we feel that there is something transcending us—it is what we call God. But we already knew this word because we were brought up in an attitude of faith . . . But I am not yet ready for God.' The following answer was given by a man in reply to the question whether the whole of Christian living was contained in commitment to others: 'You have the experience that you can do nothing by yourself, by your own powers; but there is something, like a gift, beyond you . . .' It is worth noting that this subject stated that his way of life would be in no way different were he an unbeliever. And we do notice, in fact, that for this man the basic human reality is the moral attitude; at the same time however, the way it works within him makes him feel that it is something which does not belong to him. This double experience which he has of something which he feels to be his own, and yet a gift, makes him recognize it as a sign of God.

A scientist states that looking back over things, existence taken as a whole seems to be directed, led by someone. A panoramic view gives man the impression that the succession of moments, events, and fresh beginnings is constantly animated by some unique guiding principle. Man is conscious that the 'continuity' which he recognizes in his existence 'can result from an unconscious selection which arranges concordant facts. But, in spite of everything, at certain moments, he has the feeling that there is an obvious direction in life.'

The experience of a reality which cuts across, directs, surpasses life and human efforts, is a basic sentiment: we may call it the pre-religious experience. It is not, properly speaking, awareness of the presence of God. Faith must bridge the gap which exists between the personal God and the pre-religious experience of the mystery of existence.

Of all the subjects examined, only the scientist feels that God is also the answer to the enigma of the universe: 'Scientists do not take themselves too seriously;' he says, 'we are fundamentally aware that we cannot take in the whole of creation. Science leads us to the conclusion that either the world has been made, or else it has come into being, in a manner utterly beyond our comprehension. We can say that it has been made for us, to give a certain amount of pleasure and happiness to all creatures; it has been made with love. That is the attitude of the believer . . . A scientist observes the increasing complexity of problems . . . The least we can do is to admit that creation is entirely beyond us . . . Even an agnostic scientist must recognize that.' In the strictly rational order, then, the mystery of all that exists is a factor to be reckoned with at least as a fundamental problem which will always remain irreducible. On the other hand, the meaning which can be discovered in the existence of all things leads us to feel that they have been marvellously made and that their function is one of happiness. The two experiences together open the way to belief in God. They point in God's direction without, however, openly signifying him. Among the intellectual subjects interviewed not one speaks of a symbolic and religious experience resulting from contact with nature. In face of this, we may well ask whether nature has not lost the evocative power of which so many religious texts speak. We think that it has.

Owing to the lack of empirical studies we are not in a position to make a general definitive judgement. But it is significant that another enquiry which put the question very clearly, and arranged the answers according to an attitude scale, shows that there is an experience of the cosmic sacred among working-class people that is absent in the university population. Of the sixty Italian working-class women interviewed, thirteen see the reflection of the majesty and power of God the Creater in the beauty of nature. As to this sense of God the Creator, the enquiry, conducted by means of an attitude scale, shows a very significant difference, in the female population, between the group of Belgian working-class women and university girls. For men students (aged from sixteen to nineteen years), religious sensitivity in contact with nature describes a descending curve, in the following order: farmers, labourers, clerks and shopkeepers, professional men. There is also a significant difference between the students of technical subjects (coming, for the most part, from rural and working class backgrounds) and the students of classical humanities. A detailed analysis reveals high averages in the group of Belgian working-class women for the answers which express astonishment and fear before a power greater than man. In contrast with this, two remarks made by women university students suggest that nature is desacralized in a more highly developed cultural environment: 'It is only on second thoughts that I associate God and nature.' Another girl says, 'You generally just have some sort of appreciation of a fine view without thinking very much about God.'

It should be noticed that those categories which yield high scores for 'God-Creator in nature', give still higher scores for 'fear of God'. The sense of the power of God as manifested in his works, is accompanied by religious awe. There seem to be two determinant factors for this type of religious experience: a more spontaneous bond with nature in environments less influenced by culture and technology, and the state of dependence in which a socially inferior population lives. This state of dependence fosters fear. We think that we have here evidence of the influence of socio-economic conditions on religion; an interpretation which is, moreover, confirmed by the significantly higher scores for reactions of revolt against God. Can it be that these are signs of the master-slave dialectic developed by the Marxist philosophy?

Explicit References to God

The only explicit mention of an experience of God which we have come across in the adults interviewed is that of a providential intervention in difficulties. One man wonders whether 'it is only because in such moments we realize the frailty of human existence that our attention is directed towards the transcendent. We have not yet really met God . . . but it is certainly in those moments that I have made closest contact with the Other. Everyday life does not refer us precisely to God.' A woman says, 'The fact that you quite unexpectedly manage to get out of difficulties makes you feel a certain relationship with God.' But she corrects this impression along the lines which we have already noticed: 'In general, things are all right as they are.' Another woman acknowledges that she is inclined to revolt in face of the difficulties of life. She knows that this emotional reaction has no sense, but failures and sufferings make her feel she wants to give up any form of religious living. This is an indication of the connection between dependence-frustration and revolt which we shall go into more deeply in a later chapter. The male witness we have quoted makes an important correction of his statement concerning the absence of God in normal life. Fatherhood, with all that is implied of patient effort in the education of children and the daily worry for their welfare, makes him think sometimes that divine paternity must be something of the same kind. This is the only indication which the enquiry gives of a reference to God originating in real everyday life.

The study made of adolescent subjects shows that they feel the reality of God more particularly in distressing situations. But between the ages of sixteen and nineteen years this experience gradually becomes less important.

A New Sacred?

Contemporary man seems to be discovering a new sacred, the universe itself in becoming. We have not noticed any sign of this renewal in the subjects interviewed although much of the literature published in our times would lead us to think that a religious sense is aroused by the discovery of the vast dimensions of life, space and time. We wonder whether this might not be a revival of the primitive sacred, and whether our contemporaries really are pervaded by this renewed sense of the sacred. In order to answer these questions we shall first examine two literary works and then describe the results of the enquiry into the religious influence of Teilhard de Chardin.

The new sense of God is shown up and deepened by a whole field of modern literature: Jaurès, Bergson, Lecomte de Nouy, Carrel, Teilhard de Chardin. Jaurès is one of the earliest of the writers in this field. The recent publication of his personal notes has revealed in him an extraordinarily strong, immediate sense of God. One or two extracts from his writings will clearly illustrate the new points of entry for the sacred into the world: 'Science seems to show increasingly that the universe is both infinity and unity . . . and if the universe is an infinite unity, or a single infinity, how can we fail to recognize in it the expression of what humanity has always called God?' 'If living and conscious beings have come to be through the evolution of the world itself, it is because the universe already contains in its depths both consciousness and life . . . It is in this way that evolution . . . is . . . the experimental demonstration of God. Furthermore, by this same doctrine of evolution, God is no longer a solitary abstraction . . . He acts in time, and manifests himself in history . . . Thus . . . action also develops the infinite and religion is not merely the business of monks . . .'[50] The new sense of God which arises from an active contemplation of the universe in becoming, has its counterpart according to Jaurès in the rejection of Christian dogmatics as being foreign to the historicity of the world and as alienating man by introducing an extraneous absolute into a history which should be self-constructing.

By both the new religious symbolism and the humanitarian

anti-dogmatism which we find in the writings of Jaurès, he illustrates contemporary sensitivity with admirable lucidity.

The fact of Teilhard de Chardin's exceptional reading public is eloquent in itself, for it immediately shows us one of the privileged religious spheres of our times. We shall first sketch the basic inspiration of his book *The Phenomenon of Man*[51] because it shows us very clearly where lies the naturally occurring correspondence between contemporary attitudes and religion.

For Teilhard, 'man is seen not as a static centre of the world—as he for long believed himself to be—but as the axis and leading shoot of evolution' (p. 36). He represents an ascension and expansion of consciousness. Civilization continues and perfects the vital dynamism so that the social phenomenon is a culmination of the biological phenomenon. The plurality of consciousness and individual reflections are regrouped and reinforced in the act of a single unanimous reflection (cf. p. 251). The world is unified according to the measure of its cultural and social expansion. Evolution should then 'culminate forwards in some sort of supreme consciousness . . . It is only by hyper-reflection—that is to say hyper-personalization—that thought can extrapolate itself' (p. 258). That is the famous Omega point which, because it is the term of evolution, must be an active presence in the very principle of the vital and conscious ascent. 'If by its very nature it did not escape from the time and space which it gathers together, it would not be Omega. Autonomy, actuality, irreversibility and thus finally transcendence are the four attributes of Omega' (p. 271).

With *Le Milieu Divin*[52] Teilhard's second best-seller, we are no longer dealing with an essay of scientific synthesis, but with an analysis of the communication felt between man, a corporeal and conscious being, and the divine, immanent in the material world and transcending it. Teilhard sets out to show how human activities are divinized; how man, while remaining a being-of-the-world can achieve union with the divine. God is waiting for us in the things of the world and in them he comes to seek us. The divinization of human actions is undoubtedly possible, and if there is a struggle, it is not between God and the world, but between God and the contempt of the world. 'Owing to the interrelation between matter, soul and Christ, we bring part of the being which he desires back to God *in whatever we do*' (p. 34). Man, as much a passive as an active being, adores the powers to which he submits while at the same time endeavouring to vanquish them. Religious hope and human hope are largely the same thing. 'Expectation—anxious, collective and operative expectation of an end of the world, that is to say of an issue for the world—that is perhaps the supreme Christian function and the most distinctive characteristic of our religion' (p. 148). Expectation of heaven is incarnate in utterly human hope.

The reader will not have failed to notice the extraordinary community of spirit between the ideas of Teilhard and those of Jaurès. They express one of the characteristics of the modern mentality as it has developed through the practice of the new sciences (evolutionism, social and human sciences), and through the new perceptions of contemporary philosophies.

This is not the place for discussing the theological exactitude of Teilhard's vision. The major objections put forward by certain theologians are well known: disregard for the supernatural and neglect of man's condition as a sinner. This, we repeat, is not our concern here any more than are the criticisms made by many scientists: confusion in method, naïve optimism in the synthesis of historical evolution. We take the work of Teilhard de Chardin for what it essentially is: a vision of the world and of Christianity which, after the manner of ancient myths, does away with the partitioning between disciplines common to many scientists. It is a work which takes for its theme the philosophy inherent in the practice of the different sciences and carries it over into a religious symbolism. The success of Teilhard's works is to be explained by no literary or scientific considerations, but by the religious message which they bring to a humanity refashioned by modern scientific thought. They provide a key which enables us to read the presence of God in his visible and temporal works. It seems significant, moreover, that the book by the Anglican Bishop Robinson,[53] written from a purely pastoral point of view but drawn from the same deep vein, should have stirred up the same religious reaction. The weak points of Teilhard's theology have been pointed out time and time again. But the contemporary reading public, on the lookout for new signs, has shown itself to be extremely sensitive to the appeal of an earthly Christianity; a form of Christian belief in which God is thought of in a dimension of depth rather in terms of transcendence.

An enquiry into the religious influence of Teilhard de Chardin[54] carried out among intellectuals at La Louvière has confirmed the rise of a new sacral value in a world which science has stripped of any association with the primitive sacred. The aim of this enquiry was to discover, by means of a Lickert scale, the kind of religious mentality which had prepared an unusually vast public to give such a welcome to Teilhard's works.

Of the 62% of subjects who replied to the first invitation, 46% were interested in Teilhard's writings. Churchmen headed the list, followed by educationalists and doctors, magistrates, barristers, notaries; while chemists, industrialists and business people showed least interest. It is interesting to observe the difference in interest between men and women with secondary education: the percentages were, respectively, 42 and 12·5. The population was classed according to different ideologies in the following way: Catholics 72%; non-Catholic Christians 6%; agnostics 6%; more or less spiritualist 6%; no convictions 2%; unspecified 8%. Teilhard's readers were distributed thus: *The Phenomenon of Man*, 46% read it completely; 26% partly: *Le Milieu Divin*, 32% completely; 16% partly: *The Appearance of Man*, 20% completely; 20% partly: *The Vision of the Past*, 20% completely; 6% partly. The majority of readers were interested in both types of writings, scientific and religious. Women and bachelors had more often read *Le Milieu Divin* than *The Phenomenon of Man*. Unbelievers read only the scientific works. The items of the category: intellectual synthesis (that is, implying a unified vision of the world, with the integration of faith and science) produced the greatest number of affirmative answers. However, two items, 'Teilhard spiritualizes scientific method', and 'Teilhard answers a certain need felt by scientists to open their minds to less materialistic attitudes', were met with great reserve. Second place went to the category: existential (lived) unity of the human, the world and the divine. The items with an apologetic tenor (for example, 'Teilhard offers a new kind of proof of the existence of God') had low scores. There is an important phenomenon to be noticed here and one which we constantly met with in this enquiry: it is the refusal of any idea of reaching faith through science, a denial of any tendency to find God on the evidence of scientific data, of any desire to spiritualize scientific method. The item 'T. strikes one by his sense of the psychic (interior) life of the cosmos which confers a certain spontaneity on inanimate matter (becoming consciousness in man)' received the greatest number of affirmative answers. Highly correlated with this were the item stating that every human action has an influence on the future and the item recognizing in Teilhard something which goes beyond human isolation in face of the universe—a feeling of solidarity and responsibility with regard to cosmic evolution together with liberation from a spiritually impoverished religion.

The readers questioned certainly showed themselves to be most sensitive of all to Teilhard's thesis of renewed unity between man and the universe. But, it should be remarked, this is no longer the same thing as primitive affective participation, the original conception of the primitive sacred: it is a scientific and existential vision. Teilhard's great success in African thought and in esoteric intellectual circles is sufficient witness that this new vision is rooted in those deeper strata of affectivity which, in modern man, are latent.[55] It is precisely this intense desire for a bond with the universe which causes men readily to accept a synthesis of perspectives which many philosophers denounce as mythological. A distinction should be made between primeval nature, i.e. the life force, and Teilhard's universe. True, this also is animated by a vital upthrust; but it is something more, something different. In Teilhard's world, life is constantly surpassing itself in the ascent of consciousness and in history, which advance towards universal perfection by man's scientific and moral efforts.

The poor response to the items concerned with the theme of the spiritualization of matter or of science, and those which suggested a new proof of the existence of God may be interpreted in the light of this same clinging to the mystery inherent in the universe. Readers felt that any kind of denial of this universe meant a severing of the true link, or else a call to turn away from it in order to form an attachment to some God felt as alien because too radically other.

Influence of Literary Formation on the Sense of the Sacred

The results of another enquiry[56] supply us with information which is very useful for the light it throws on our problem. The basic material of the enquiry was a series of lantern slides showing either nature scenes (mountain, sea, storm) or existential themes (birth, human love, death). The results provide complementary information about religious sensitivity. Eighteen years was the average age of the subjects and they were divided into two groups on the basis of their previous schooling: classical humanities and technical studies. Subjects in the first group imagined heroes who were more acutely aware of their insignificance in face of the elements; they had a greater sense of participation in the universe. Furthermore these heroes often viewed the elements in a perspective of the characteristic polarity of the sacred; fascination and fear. This was particularly noticeable with the picture showing a man standing alone on a hill during a storm. But on the whole the religious associations aroused by these slides varied only slightly for the two groups. One exception to this generality was provided by the picture of a dying person. The subjects from the classical humanities group gave a greater number of religious replies than did subjects of the second group. When we compared the two groups for religious association content we noticed a correlation between sensitivity to symbols and the frequency of religious association. Religious association had a slightly higher frequency in the group showing greater religious sensitivity in face of nature (insignificance, participation, fear, fascination). The results of this enquiry might seem to contradict the positive data quoted earlier. It may be asked whether these results do not prove the existence of a constant connection between the sense of nature and the sense of God. It may also be asked whether this link is not to be found precisely in the more cultured milieux.

There are no well-established data to help us answer these queries. The very minor differences observed between the two groups are insufficient evidence to justify a change in the conclusions arrived at earlier. They do, however, show a connection between religious association and some sort of sensitivity to the sacred in nature. It is significant that the subjects who produced the greatest number of symbolical associations and religious answers attributed to the heroes of their stories many more self-centred attitudes: 'closed in on himself'; 'thinks about his past, his future, his life'. Often these heroes were shown as being silent and in communion with nature. Many responses to other pictures betrayed a particular form of sensitivity which could be described as passive and narcissistic. These subjects allowed themselves to be impressed and frightened. They wanted affectionate intimacy and contemplative union with nature; they painfully kept alive within themselves a nostalgia for family intimacy. These associations, nature-sacred or nature-God, might be called the result of separation and longing for union.

It seems that adolescents who have received more training in interiority are more sensitive to the poetry of nature. They are led to recollection and the characteristic sentiments of the sacred are aroused in them by the fact that they are well-disposed to nature; the nostalgia which it stirs up makes them receptive to the sacred. The type of situation which they evoked in response to other pictures betrayed the same sensitivity to the values of intimacy correlative with feelings of being forsaken and isolated. This phenomenon is similar to the one we met in the mystery religions: a developed sense of participation which predisposes to religious experience; in the case of the adolescent subjects of our enquiry, participation was less direct, more interior; it was thus marked with the negative sign of separation. It is our opinion that this is a restricted phenomenon characteristic of adolescents formed in a very well-defined type of symbolic culture. Nothing allows us to conclude from the observations we have made that these adolescents will have the same sensitivity once they have become adults.

There are other types of religious experience and those engaged in pastoral duties would certainly be able to supply complementary information. There are people who are convinced of having had, in particular and definite situations, an immediate and almost tangible experience of the presence of God, or at least of a certain divine world. We can only give a single example here as it was told to us by the subject himself. Having received a Christian education in his childhood he fell into rationalistic unbelief. After long years in this state he became more or less of a believer. He fell in love with a girl during one of their first meetings and he found himself sitting beside her at the station just before leaving. In two brief moments of intense lucidity he had the indefinable impression that life cannot end, that it goes on for ever and participates in an unfailing transcendent reality. That would seem to be, in quasi-metaphysical terms, a religious experience cutting across the experience of love. In his book on religious experience James gives numerous examples of this type.[57]

Are such experiences frequent? Do they fix themselves actively and lastingly in the memory? If we may trust to our own limited experience, we would say that such experiences are relatively frequent; they suddenly open up a dimension in depth where religion takes on an existential density. But, an isolated experience does not leave a lasting impression if it is not backed up by a more objective experience. Studies that have been made on the problem lead us to think that, in general, people do not consciously refer to such experiences once life has found its orientation in social and professional commitments. Therefore they will not be taken into consideration in the conclusions which we are now going to list. It is quite possible that religious faith is stirred up by such experiences but it is not based on them. Once more history is a forgetting of the past.

Conclusions and Reflections

At the close of this enquiry we feel that we may point out the continuity between religious experience of ancient time and that of our contemporaries as well as the very obvious gulf by which they are separated. However scattered and deficient may be the enquiries into religious experience to which we have referred, they nevertheless allow us to pinpoint a few basic characteristics. From these it should be possible to outline a coherent religious profile which will correspond with the teachings of sociology and philosophy on the cultural situation of contemporary man.

The Primitive Sacred

Formerly the sacred was present in a perceptible and yet diffused manner. The divine appeared to be immediately linked with the mystery of life celebrated by primitive religions. Wach[58] points out that in ancient times 'the sacred represented less a fourth value added to the Good, the True, the Beautiful, than the womb where these values took life. It was their form and common origin. To use an image we can say that religion was not a branch of a tree, but its trunk.'

From the arborescent power of the sacred many religious forms came into being and often veiled the primary theist experience. Ancient religions set up a dialectic between the sacred and the sense of God. As long as humanity remained in cultural childhood it regarded the world as God's realm, and God was thought of as a benevolent Father and the Author of life. This form of religion may be called theist because it expressed the direct intuition that existence and the world belongs to the Other and are placed by him at man's disposition. But from this vital link between man and the world there soon arose an attitude of participation. The world became the place of strange and fascinating signs in which the sacred was embodied. Affectivity asserted its mythical powers and haunted the universe. By his perception of things as symbols of the drama of life and death, of sex and of power, man made them repositories of the sacred. The divine mingled with the mystery of life, was compromised and tended to lose itself in it. It is by a hard and sustained effort of spiritualization that man wrests God from the sacred. Monotheism is a conscious and deliberate rediscovery of God, already recognized by simple consciousness before any speculation arises or any development of participative affectivity. A religion of this sort can only be very precarious, constantly threatened with absorption into bio-cosmic forces.

Religious experience is polymorphous: a fact which is too frequently forgotten by different phenomenologies of the sacred. Properly speaking, when considering ancient religions we must distinguish at least two forms. In the first place primitive experience consisted in the direct intuition of the world and of existence as gift and property of a Father recognized as being the progenitor of humanity. This intuition was felt as an immediate perception coming before any intellectual query and untainted by affective cosmo-vitalist involvement. The experience of the sacred and the speculations of deist religions are proper to a more highly developed psychology. However, the fascination of the mystery of life and the magical domination of the world did not always imply the stifling of the perceptive intuition of God as Father. This is amply proved by the coexistence of a variety of religious forms.

The religion of the sacred can be found in widely differing cultures, sometimes side by side with strict monotheism. It arises from a symbolist attitude and from a culture where man feels he is in symbiosis with life and the world. The fact that throughout the Middle Ages every terrestrial value—life, health, sexuality, authority, justice, peace—was rooted in the sacred leads us to wonder whether the Christianity of Constantine which was prevalent in western culture during this whole period, was not just a new form of integration of the profane with the religious.

Remains of the Sacred

The practical research work which we have carried out shows that there are still traces of a certain sensitivity to nature very much akin to the mentality of participation; it also draws our attention to the fact that nature invested with sacral values can continue to be a direct sign of God. Mountains, starry sky, storm, sunset all have power to evoke the power, majesty and anguishing mystery of God. This poetic perception of the nature symbols of

God has been met with in certain well-defined groups; members of the working class and adolescents educated in a literary culture. We noticed that their reaction to the symbolic world was not identical. The adolescents showed a more interiorized affectivity and a longing for union.

It is possible that if an enquiry were to be carried out in artistic circles we should discover a particular sensitivity with regard to sacred values. How many artists, we may wonder, turn to art for a religious experience which they cannot find in institutionalized religion because, often, the symbolic forms are debased in sham devotion? In these circles the tension between the sacred and religion intensifies the dialectic which has always been at work in the heart of religions from the earliest times. We frequently discover here a conscious opposing of sacred and religion and a seeking after the infinite in aesthetic values. Humanist tension has increased the ruptures which the modern world has brought about between the divine and the human.

Rupture and Desacralization

Formerly the border line between the sacred and the profane was in doubt but it has now become more definite. The progress of scientific culture and the affirmation of the transcendent God of Christian revelation have caused estrangement between the sacred and the God of nature and life. We may say that the world has become a-religious, or a-theistic in the privative sense of the term. It is no longer haunted by the divine omnipresence. It has found a kind of stability in complete acceptance of its relativity and its reality as specifically man's domain. Taking the word in its etymological sense we can say that the world has become 'humanized'. It is no longer directly perceived in a perspective of eternity. It has come to be more than a mere object of contemplation and religious celebration; it is something offered to man in order that he may build it up.

The desacralization of the world and the rise of the universe as history are cultural facts which have profoundly modified religion and they themselves cannot but respond to this religious change. In proposing the world as man's particular domain, the absolute

transcendence of the Christian God has stamped western civilization once and for all. Various elements enter into this new
situation: a reflective awareness, the rise of the scientific era, the
distinction between the temporal and the religious. Their dialectic
results in an autonomy of the subject who, on the one hand,
liberates the ego from its inherence in cosmo-vitalist principles,
and on the other, eliminates the sacred from the universe. R.
Guardini has underlined this destruction of primordial unity
which is the price modern culture has paid for its concepts. Since
the end of the Middle Ages man has become freer, more independent, a more interior being. But his interiority is a 'separated
interiority'—man has disintegrated himself. 'On one side we
have reason working abstractly, manipulating concepts; on the
other, a physiological apparatus of sensations capturing impressions. Between the two and strangely uprooted, is a purely
emotional feeling.'[59] Modern man, according to Guardini, has
forgotten how to see God in nature and history: 'The symbolic
power has been degraded.'[60]

A psychologist should be impartial when faced with cultural
evolution. For this reason we share neither Guardini's hankering
after a world unified on the plane of symbols, nor his pessimism
about the degrading of affective and symbolic powers. Certainly,
a scientific rationalism can shrivel man's affectivity and stifle his
capacity for symbolic perception. This has often been noticed.
But, the extraordinary efflorescence of symbolical and even
mythical thought in modern times seems to show that man today
refuses to be reduced to mere intellectual faculties. The discontinuity introduced between man, the world and the sacred has
not led him to lead a worthless egoistic life. It has, on the contrary,
liberated his imaginative and symbolist powers. We often assist
at the revolt of the irrational against the orderings of reason.
But this is just because man is struggling towards a new form of
understanding which will integrate every level of existence. The
real cleavage is not between reason and emotion, but between
the world and the sacred. Symbolic culture has also been desacralized. Formerly symbolism was a direct contact with the sacred
but now it is simply the exploration of the ever-widening human

sphere. The renewed sense of existential depths, however, opens man up to the divine mystery. Claudel's first conversion was an experience of the 'supernatural' occasioned by the reading of Rimbaud's work which tore open the low ceiling which rationalism had built over his head. But he had to discover God before he could grasp the religious import of human symbols.

Everything happens then as though man, having acquired his own independence and gained mastery over the world, had come to a cross-roads. Either he must seek an absolute in the intensity of his experiences and human activities, or he must follow the references which urge him forward, pointing towards a divine Other.

It is not our intention to depreciate experience of the sacred simply because it is poetic and participative but we wish to respect the genuineness of different attitudes. It is our business to disentangle the theme of religious experience from ambiguities and to dispel any confusion which may possibly arise from nostalgic longing for fruitful dialogue between Christianity and pagan religions.

We have no wish to pass hasty judgement on the religious evolution of non-western civilizations. No one can foresee what will come out of the melting pot of western techniques and ancestral traditions, 'pagan' religions and Christian missions. It is nevertheless true that western civilization, in promoting science and the economies of production, carries to the rest of the world ferments which attack the foundations of civilizations and traditional religions.

Pre-Religious Experience and Faith in God

The intellectuals interviewed by our research-workers deny religious experience but acknowledge certain personal experiences which we have defined as pre-religious. The direct object of these experiences is not God—neither the divine nor even the sacred in the strict sense of the word. Thus the terms 'religious experience' and 'experience of the sacred' are inadequate. Were we to use them at this point, we should risk stretching their meaning more than would be reasonably acceptable, and we should lead the way to many ambiguities.

These pre-religious experiences refer to the world and to existence—to the world as a totality; to existence seen as something supported and penetrated by a transcendent.

Scientific thought is conscious of its natural limitation. It does not explain the existence of the universe. The enquiring mind is led to the ultimate question: why do things exist? The world is silhouetted against the horizon of a reality of a quite different order which remains, for scientific reasons, a mystery wrapped in silence; man, instructed by a religious tradition, invests it with meaning: the mystery of a God-Creator. In so far as it is the realm of mankind, the world suggests a final perfection preventing the totality of human travail from slipping back into absurdity and nothingness. For human activities themselves are outlined against the horizon of another world, an eschatological horizon beyond time in the making. The Other only reveals his real identity after he has been deciphered by religion as being the utterly transcendent God.

Existence is not felt to be in complete possession of the principle of its own being; this is something it has received. We may take this perception as the grasp of a dimension in depth. Existence is profiled against the horizon of an Other; religious tradition has taught us to give this the name of 'God'. Existence is seen as basically good, and in spite of every vicissitude, change and contradiction, it offers mankind a chance to grasp at a thread of significant continuity; it appears as a gift of love. However naïve may seem the evidence of the subjects we questioned, we think it worth quoting them here, though it is possible that some readers will set against us the impression of meaninglessness, which so many have, of existence and the world. Our witnesses also have had experience of meaninglessness; but it is secondary and less important. The subjects who took part in the enquiry on Teilhard state that the existentialist theme of the absurd does not convince them.

Generally man feels his ethical quest to be the most personal of his works, and also as the work of some presence entirely beyond him, while the gift of existence has particular significance for his quest. We call this awareness experience, because it is an immediate perception of the nature of the world and of its foundation by another. It is a pre-religious experience because the Other is only known indirectly, through the medium of the visible upon which all awareness is founded, and in which it finds its origin and its perfection. The subjects of our enquiry tell us that in order to discover God in the visible, man must have learnt to recognize him. This recognition implies a leap beyond the barrier of immediate intuition.

Nature has been desacralized. But the universe as a whole, existence as such, have become indices of an Other, which is not just pure negativity, but rather the foundation, giver, perfection, and inspiration of the good.

The different moments of pre-religious experience can acquire heightened intensity. In a loved person, man takes hold of a gift so unique and so marvellous that reference to the Other becomes more urgent. Similarly a rift may develop between the ethical quest and its basic inspiration. Many people discover at certain moments in life an urgent need to be saved by a power which gives them, as it were, a 'soul supplement'. Pre-religious experience is modified by such particular and naturally intense experiences. Though fugitive, they are persistent and usually give deeper meaning to the common pre-religious experience.

The repercussion on our times of the message of Teilhard and other such writers indicates that modern man wants religious truths to be inscribed in human reality according to the cosmic, historical and humanitarian dimensions of his vision of the world.

There appear to be three essential traits which determine the modern intellectual outlook. In the first place, man rejects any individualism of inner consciousness; his aim is to re-objectify consciousness; he knows how deeply it participates in the action of natural forces working within him. Undoubtedly the displacing of man as centre in favour of the world risks leading him to a naturalism which would deny the specificity of consciousness, reducing it to the law of universal matter. But it may equally lead him to conscious self-insertion in the universe-in-becoming whose abysmal depths in space and time have been unveiled by the sciences. Man's participation in the advancing human collectivity is another dimension of his displacement as centre.

A second characteristic of the contemporary mentality, illustrated by Teilhard, is to be seen in man's entirely positive appreciation of the world and humanity; this is often a stumbling-block for the different forms of 'spirituality'. Modern man accepts his displacement as centre, he is willing to sacrifice his individuality but he also claims a conquering independence which henceforth will be exercised on the scale of humanity as a whole.

The third characteristic is the refusal of a sacred which would be alien to the world, separated from it, in conflict with it; a sacred which would be an outside intruder abolishing human history, setting up an exclusively vertical relationship.

Teilhard's synthetic, almost mythical, vision is a religious reading of the world which brings pre-religious human experiences into the religious discourse. Many, believers and unbelievers alike, are hesitant with regard to Teilhard's vision; those who accept it discover meanings which enable them to tie up the human with the religious. The concept of God is charged with an existential density; the divine reality stamps the mysteries which point towards it; the breach has been partly repaired. This twin element in Teilhard's vision explains the fact that it irritates and frightens as much as it fascinates. There are many people who fear that the human will once again be engulfed in the divine; others are worried lest the divine be reduced to the rank of idols and myths.

Note on Religious Experience as an Inward Experience of the Divine

In the foregoing conclusions we have used the term 'experience' in the sense of an intuitive perception of the signs of God. But for many contemporaries it conveys the idea of an immediate and affective contact with the divine; it still has the meaning conferred on it by irrationalist religious philosophy and inherited from Schleiermacher. For this reason the term 'religious experience' is the object of telling criticisms which attack its ambiguities. It is pointed out in the first place that God does not allow himself to be seen visibly; in a world which has been stripped of the primitive sacred, God is no longer immediately apparent. It is not possible, then, for us to have objective experience of God.

There remains the refuge of interiority. Man, withdrawing into himself, can foster the sense and taste for the infinite in the way described by Schleiermacher, finding its reflection in all surrounding nature. We may query the legitimacy of an affective experience of this type. Psychology points out both the sincerity and the illusion inherent in it.

In order to understand religious experience and make a psychological evaluation of it, we must first go into the question of the significance of affectivity. Sentiment links the totality of existence to the totality of the universe;[61] in faith and in anguish they both appear as either the gift of happiness or the brink of nothingness. Sentiment is a mode of comprehension of the universe and existence. When I am happy, I do not see the world as the place to which it should be possible to adjust my projects; on the contrary, it appears to be adjusted to them. Similarly the erotic experience discovered in the other body is at once the knot tying together all the values of the universe. Each experience sums up the universe and appears to drain it of every other meaning. The alternation of joy and sadness, erotic emotions and political passions, is enough to bring us up against the suspect nature of this apparently absolute intuition: is it really a valid revelation and possession, or is it nothing more than deception? The same absolute character helps us to understand how it is that every human value, political, scientific, erotic, aesthetic, may take on the aspect of a 'religious' value. Man gives up his whole existence to any such value with a fervour and exaltation which appear to some observers as the residue of forgotten religion. We should have to go into this more carefully before being able to say whether it is a matter of unrecognized or of repressed religion. For the time being let us simply bear in mind that, of its very nature, emotion has this character of the absolute.

The equation linking affectivity, the absolute and religion suggests the possibility of delusion. But it also indicates a possible emergence of religion in emotive experience that always offers a universal value. This implies that affectivity opens man up to the religious universe which, possibly, is conjured up as a mirage to fill a human void. Whatever the case may be, the avatars of affectivity largely determine the becoming of religion.

Secondly, affective experience is a direct hold on the world. To the guileless seeker experience appears to be a mode of awareness of the world, a way of living in it and, conversely, of being haunted by it; of giving oneself up to its pervadings. Phenomenologists are right, then, to return to things in themselves; in so doing they point out the intentional character of affectivity[62] as it reveals the world's qualities. In times of joy the world is seen to be in harmony with my desires; in anguish it reveals itself as built on nothingness. Religious experience is also a reading of the totality as the ultimate value of the whole of existence. This does not solve the problem of delusion. I may be sure, in religious experience, that I am rooted in the totality of existence; but once I start asking myself questions this certitude is shaken: am I not, finally, the subjective source of this apparent salvation? Is it not just 'projection'? If affective illusion is possible, where shall I find the guarantee of my religious experience? Does not magic bear witness to the possibility of a false reading of the world? Therefore experience is insufficient. We must, however, recognize its intentional character which is to make me aware of the qualities of the world and to show me its values.

The third characteristic we find in experience is its power to shake us up; it gives a jolt to our whole existence; the pathic nature of experience constitutes man's potential energy. Psychological theories are not in agreement over the question of the link between sentiment and action. We hold that the emotion manifested by the affective perception of a value (the hateable, the lovable, the dangerous, the sacred) is at the same time an appeal for a certain kind of behaviour. It is a tension of the subject who is shaken in his needs, his drives, his desires. Emotion is the functional bond between things and his tendencies.[63] The thorough analyses made by Girgensohn have brought out this basic unity of religious experience; a unity which is something far beyond any division of the soul into faculties. The dynamic aspect of affectivity will be dealt with at greater length in the next chapter.

To bring this summary of the psychology of affectivity to a close we can say that it is the natural seat of religious experience in the strict sense of the word. Religious affectivity carries man towards an undefined infinite which may equally well be an earthly, pantheistic, or even diabolic infinite. It is not surprising then that in our a-theistic culture, religious affectivity manifests itself mostly in earthly mysticisms. It is no longer the basis of a truly religious faith. We shall come back to this in the section on mystical tendencies.

The suspicion with which religious experience is regarded does not exclude adherence to pre-religious experience; the divine is not the object of this experience. In a desacralized world which still carries signs of the Other, God becomes silence; Bernanos has pointed out that silence is a divine quality. The gulfs between man, the sacred and God, leave room for another presence; that of the word of the Other. Religious discourse, whatever its nature, allows man to recognize in the Other a personal God. There would be no faith if the discourse held no reply for those awaiting one. The word can only pervade a place which already declares the Other.

In this personal relationship with the Other, the ambivalences of the sacred show up in another way. The *tremendum* and the *fascinosum* are personalized as reverential fear and acknowledgement of a God of grace. These themes invite us to make a step forward in our research and lead us to the symbol of the divine paternity.

The breaks which mark religious history have led us to discover a certain continuity; the same mental pattern relates actual pre-religious experience to genuine theist experience: the perception of existence as gift and as grace, and the consciousness that the universe is held in being by the Other. But modern consciousness of historicity, and the apparent efforts to accomplish some ethical work, introduce new, more dynamic elements. In the course of conflicts, critical reflections and experiences of all kinds, man has gradually come to purify his original intention and to adopt it consciously.

1 A. Lalande, *Vocabulaire technique et critique de la philosophie*, Paris 1947, 309–10.
2 We use this term in the sense of that which always underlies the voluntary: emotions, drives, etc. See P. Ricoeur, *Philosophie de la volonté. Le volontaire et l'involontaire*, Paris 1949.
3 See E. R. Dodds, *Les Grecs et l'irrationel*, Paris 1965.
4 *Discours sur la religion*, Paris 1944, 151.
5 *Der christliche Glaube*, para. 3.
6 *Discours sur la religion*, 152.
7 *The Idea of the Holy*, Penguin 1959.
8 *Vom Ewigen im Menschen*, Leipzig 1921, 550.
9 *Ibid.*, 360.
10 *Traité d'histoire des religions*, Paris 1949, 17, 18, 343, 344.
11 *La religion dans son essence et ses manifestations, Phénoménologie de la religion*, Paris 1948, 9–10.
12 *Ibid.*, 452–3.
13 The opposition between liberal Protestantism and Catholic modernism is described by E. Poulat in *Histoire, dogme et critique dans la crise moderniste*, Tournai—Paris 1962, 89–102.
14 The principal exponents of this view are F. Schleiermacher, F. Frank, R. Seeberg and G. Wobbermin.
15 *L'essence du christianisme*, Paris 1902, 152.
16 'Die Methoden der religionspsychologischen Arbeit', *Handbuch der biologischen Arbeitsmethoden*, VI/1, Berlin-Vienna 1928, 1–44.
17 *The Individual and his Religion*, New York 1953.
18 *The Psychology of Religion*, New York 1958.
19 See R. Aubert, *Le problème de l'acte de foi*, Louvain 1945, 703ff.
20 For a description of Christian experience see J. Mouroux, *L'expérience chrétienne*, Paris 1952.
21 *Pages de prose, recueillies et présentées par A. Blanchet*, Paris 1944, 277.
22 B. A. Baker, *Vers la maison de lumière*, Paris 1917, 239. See also *A Modern Pilgrim's Progress*, London 1906.
23 *Der Begriff der Angst*, ed. E. Hirsch, 144.
24 *Journal métaphysique*, Paris 1927, 57–9.
25 *Traité d'histoire des religions*, 15, 24–5.
26 *Ibid.*, 40.
27 M. Eliade, *Le sacré et le profane*, Paris 1965, 21 ff; K. Goldammer, *Die Formenwelt des Religiösen*, Stuttgart 1960, 190 ff.
28 This is the position of K. Goldammer, *op. cit.*
29 J. Goetz, 'Les religions des primitifs', in F. M. Berganioux and J. Goetz, *Les religions des préhistoriques et des primitifs*, Paris 1958, 113.

30 J. Goetz, *op. cit.*, 94 ff.
31 P. Schebesta, *Les pygmées du Congo Belge, ces inconnus*, Namur 1957, 173–4.
32 J. Goetz, *op. cit.*, 113.
33 M. Eliade, *Le sacré et le profane*, 15–17.
34 *Op. cit.* 22–3.
35 *Confessions*, XI, 9.
36 See A. Descamps, *Les justes et la justice dans les évangiles et le christianisme primitif*, Louvain 1950.
37 *La métamorphose des dieux*, Paris 1958.
38 *Der seelische Aufbau des religiösen Erlebnis*, Gütersloh 1930, 312.
39 See T. Reik, *Probleme des Religionpsychologie, I, Das Ritual*, Vienna 1919, 59 ff.; R. Caillois, *L'homme et le sacré*, Paris 1950, 125, 168.
40 M. Eliade, *Traité d'histoire des religions*, 29.
41 Goetz, *op. cit.*, 113.
42 *Les carnets de Lucien Lévy-Bruhl*, Paris 1949, 76.
43 M. Leenhardt, *Do Kamo*, Paris 1947, 50.
44 *The psychological structure of religious experience.*
45 *Ibid.*, 492.
46 *Das Gotteserleben in der Betrachtung*, Munster 1949; II, 83; XVIII, 5, 6, 20.
47 *The Individual and his Religion*, New York 1959, 13–14.
48 These interviews were made by G. Vercruysse while preparing a study on the faith of intellectuals. In these interviews the aim was to obtain answers to the following questions: what is the concrete significance, for intellectuals, of 'religious faith'? Do they practise what we might call the engagement of faith, and if so, how do they practise it? Is there tension between autonomy and faith? Is it possible to integrate them? A question on religious experience, in the sense that we take this expression, was also set. These interviews were intended as a preparation for further enquiries conducted according to other methods; as these are only as yet taking shape, we cannot use them here. We are well aware that these interviews give us a very restricted basis of information. However, for want of more complete data, we have considered it advisable to make use of the little we have, rather than trust entirely to the impressions we have formed as a result of contact with believers. We are encouraged to work like this by the fact that there seems to be a convergence between the two approaches: many conversations on the subject confirm the results of our interrogations and at the same time they show an attitude which written testimony amply illustrates. Moreover, it is our firm conviction that a few seriously conducted interviews of subjects who are representative of the spirit of the times are enough to give a vivid picture of the way in which the different elements of human experience and religion are inter-connected.

49 We give here extracts from three enquiries carried out with a view to obtaining the Licentiate in Education and in Psychology, and which were made under our direction and presented at Louvain University in 1963. The enquiries appeared collectively under the title *Contribution à l'étude objective de l'attitude envers Dieu. Construction d'un questionnaire et son application à un groupe de jeunes gens d'humanité* (G. Barelli), *à un groupe de l'enseignement technique* (J. Hermans), *et à trois groupes de jeunes filles—ouvrières, universitaires et élèves de l'enseignement secondaire* (G. Stickler).

50 *La question religieuse et le socialisme*, Paris 1959, 45–6.

51 The revised edition of 1965, translated by Bernard Wall and published by Collins, is that quoted here.

52 The Collins edition of 1960, translated by Bernard Wall, is that quoted here.

53 *Honest to God*, London 1964.

54 Michael Simonis, *Teilhard de Chardin et son public*, thesis for the Licentiate in Psychology prepared under our direction and presented at the University of Louvain in 1964.

55 See Léopold S. Senghor, *Pierre Teilhard de Chardin et la politique africaine*, *Cahiers P. T. de Chardin*, Paris 1962, 19, 40.

56 P. De Meuter, *Images-situations d'aperception thématique*, thesis for Licentiate in Psychology, Louvain University, 1964.

57 See *The Varieties of Religious Experience*.

58 *Sociologie de la religion*, Paris 1955, 19.

59 *Die Sinne und die religiöse Erkenntnis*, Würzburg 1950, 52.

60 *Die Bekehrung des Aurelius Augustinus*, Munich 1950, 72.

61 M. Arnold, in his *Emotion and Personality*, New York 1960, 1, 142, 171, insists upon the intentional nature of emotion, which is always appreciation of an object. M. Heidegger has developed the idea that the affective disposition (*Stimmung*) links us up with a set of beings; see *Vom Wesen der Wahrheit*, Frankfurt 1943, 18, 31.

62 Sartre has strongly developed both the thesis of the intentionality of emotions, and that of their magical deceptiveness; see *Esquisse d'une théorie des émotions*, Paris 1948.

63 This is the thesis of A. Michotte and K. Lewin, see M. Arnold, *op. cit.*, 164, 178.

CHAPTER 2

RELIGION AND THE PSYCHOLOGY OF MOTIVATION

The religious man asks himself a question: does the name 'God' which he gives to the mystery and gift of religion cover a personal reality? Is heaven anything but a void? The believer realizes, much more than does the unbeliever, the immense abyss which lies between his intention and the Other to which it refers. All things considered, nothing is absolutely guaranteed. How could it be otherwise? Certitude is a subjective state corresponding to the evidence of the object; but 'faith is of things unseen'. The problem of illusion lies at the very heart of faith. Not that faith is uncertain, but it is always question and assent, constantly renewed in the obscurity of the unseen. In order to define the precise status of religious faith we should need an epistemology analysing in detail the different forms of doubt and certitude. It could be based on the epistemology of the relationship with others as this is achieved in speech and in love. Philosophers and psychologists know how difficult a task this is.

We have a more restricted aim. It deals solely with the question: why is man religious? If the religious man does not read the design of Providence in things, with the certitude of evidence, why does he go beyond the confused signs of the world? What is the psychological movement which carries him beyond the evidence offered by the world toward its perfection and its foundation in God? Or is this faith rather a result of some intellectual approach?

It is from the standpoint of psychology that we ask the question 'why'. The query about faith is indeed a double one. The believer has motives based on reason; faith rests on these motives. But if faith transcends them, it is because its motives are not merely theoretical. They relate to desires, wishes; to things which belong to the order of 'values'. If this were not so, God would only be the supreme speculative abstraction whereas in fact, the God of religion is both the God whom man affirms with his reason, and the God who gives meaning to his existence. But what is the significance of the words 'meaning to his existence'? This is the very question upon which the psychology of motivation would shed some light.

The scientific question posed by the psychologist concerning the motivation of religion links up with the question asked by the religious man. However, in so far as the believer's question is asked within the framework of religious faith it does not take the same form as the psychologist's question. For the religious man, the question is contained within the bounds of his conscious intention and his religious quest. It is inspired by an active seeking after truth. It is not neutral, though it may mean to be quite clear. On the other hand, the psychologist puts brackets around the question of religious truth. He aims at being an objective and neutral observer. By that fact he goes beyond the scope of the question as the believer poses it. He examines subordinate problems, and influences of which the believer, in his conscious intention, is unaware. Nevertheless, psychologists would make a mistake if they were to ignore the believer's motives; they are intrinsic elements of lived religion. Nor would the psychological gaze be any more objective if it remained aloof from the religious attitude and its motives.

These antinomies, outer and inner, objective and subjective, unconscious and conscious, contribute to the extreme complexity of the psychological term, motivation. The real answer lies beyond both behaviourism and introspectionism. We are led, then, to the necessity of clarifying the term, motivation; we have to justify our idea of it and the limits which we think should be set to the attempt to explain religion by studies in motivation. Only then shall we be able to tackle our own problem.

I.   Psychological Theories of Motivation[1]

The aim of psychology is to observe outward manifestations of psychic phenomena and to understand them. To understand is to know the reason why, the motive: the origin and the goal. Motive may be briefly defined as a specific force which is both directed drive and directed attraction.[2] Motives justify every human activity because, even from birth, man forms projects. The dynamic unity of the human being has been defined according to logic by the tripartite division of human faculties into knowing, feeling, willing; a distinction first proposed by Wolff and Tetens. Feeling is a pathic element and is only one aspect of the exchange between the subject and the stimuli of his inner and outer environment. It is the inner repercussion, the intimate appropriation of the stimuli felt by the subject and to which he responds by an active movement. The stimulus provokes the feeling, sets off a corresponding mode of behaviour. But will is something much more than conscious and deliberate movement. Acts of willed decision are only radiating centres in the confused mass of involuntary movements towards others and towards the world. Moreover, no deliberate act could be effected if it were not based on the projects which precede and feed it. The complexity of motivation arises from the dynamic relationship which is established between spontaneous movements, the ego and the world. In me every action is first done of itself; it precedes me. However, because it is within me, I participate in it; I accomplish it; I make it mine, even if in the first place and to a considerable extent I undergo it. On the other hand, my action is directed towards the world; I belong to it and in it I realize my projects. But I also receive these from it, since through its stimuli, the world rouses me to awareness of my projects and of myself.

The term 'motive' is as old as are ethical considerations; it designates the explicit intention which releases and directs behaviour. Recently, it has been given a scientific status by Anglo-Saxon psychology. The concept 'motivation' has become an objective term expressing not only conscious processes, but also those which precede, condition and determine conscious intentions. And, as always, in science, an operative concept—in our case, motivation—acquires numerous meanings according to the theoretical systems to which it is annexed and according to the method used.

The Images of the 'Religious Need'

The scientific psychology of motivation was born of a double reaction—against introspectionism, and against the reduction of motive to the sole conscious project. It sets out methodically to observe and interpret modes of behaviour as objective facts. In this perspective, motives are deduced from external behaviour and from the conditions of observable stimuli.

Influenced by behaviourism, the objective psychology of motivation even tends to exclude from its field anything which is not strictly observable. Such, for example, are the psychic processes which clinical psychology, particularly the German schools, have analysed with great precision: drive, feeling (*Stimmung*) wish, desire, project, decision. Combined with the predominant influence of McDougall's hormetic theories, the objective psychology of motivation tries to define the whole array of psychic dispositions which activate the subject and direct him towards his various objects. These are the needs or specific aspirations such as hunger, thirst, sexuality, self-assertion, sociability, parental instinct, need for rest and so forth. Thus the study of motivation becomes the study of the types and varieties of motives, of the conditions of their release and of their objectively verifiable intensity.

Since the majority of adults are religious and since religious behaviour seems to be a genuine entity, observable, measurable in its external manifestations, we are obliged, in accordance with this motive psychology, to invoke a religious need or aspiration. The religious need is, then, one of a dozen or more fundamental needs which make up the psychic apparatus of the normal adult.

Far be it from us to depreciate the strict analyses which try to detail the spectrum of patterns of human behaviour, to measure their intensity and discover the correlations by which they are dominated. There does, however, seem to be a danger that the new psychology of motives, in a display of fine words, will simply relay the old static faculty psychology. Observable phenomena are only legitimate sources of psychological knowledge if they do not immobilize human dynamisms in needs, aspirations or faculties conceived of as being little automatons at work within us. To fall back on the religious need as the final psychological explanation would be to lay ourselves open to the sarcasm which *virtus dormitiva* inspired in Molière.

Certainly, motive psychology is aware of the exchanges between the subject, led on by his needs, and the environment which conditions him. But, marked as it always is by behaviourism, it tends to reduce these exchanges to mere learning, as we can see from the elementary imagery which it uses. It speaks of the canalization of needs, of their following the route traced by learning. This suggests that needs, basically undirected, are orientated by education, acting as a sort of a pipe-line, in the precise directions we observe.

This psychology is still very dependent on unconscious dogmas inherited from ancient genetic mythology. The verifiable fact of religious behaviour in no way authorizes us to postulate a natural religious need. Either the religious need is nothing more than a label for a certain type of observable reaction, or else we consider it as a phenomenal and puzzling fact about which we have to acquire some psychological understanding of its origin and its exact nature. But to confer upon it the status of a self-contained motive on the basis of actual patterns of behaviour observed as external facts, is to imagine the existence of an original psychic entity. And thus we bar the way which motivation psychology aimed to open up.

Moreover, do religious subjects practise their mode of behaviour as arising from a specific need? So far, investigation has never been able to confirm this—quite the contrary. It can of course be pointed out that objective psychology does not have to bother about conscious intentions since these motives do not fall within its limits of felt introspective experience. Even so, it would be very strange if the concepts elaborated by psychology had nothing to do with real behaviour. There is no difficulty in speaking of the need for food or rest; in these cases psychology is based on actual experience and is able to observe its immediate presence in the pattern of behaviour. This shows, surely, that the supposed motives, or the irreducible needs, are thought out from instinctual needs, simple in origin and limited in bearing, directly observable both in their content and in relation to the stimulus. But the more human motives, such as the supposed religious need, do not produce evidence of an instinct. They are integrated into the totality of the developing person. Here we are no longer dealing with permanent elements which can be bound together to make up the psychic apparatus. Furthermore, the fact that man may become religious, remain a-religious, or pass from religion to atheism, without harming his psychic apparatus, makes the probability of an inborn specific religious need all the more doubtful.

The Danger of Monist Psychology

The psychology of operational motives may be set up against a psychology which considers the person as a dynamic unity. Less scientific in its operative concepts, less subject to the demands of an illusory ideal of pure objectivity, the latter nevertheless aims at remaining faithful to strictly psychological objectivity and thus accounts for behaviour by the study of fundamental tendencies emanating from the centre of the subject. This in no way means that man is identified with his explicit consciousness. To dissipate any misunderstanding on this subject, it will be enough to recall Freudian psychology.

The psychology of the person has a long tradition: Nietzsche, Freud, Adler. But these names alone warn us of the danger it carries with it: the danger of monism. It has a tendency to explain every mode of behaviour by a single fundamental dynamism: will to power, desire to impose oneself, etc. We could speak of an arborescent psychology. Even Freud did not escape the reproach —quite unjustified—of pansexualism. And there are certain religious thinkers who are inclined to regard all human activity

as solely the masked or derived manifestation of desire for God.
This gives us a metaphysical interpretation of man made familiar
to us by the Platonic tradition and transposed here into the terms
of psychology. Certain psychologists of today would even claim
that mental illness derives from a religious factor which is active
by its absence. God, it would seem, is the real unconscious
demanding recognition by the subject on pain of exposing a lack
of religion by mental disorder. The connection between mental
health and religion can be justified, so they say, by theological
roots in the unconscious. To be sane one has to be a saint. Thus
the theme of the religious need is given a sort of mythical magnitude and its vagueness helps to give an appearance of profound
psychology. From the point of view of psychological science this
type of monist interpretation smacks of pre-scientific mythology.

We must try to find a middle way between the positivism of
motives conceived of as entities, and the monist tendency to
explain man by reference to some ultimate power. G. W. Allport[3]
vigorously condemns the arbitrary nature and the inanity of the
various lists of instincts which have been attempted. He quotes
the instance of the psychologist C. C. Bernard who, as early as
1924, had made an inventory of fourteen thousand different
instincts mentioned in the psychological literature of that period.
Allport credits them with nothing more than an entirely pragmatic
utility. Adopting the theories already set out by Goldstein and
Maslow, he believes that one can only fully account for personality by reference to another principle underlying the action of
each separate motive: the principle of self-fulfilment, closely
bound up with the independence of the ego. This alone will allow
a psychological growth unhampered by any conflict; this alone
enables us to understand the functional autonomy retained by
the different active tendencies in relation to their origin.[4] And
when psychologists emphasize the specifically human lack of
direction, and the human quality of openness to the world,
they echo anthropologists who consider man to be the least
'programmed' being of the biological kingdom.[5] Existential
philosophers, setting out from an entirely different point, state
that the nature of man is to be without any specific nature.[6]

It is not our intention to resolve this contradiction; all contemporary psychology of personality is centred on it. But it
assumes such importance in the realm of religious psychology
that it is necessary to hit upon some solution, however hazardous
it may be. What is the basis of religion? Nothing is to be gained
from postulating a hypothetic 'religious need'. But if religion is
nothing else than one of the many possible expressions of a more
general tendency underlying all the others, we are no better off,
for this would deprive religion of all character.

The psychology of C. Rogers provides an eloquent proof of
the ambiguities entailed by every recourse to a basic psychic force
defined solely by its power of growth. Rogers suggests that there
exists some 'flow of experience' which bears the subject forward
in his different activities.[7] He believes that the essential therapeutic
process consists in overcoming fear and in progressing by direct
experience and by the expression of the 'flow of experience'. In
order that experience may develop and express itself fully the
therapist must constantly refer to it. If the circumstances favour
the therapeutic dialogue which, according to Rogers, is in fact a
monologue, the subject develops in a constructive process. We
do not deny the value of 'client-centred therapy' but we wonder
what is explained by this sort of psychology. What is to be learnt
by calling upon a vague, indefinite force which may lend itself to
anything? But this determined way of centring everything round
an immanent principle of growth and experience is part of
Rogers's religious agnosticism. He himself, moreover, drew the
consequences of his theories: having discovered that honest folk
can have widely differing beliefs, he abandoned the religion of
his parents.[8] There is nothing extraordinary about this discovery,
but the conclusion Rogers comes to is significant: since nothing
counts but inner sincerity, what is the importance of convictions
and the structuring of behaviour? If the only thing that matters
is the expression of the 'flow of experience' why should we face
reality and its structures?

Monist psychology, at least as far as its applications to religion
are concerned, joins motive psychology. It sees religion as an
emanation of the subject himself, a spontaneous realization of

some psychic force at work within him. That is exactly what we may well call psychologism; a sort of psychological idealism, younger brother to epistemological idealism.

Towards a Genetic Psychology

Religion can be explained on the plane of motivation neither by an autonomous function (the 'religious need') nor by a single process (the self-realizing ego or the expression of interior experience). In order to avoid the rift between the too general and the too particular, certain psychologists make use of the concept of situation, while others use the concept of drive. This is the solution proposed by the psychologist Lewin and by psychoanalysis. There are many other psychological theories which could be quoted, but we shall have to restrict ourselves here to directing our research and its perspective.

Lewin[9] aims at reintroducing into psychology the concepts of end, of teleological activity, and tries to link them with the idea of situation, defined as the total assemblage of those facts of the 'outer world which are able to call forth a response from the organism'. This does not mean that the situation is an independent variable; it is the outcome of an exchange between the interior experiences of an organism and external factors. Thus, if the directed action of the subject is bound up with his concrete situation, scientific psychology must avoid the elaboration of general concepts which would merely take over from Aristotelian essences. It must turn to concrete, individual facts and build up genetic conditional concepts able to qualify homogeneous fields of psychological facts. Consequently, leaving aside the 'religious need' which can be justified by no scientific approach, let us examine the situations and the concrete facts of religious activities; let us try to discover their purpose and elaborate concepts which are able to express the homogeneous fields observed.

The situation is part of the definition of religious dynamic development; it results from the interior experiences and structures in which the subject engages himself. These concepts can be explained more clearly by an example taken from the preceding chapter on religious experience. The food-gatherers, members of the most primitive of known societies, pray to God as Creator and benevolent Father. When the economic situation changes, when the horde becomes a clan of shepherds, then religion is greatly changed too; the religious sense adapts itself in conformity with the new situation. And this, in its turn, creates a new religious sense. In their new situation, the subjects engage themselves in other structures.

There is, then, only one way of following up our study on motivation: it is to study the link set up between directed religious activities, that is to say their intentions, and the situations by which they are conditioned.

We consider motivation as something which includes the subject's history; this leads to a genetic study of motives. Aims are moments in a process of becoming. This genetic study can be pushed very far; no one has ever gone as far as has Freud in the search for human motives and their developments. Led by his clinical experience to go back to the breaking-point between the normal and the pathological, he has elaborated a psychology of anthropogenesis: by what dynamisms and structures does man, a being made up of drives, develop into a human being? Were we to speak of pansexualism here we should, to say the least of it, take a surprising short cut. Freud acknowledges the multiplicity of human interests and motives; but, in trying to understand their interaction and vicissitudes he comes upon the fundamental dynamisms: the two or three elementary drives (libido, self-preservation and death drive) underlying all the numerous motives which, adapting themselves according to the laws of the conflicts and exchanges of the situations they go through, produce the sentiments, the desires, the multiple tendencies of the healthy or the mentally ill person. Normal human becoming is carried out in dynamic structuring; through conflicts, identifications and sublimations, a personality is born, and the ego in act emerges from impersonal forces: 'there where "it" was, "I" shall become'.[10]

No one who gives a moment's thought to the major themes transmitted by religious tradition—happiness, guilt, anxiety, the prohibition of homicide, the desire for immortality, and especially the father symbol, knot of every dynamic structure in man—can possibly doubt that religion has to do with drives and their history. But this still does not imply that a study of depth psychology must necessarily give us the final answer to the reason for the religious phenomenon.

In our study of motivation we shall proceed in two stages. First we shall pass in review some of the studies which have been devoted to apparent, observable motivations. In a subsequent chapter we shall tackle the more radical question of the profound genetic explanation.

The religious man turns to his God for what he expects of him: protection, immortality, happiness ... Man also speaks to God, of course, because his presence cannot be ignored. Respect and request, worship and desire are the two aspects of the religious attitude. They are closely intertwined and lead to the many phenomena whose morphology we can track down. But where is the predominant movement? Where is the first dynamism? At the beginning of the century many theories were put forward to explain religion. The theory of motivation makes a contribution without pretending to be exhaustive. Religion, it is true, is a psychic act and therefore has something more before it than an object (in the psychological sense of the term, an objective unity directing behaviour); it also results from the tendencies which surge up within the subject. The object in view corresponds with the intentions of the subject. The question arises: do active intentions determine the object? Or is it rather the contrary which happens? Or, again, since the religious man lives his relationship with God as an encounter, are both possibilities true? That is to say, God arouses active intentions in man and at the same time man's requests and desires actualize a certain presence of God.

The question of motivation, it can be seen, opens out on that of the illusion or the objectivity of religion. Often the problem has been obscured by the unscientific use of badly formulated or indefinitely extended psychological concepts, such, for example, as the concepts of projection, archetype, etc. Any attempt to provide an answer will have to define the concepts used and state precisely in what measure they account for religious phenomena.

This principle underlies the analysis which follows. We shall examine successively the different vectors which determine the religious dynamic and which are expressed in theoretical concepts. The question of illusion will crop up of itself when we attempt to regroup the major themes running through the religious field.

The observable motivation, we have said, is defined by the concrete relationship set up between the object followed and the given situation. A religious mode of behaviour is an activity transcendentally directed in response to a definite human situation. Is there a dynamic vector common to the different religious orientations and specified by their respective situations? Perhaps. But we must not begin by reducing the more complex facts to a pattern which could appear too simple.

Our method is determined by our conception of motivation. What the subjects themselves say is indispensable to us for it is that which will tell us the direction they take. This does not mean, however, that we are falling back into a psychology based on introspection; the verbal witnesses are placed in the concrete context of their situations. In other words, the subject is no more explicitly conscious of the motives for which he addresses God than is a child of the reasons for which he loves his parents. Psychology is not out to collect avowals, to record and classify them into categories. It is an interpretative science. In linking the lived situation with the quality of the object aimed at in a given situation, it brings to light the unreflected motives underlying behaviour.

II. Motives Underlying Religious Behaviour

RELIGION: RESPONSE TO FRUSTRATIONS

The Stoics of old knew that the non-satisfaction of desire, whether desire of possession, of lasting love, of personal recognition, or any other, is the fundamental suffering of human existence. They also knew how insatiable man is and they proposed a remedy of inner liberty based on renunciation. Religious apologists, similar to the Stoics in some ways, and yet very different, claim to offer the real solution: all that man can desire is to be found far surpassingly in God. And as few men really do desire God, they are told to learn to desire him; God is the hidden object of their desires and so they should seek to convert their too human desires into religious desires.

For the psychologist who does not think of the human reality in metaphysical terms, human desires retain their importance. He remarks that man can become religious in order to find a response to desires which are first of all purely human; they have an earthly aim; they are not directed straight to God, but take a vertical direction in the hope of finding some human satisfaction in it. Thus the religious attitude would seem to be born of human dissatisfaction. In this case then, considering the link between the first intentions and the objects of their search, we might ask whether religion is not exhausted in this deflected human quest. Does not the conversion of the human aspirations into religious demands engender a purely functional religion, a religion stripped of any autonomous consistency and value? It is all very well for certain psychologists to say that their explanation leaves room for a metaphysical justification;[11] it remains true that in this case, religion, born of frustration, is marked with the stamp of inauthenticity. This is the brutal conclusion which Freud and Marx have drawn from their theory and which they treat as being henceforth a firmly established fact.

Frustration may be defined as the absence of response to a need or a human desire. Strictly speaking, frustration is the term given to an active agent, one which deprives the subject of something which is due to him. The word was brought into the technical language of psychology by the French and English translators of Freud in order to render his *Versagung* which forms an antithetical pair with *Befriedigung* and expresses the refusal which the reality, the situation, or a person may bring to bear on the satisfaction, the pacification of a drive. The dissatisfaction is not merely occasional, it is coextensive with the drive. This is open and can be matched by no object; without being arbitrary, since it is directed, the drive finds no adequate object which could gratify it with full satisfaction. Thus, by its very nature, the drive introduces into man an essential dynamic which, though directed, is never polarized by an adequate object.

It is not surprising then that man's basic dissatisfaction is the hollow into which religion fits. No one has expressed this better than St Augustine: 'My heart is restless till it rests in thee.' But, for St Augustine, this essential emptiness has a purpose; it is God himself who hollows it out in man by his hidden presence: St Augustine attributes to him these words: 'You would not seek me had you not already found me.' But before we tackle the problem of basic dissatisfaction, we must consider its special manifestations; they are more evident and more openly determine religious behaviour.

These few lines on frustration will help us to avoid the pitfall of anecdotal explanation which lies in the path of every psychologist. Frustration does not arise from an occasional accident in life's course. Even in the very special field of well-defined desires it is always the fundamental frustration which comes to the surface. Like the drive itself it has a thousand faces which haunt us like the masks of a James Ensor.

Distress and God as Providence

We introduce this theme with an argument taken from Freud. It expresses very well, clearly and distinctly, the religious act which proceeds from a feeling of frustration experienced in moments of great distress in life: 'We understand how a *primitive man is in need of a God* as creator of the universe, as chief of his clan, as personal protector . . . A man of later days, of our own times, behaves in the same way. He, too, remains childish and in need of protection, even when he is grown up; he thinks he cannot do without support from his God.'[12]

According to Freud there are two kinds of frustration particularly mortifying to human desires: society inhibits drives and nature opposes them with the inexorable law of fate. Man himself constitutes society and in that he finds his humanity. But at the bottom of his heart he is always in revolt against it. Contrary to Marx, Freud does not believe that a complete reconciliation between man and society is possible. Man will always feel cheated in his desires and his liberty.[13] One wonders whether the theme, so often found in literature, of the man who finds he is an outsider in relation to society, has not, in fact, shown that Freud was right. Moreover, he justifies his realistic observation by retracing the genesis of the individual from the moment when the tie linking him to the sources of life and plentitude was cut. Society has nothing to offer in compensation for the resulting conflict and privation but the promise of religion. In the life to come the individual will receive a hundred-fold in return for his pains here below. Furthermore, religion offers the only possible refuge for man in his helplessness in face of all-powerful nature. Illness and every kind of failure urge man to ward off his fate. He does so by masking it with the tender and comforting features of an all-powerful human being. He attributes consciousness and intentions to nature so that he may pray to it, implore it, ask of it protection and satisfaction. Such attributions are furthered by certain psychic processes. In moments of distress, for example, man becomes a child again and primitive tendencies re-awaken in him. Spontaneously he attributes human intentions to nature, which he submits to the conjuration of incantational prayers. Returning thus to the affective state of childhood proper to certain primitives, the religious man believes that his need for protection and reward is effectively answered by means of the intervention of an all-powerful Father. He transfers his own magical inclinations to God who will do what man has discovered himself to be personally incapable of doing.

Freud is well aware that in this theory he is following along the lines of a long tradition of criticism. But he renews the criticisms of classical rationalism by basing them on the data yielded by psychological analysis.

Certainly, there are many religious forms which do not effectively correspond with this analysis. That has always been known. But we must take into consideration both the truth and the limits of an explanation of this sort based on motivation. Practical studies of the religious attitude in distressing situations will help us to see the question more clearly.

Stouffer[14] has observed that during the last war, in the thick of the fray 75% of American soldiers found help in prayer. The recourse to religion dominated every other thought: hatred of the enemy, the outcome of the battle etc. . . . Those who prayed the most were those exposed to the greatest danger: infantry-men, those who in the out-posts were under cover of fire from their own batteries, or soldiers posted to a new unit. It is significant that the percentage of those who most feared being killed followed the same pattern. The intensity of prayer in distress is not affected by differences in education.

These statistical facts will not surprise anybody: they merely serve to confirm a common experience. Prayer is often the cry of a threatened man. The same enquiry showed that religious intensity follows the danger curve to a certain extent. When ex-soldiers were asked if the war had made them more religious their answers varied according to these percentages: more religious, 29%; less religious, 30%; no difference, 41%. The replies of soldiers who had had no fighting experience were respectively 23%; 35%; 42%. On the other hand, for 79% of the soldiers who had been on active service there was an increase of actual belief in God; while for 17% there was a decrease; for 2% of the soldiers in this category there was no change. The figures for soldiers having no experience of active combat were respectively 54%; 17%; 29%.

We should note the ambivalence of these experiences of distress. On the whole, the group of subjects showing an increase of religion and the group showing a decrease balance each other. But belief in God has considerably increased. A discrepancy of this sort can be understood if we admit that 'more religious' means more actively religious, attending religious services and praying more. Another enquiry undertaken by Allport[15] throws some light on the ambivalence of the effects resulting from an experience of distress. Soldiers who had become less religious said that the death of practising believers and the horrors of war made them sceptical; the others felt that prayer helped them. Allport concludes that the experience of war weakens traditional church religion but intensifies the basic interest in religion.

We propose the following hypothesis: an equal number of

subjects experience the efficacy or the inefficacy of their prayers. The efficacy of prayer corresponds either to the impression of having been effectively protected against danger from without, or to the experience of regained tranquillity; these two ideas are more or less connected. As to the experience of the inefficacy of prayer, it is clear that it refers to a non-intervention of Providence. It is then an effective intervention for which the subjects had hoped. Frustrated in their religious hope, they abandon all religious practice. And yet, more often than not, their belief in God is strengthened. What else does this mean but that their basic religious conviction not only is unaffected by the negative experience, but that it even gains in depth? It seems then that religious practice corresponds to an almost miraculous idea of divine Providence. Is there any connection between the two phenomena: disappearance of a rather magical idea of Providence in times of distress and deepening of faith in God? We find here a purification of the religious attitude and there is nothing anomalous in the fact that the deepening of personal faith in God is accompanied by a decrease in religious practice. Religious orientation takes precedence over practices which are meant above all to compensate for, and overcome, a feeling of frustration.

We shall have to conclude, then, that faith in God must have other sources than magic belief in Providence, even if, in its early stages, this belief should give some concrete shape to the idea of God.

A second type of study can check the theory that religion is an answer to frustration; the study consists of enquiries made by means of attitude scales in which the items describe different existential situations; the replies express the degree of religious intensity felt by the subject in these different situations. We have already mentioned this questionnaire which we elaborated and applied with the help of our collaborators.[16]

The questionnaire comprises a scale to which we have given the title: 'God as someone who gives material aid.' The pre-enquiry had already thrown some light on the question. 50 Italian working-class women who were interviewed provided the following frequencies: of a total of 84 spontaneous evocations of God 40 look upon him as material aid and protection in distress, (the words 'Providence' and 'Father' appear respectively 9 and 3 times); 13 spontaneous evocations concern the moral help given by God; 13 mention the power and majesty of God the Creator. The same question set to 180 students of classical humanities (11–18 years) gave the following results: 15% speak of material difficulties; 41% of moral difficulties; 4% of happy circumstances; 7% of moments of joy; 7% of beauty of nature. It should be remarked that happy circumstances are almost always mentioned with unhappy circumstances, in the same sentence, but generally in second place. One has the impression that even here it is distress which starts off the spontaneous religious movement and that, after avowing as much, the subject tries to cover up by adding the association, joy—God, in order to conform to the nobler religious attitude which he has been taught.

The enquiry as a whole does not bring out the predominance of the category 'God as material aid'; this does not prevail in any group. An attitude scale should, of course, reverse the hierarchy of percentages; it does not deal with modes of spontaneous religious behaviour but a more lasting disposition. Within the category 'material aid', the varied responses nevertheless remain significant. In the Belgian female population, the highest percentages are spread out in decreasing order from workers to technical pupils, then from pupils of modern humanities to those of classical humanities and, finally, university students. Belgian working-class women, who enjoy easier conditions than the Italian women, give less emphasis to the material help given by God. Boys from technical schools give it more importance than do students of classical humanities. We can say, then, that the material conditions of life determine the importance which subjects give to the providential intervention of God in material difficulties. And it is in situations of material hardship that the religious sentiment is most readily provoked.

In order to test the theory of frustration we also used, in collaboration, a semi-introspective technique inspired by Welford's works.[17] The subjects were invited to let their imagination react to ten given situations: four pleasant, four frustrating, two ambivalent. For each situation they were asked to note different psychological impacts: the intensity of the emotion, the first reaction, the reference to another, the intensity of tendency to prayer. In the Belgian group, both for the men and for the women, the difference in the averages between the intensity of tendency to prayer in pleasant situations and in unpleasant situations was mimimal. The Latin-American group, however, showed a marked tendency to pray more in frustrating situations. For the men, the combined average of intensity of tendency to prayer was 2·34% in pleasant situations and 3·17% in frustrating situations. For the women the figures were respectively 3·70% and 4·28%. Men of the Belgian group rated 3·13% and 3·38%; the women 3·30% and 3·40%. But all the subjects put the same three frustrating situations at the head of the list and in the same descending order: (1) a drowning at sea; (2) a woman waiting at the head of a collapsed coal pit where her husband has been working; (3) a father beside the bed of a dying woman. It was also in the situation of drowning at sea that the greatest number of subjects said they would think of God: 8 out of 37 in the Belgian group, 15 out of 71 in the Latin-American group. At the bedside of a dying woman 7 out of 87 Latin-Americans would think of God; none of the Belgians would do so.

With all the subjects, the strongest tendency to pray was shown in situations of very great distress, when they were faced with death, especially their own death, or were in mortal danger. And here, prayer was not a substitute for human action. Among the subjects who showed a marked tendency to prayer, 54% expressed an active reaction (struggle, for example) in face of danger; 29% expressed a subjective reaction (hope, resignation); 17% expressed a passive reaction (despair). Among the replies showing a weak tendency, or none at all, to prayer, there were 33·5% expressing active reactions; no subjective reactions; and 66·5% expressing passive reactions. Prayer is, then, first of all a cry for help coming from a struggling man; it is very much less a process for subjectively changing the situation by resigned acceptance.

We may draw the following conclusion: the frustrating situation is not the only one to arouse a religious response. However, with all subjects, danger of death provoked the most frequent tendency to pray, that is to say, to call upon supernatural help capable of supplementing failing human forces. If we consider the situations taken as a whole, pleasant and frustrating, religious impact varies with the nationalities; education and cultural climate would seem to have a great influence on the religious attitude.

All the enquiries confirm an individual experience: situations of extreme mortal danger, and more generally, human helplessness in presence of material distress or sickness, are the most powerful pistons of spontaneous religious behaviour. Religion plays the part, among other things, of compensation in relation to frustrating experiences. Prayer is largely a cry for help. In the measure that man feels himself to be threatened in the realization of his most primitive desire, the will to live, he tries to ward off fate by an appeal to an all-powerful Father. Even the sceptical are tempted to pray in moments of dire distress.

Such behaviour is not to be despised, but we can attribute to it little religious significance. It is just as simply natural as the will to live. Shaken in his most primitive feelings, as soon as he sees he is forced into a situation which has no natural issue, man rushes into the supernatural world. Freud saw that very clearly; distress wakens in man the magic belief in a Father who is able to do everything and who supplements human helplessness. When man is at bay he rediscovers his all-powerfulness by proxy, so to speak. Debased religion? Shall we say rather: the most primitive spring of religion. It is only debased if man is caught in his own trap. The danger is real. Does not the concept of God as Providence evoke for many religious people the idea of a Father who saves in every extreme situation? How many Christians have thought out divine Providence in the strictly evangelical perspective of Christ? Extreme situations can awaken in man the profound sense of existence utterly dependent on God. In the abyss created between desire and satisfaction, man can discover his finitude. When his existence crumbles he feels that it has no foundation of its own. But the trial is affective and of the nature of a drive. And so is the first reaction: affective belief.

Let the distress cease; the desperate appeal risks being immediately forgotten. The behaviour resulting from such drives does not, of itself, lead to the recognition of a personally accepted God. Between the cry to God and a personal religion lies the same long distance as separates the first falling in love from formal engagement.

The close connection between basic drives and such prayers is also shown up by the reaction of revolt or indifference which may be provoked by what is seen as an eventual deception. We have already mentioned the religious scepticism observed among American ex-soldiers.

This analysis has been confirmed by our own enquiry.[18] We noticed a marked decline in religiosity between the ages of 16 and 19; for 6 of the 9 categories (or sub-scales) there was a significant difference of 1% for the average between 16 and 19 years. The categories: fear, revolt, belief in God as Creator, remained unchanged. And for the items concerned with recourse to God as Providence when in difficulty, we noticed that the older subjects did not easily admit the intervention of God. The ambivalence of their feelings was clearly revealed; many still admitted the principle of a prayer of demand, but they confessed that they practised it very little. They hesitated between the desire for independence and the need to be helped. Let us recall at this point that the adult intellectuals who were questioned, formally denounced this kind of religious behaviour.

The results obtained under the heading 'revolt against God' are also eloquent. In the female population we noticed a very significant difference between the two groups whose answers about God as a source of material help were especially notable: the workers and the university students. The former subscribed frankly to the items expressing feelings of resentment towards God when they met with suffering. Revolt is a negative expression of the imperious expectation that God will intervene since he is supposed to be good and all-powerful. Prisoner of a primitive religious emotion, the subject can just as easily turn against God as towards him. In reality, true religion can only be the fruit of purifying reflection.

Social Alienation and Belief in Another World

Freud denounced 'the discontent in civilization' (1930)—civilization which never fully succeeds in being reconciled with man even though it is his work. By his psychology of drives Freud makes the Marxist critique an absolute. For him mutual recognition among men will not eliminate the essential discontent in civilization, because it has its source in the dialectic of drives. That is why, in the Freudian perspective, the institution of a perfect society will not do away with the conditions for the rise of religions and their development. According to Freud a secret and profound discord between society and the individual will constantly create the void where, so long as man has not stoically accepted the necessary frustration drive, religion can always appear. It springs from the essential insufficiency of the primary drives in relation to their objects. In his will to live and be happy man inevitably comes up against the refusal of nature and the restraint of society.

Marx and Freud agree in recognizing religion as a solution of evasion and substitution; they diverge, however, in the way they account for its formation and its real meaning. Freud sees that religion has a doubly pacifying function; by setting up an ethical code it reconciles man to a certain extent with society and offers him consolation with belief in another world, heaven. For the moment we shall deal only with the second function. Marx regards the life of religion as an imaginary realization of heaven on earth; a visionary realization of the human essence. Cut off from effective communication with men, for actual recognition the believer substitutes an ideal, imaginary communication. Religion will disappear when man has broken down the alienating factors of society and set up the reality of true human relations. The Marxist society will be the realization of aspirations to which religion gives imaginary expression.

The two theories conceive of very different forms of the processes of substitution. For Freud, the man who seeks the satisfaction of his drives and absolute liberty is not bent solely on recognition and the establishment of peaceful relations. Deep down in his being he conserves veiled consciousness of his revolt.

Thus, he transposes into an entirely different world the desire for a harmony which will satisfy all his contradictory aspirations. Freud regards heaven as the recompense for every frustration. Marx, however, does not attribute to heaven any major importance. For him, religion is the ideological anticipation of the sole aspiration at work in man: peacefulness in social communications.

We are faced, then with two very different theories of religion as a phenomenon of substitution arising from a sentiment of social frustration. Common human experience, however, has not failed to recognize the merits of Freud's thesis. It is very much easier for mankind to count on the consolations of a world to come than to face present reality as it shows itself in the precarious conditions of living, in trying human environments, in constant exposure to sickness and the threat of war. But we must acknowledge the ambivalence of such frustrations, for if it is possible for them to metamorphose into hope aspiring heavenwards, they can just as well lead man to revolt against God. However, Freud's analysis does not stop there; it discovers in religious experience some hope of a transcendent recovery of all the good things which have to be given up in the present life; God, judge and rewarder, will do this for us. In the absence of detailed studies on this element of the religious attitude, we can put forward a criticism arising from the earliest Christian tradition; amongst others, the parable of the workers of the eleventh hour exposes this form of religious hypocrisy. And, since Nietzsche, it has become a commonplace to decry the mercenary spirit of pious folk for whom heaven is bought with religious devotions. But we may well ask ourselves just how far this instinctive expectation can go—of winning a reward from God at the cost of numerous frustrations which we have put up with by conforming to the ethical code of life in society. We must not forget that resentment is one of the most violent of forces and one of the hardest to uproot. To see this we have only to record the spontaneous reactions to a theological reflection on the meaning of the parable which we have just mentioned: 'What is the use of religion, then? Is it still worth sacrificing oneself for? Why try to rise above the good things of this world if God seems so indifferent to good and evil?' This exacting demand for divine justice is, without any doubt, one of the most powerful levers of religion, and we cannot deny that in the early stages of development the experience of frustration and the hope of recompense do play a functional role.

The sociological data of religious behaviour is too complex to lead to a conclusion, on the sole basis of such statistics, for or against the thesis of either Freud or Marx. If Marxism had been able to set up an atheist society without having recourse to violent persecutions, history would perhaps have been able to provide an outstanding argument in favour of the theory of Marx. Unfortunately, the Marxist leaders have shown no faith in his thesis of religion. The differential studies on religious practice make interesting contributions and oblige us to go further than the over-simple Marxist schema. Let us mention only two undeniable facts: the most actively religious populations in America are drawn from the middle classes: in England from the upper classes.[19] These sociological facts do not, of course, exclude the possibility that Marx's thesis may have some application in what concerns the religion of the lower classes. But, whatever may be the case, social frustration does not suffice to account for religious phenomena; there are other relevant factors. We must take into consideration, for example, historical and cultural traditions, education and, possibly, as we shall see later, psychological motives bound up with the maintenance of social order.

Marx's thesis, moreover, does not lend itself to ready use in psychology, because it presents a metaphysical interpretation of religion: it outlines a consciousness which has not yet arrived at the truth of its intuitions. If the establishment of a perfect social order were to uproot religion decisively, then we might possibly recognize in it a verification of the Marxist theory. But, again, we should first have to refer this fact, as did Marx, to a Hegelian framework.

Considered as an incomplete point of view, Freud's thesis of religion as a response to social frustration lends itself more directly to objective verification. It does not involve the subconscious taken in the fullest sense; and it does not offer symbolical interpretation on the metaphysical plane. In order to check Freud's thesis it would suffice to measure precisely the weight given by the belief in a God as rewarder to the religious attitude as a whole. It is regrettable that no such study is available to us. The doubts which afflict many subjects when the question is openly brought up, and the temptations which they then feel to abandon any religious practice, incline us to give considerable importance to this primitive motivation of religion. Man willingly makes a contract with God on the basis of strict justice. And for Christian theology the notion of divine justice is very complex; there is, finally, no purely logical synthesis of the facts of revelation to contain it.[20]

There is a certain type of religious sect which offers us an interesting field for study in that it combines social frustration, belief resolutely fixed on the beyond, and the setting up of a new brotherhood. It is not our intention to give a comprehensive explanation of the religious sect. There are various studies which have more or less established its typology in pointing out its multiple ties. A sect always appears as a dissenting and charismatic religious minority, but the causes of its formation may be numerous. Milton Yinger[21] classifies them as follows: (1) personal factors; (2) variations in political and economic factors within the group; (3) national and racial differences; (4) profound and fast-moving social changes overthrowing established order; (5) differences resulting from the development of the religious system itself (doctrinal and liturgical conflicts, for example); (6) the presence of the leader in crucial decisions.

After the differentiated sociological analyses, the theory of Weber, Troeltsch and van der Leeuw, who regard sects as regroupings of the religious élite, is only one possible view. There is no doubt that a sect is a charismatic reaction against the institutionalized Churches. But we must also grasp what it is that the charismatic mind seeks, and what it refuses. Some sects instruct Negroes simply to continue living out their ancient, more emotional and more spontaneous cultus on the outskirts of society. Their own sensitivity and their ancestral memories keep them away from the main Churches whose rather obsessional institutions and rites prevent emotions and religious traditions from creating appropriate forms. But there are some sects in which psycho-social elements give a characteristic role to the charismatic mind. In the United States sects have multiplied as a result of the mingling of races and Churches, and under the influence of wars and economic crises.[22] Similar situations in our times are causing the same phenomenon in Latin-America. Several writers[23] have shown that the sect is able to provide immediate relief where there is social distress, but more often than not, in segregating its followers, it diverts their attention from real social problems. By way of example we can mention the case of the Puerto Ricans who, on arriving in New York, join the Pentecostists en masse.[24] For these unadjusted aliens the sect is a community which saves them from the deep anxiety of anonymity; there, at least, they have the opportunity of belonging to a society. Simple ritual, a common tongue, fellowship discovered in the experience of the same suffering, these provide the elementary setting where they can find a means of identification. Furthermore, in organizing themselves on the fringe of official societies and their big churches, they receive a religious indoctrination which makes a theme of, and justifies, their separation from a decadent and perishable world. Among the followers of Krishna, 'son of God', Catton has distinguished two groups of listeners: the curious, and those who are seeking truth. The latter frequently read the Bible and often think of the next world. Generally they are people who have suffered greatly from the war or economic crisis; socially isolated people, tried by personal and family failure. Detailed studies of the 'sectarian' personality have underlined the affective springs of this sort of belief. Cohn[25] speaks of a fixation of adolescence manifested by the excesses, the instability and the insecurity of this type of personality. Their rigidity has been described. Delay[26] remarks that he has noticed in a group of 'Christ's Witnesses' an extreme rigidity towards self, a strong defence against their own pathological deficiencies. To social isolation, these characteristics add a more or less morbid psychological dimension.

The relationship between the social situation and this type of belief is clear enough in the case of sects for us to be able to check the theses of both Marx and Freud on the link between social frustration and religion. Does the sect not offer its followers a world of the 'heart' which they cannot find in their natural environment, and compensation for earthly frustration in directing hope to another world? Truth to say, neither of these theories is entirely applicable to the sect type; but we chose the sect as illustration because it offers the closest conformity with the situations envisaged by Marx and Freud. The sect is typical of a form of religion which is not compatible with the great religions and is set up in opposition to them. A sectarian is one who decides against the Churches. He gives his religion a meaning which it does not have in other cases: that of an opposition to the world. Rejected by society, deprived of economic sufficiency, socially ignored, this type of sectarian offers a model religion for the application of the Marxist schema. It also illustrates the process described by Freud: the expectation of heaven is a recompense for the social hostility by which the sectarian is taunted. But it should be understood that sectarians seek a human bond in an actual group just as much as, and even more than, they hope for satisfaction of their desires in heaven.

Social frustrations have some part to play, then, in the case of certain specific religious phenomena. More generally we agree with Freud in thinking that the secret hope of a reward in the next world for every restriction which man suffers for the sake of making society viable, is a powerful factor in belief and religious behaviour. But the impact it has seems to vary with different historical situations and in relation to religious education and the critical spirit. In our age there are many, even among Christians, who reject as unworthy the idea of a God who rewards good and who takes revenge for evil.

In order to judge the psychological significance of the Marxist thesis we should need a comparative study of sects and Churches. We do remark, in fact, that the Churches, in their relations with the world and society, are the opposite of sects. These, moreover, never cease reproaching the Churches for this difference. Churches aim at universality, they want to be integrated with social and national structures.[27] They put a value on the world and thus appear to the sects as a detestable compromise. Whatever may be the case, the incompatibility between these two attitudes destroys the apparent links of causality which Marxism claims to recognize between social failure and religion. It also allows us to judge the concepts of religious alienation and illusion. If the relationship set up between the Churches and the world is not mere concession to weakness, but militant truth, it becomes clear that the faith of the Churches does not seek to substitute itself for the reality of world and society. It fits in with it, acknowledges and furthers it while endeavouring to contain it within temporal bounds. The theme of withdrawal from the world which was so prevalent in primitive and medieval Christianity, does not arise from social frustration, but from the much more deeply-rooted movement of religious desire to which we shall devote a later chapter.

Moral Misery and God as Consoler

In the series of writings which Freud has devoted to religion, *The Future of an Illusion* is a sort of interlude of a rather more rationalist type than some. In this work Freud follows Hume's *Dialogues Concerning Human Religion* which opened the way to the criticism of the Age of Enlightenment. In his other writings Freud adopts a more strictly psychoanalytical line of research; religion is presented as being, up to modern times, the most suitable means by which man can assume his guilt.[28] We shall take up, in the next chapter, the discussion on the genesis of guilt and the emergence of the father symbol which is connected with it. In this present section our starting point is the guilt which dominates the human world. We should like to ask in what measure it requires a remedy of the religious order? The links between religion and guilt are certainly dialectic. For Freud, guilt is as wide-spread as humanity. Being connatural to man in his work of humanization, it weighs on every human existence. Structurally, guilt precedes religion of which it is one of the genetic foundations. Once it has established itself and given rise to religion, then religion in its turn liberates from guilt. Symbolic warden of a guilt which is connatural to man, religion may well crush its followers beneath the weight of repressive legalism. But these possible excesses must not lead us to ignore the powerful means of salvation which it offers.

On the level of established religious conscience, the Freudian theory provides an explanation of religion by referring it to conscious guilt. Leaving on one side, for the moment, its profound genesis, we need only remember that guilt is one of the psychological motivations of religious behaviour. Educationalists, pastors and clinical psychologists will certainly not dispute the truth of this thesis. Furthermore, practical enquiries have been able to measure the incidence of psychological guilt in religious life.

Researches carried out by Gilen into the psychology of adolescents have very shrewdly brought out the sentiments which go to make up guilt.[29] They are, in order of importance, a feeling bearing down upon the subject with the force of a weight he is compelled to carry; an oppressive anxiety urging the subject to self-expression and self-liberation; a remorseful conscience; fear and anxiety, chiefly about being found out, which give rise to a tendency to run away and hide; and depression, which often goes with solitude. The reference to God is decidedly less frequent than reference to self and to society. There is nothing surprising in this; guilt as most people experience it is the psychological and moral guilt of a subject up against standards of behaviour taken from surrounding society, and from which he builds up the ideal of his ego. Guilt appears in the first instance as a state of mental laceration, or inner discord.[30] Because of his faults, the subject feels he is condemned by both his own moral prompting and that of society. Summoned to appear in this twofold court, he feels anxious, forced to confess, to make reparation or to escape to depressive solitude.[31] For believing subjects, the moral authority of society is above all embodied in the religious order because, in the long run, it is founded on God's law. The reference to God is, then, indirectly present. It would, however, be a mistake to speak of a strictly religious guilt as long as man has not the explicit consciousness of sinning before God. Sin, the religious fault, is judged according to the criteria of divine holiness; this is both demanding and merciful; purifying and always ready to forgive, to renew the covenant of love. Let us not make any mistake about it: true religious guilt is the end of a long spiritual journey. At that stage it is free from any affective burdening which, on the merely human plane, paralyses and isolates. A clinical and phenomenological analysis would show up the immense chasm separating the sense of sin from the narcissitic wound inflicted by psychological guilt.

Gilen's enquiry shows that confession seems to many to be the most adequate means of reparation, it has the highest ratings for religious references. We cannot see from the texts quoted whether, in this instance, the idea of God as eternal judge already enters into the sentiment of guilt; it is very probable that it does. But what does come out very clearly from this enquiry is the idea of liberation and reparation by means of confession. Religion is seen to be, then, the foundation of moral laws, and the means of pardon and rehabilitation. Practical psychology can never verify the Freudian thesis according to which guilt is the source of religious belief; but it does confirm that the experience of guilt is a powerful factor in religious practice.

To bring this survey to a close, we must once again go back to the enquiry which we ourselves carried out in Belgium among several hundred adolescents. The results throw light on another aspect of the relationship set up between moral wretchedness and religion: recourse to God's help. The enquiry does not enable us to compare witnesses to belief in divine Providence with evidence of the passage from psychological guilt to religious remedies. But at least it has allowed us to pinpint the fairly noticeable factor, God as moral help, in the general picture of the religious attitude.

The pre-enquiry already indicated the importance of this factor. The question, 'Do you think of God at times when nobody is speaking to you about him?' was set to 180 boys and girls, students of the classical humanities. The positive answers given were in the following percentages: in moral difficulties, 31%; in material difficulties, 15%; in happy circumstances, 11%.

In contrast to these results, of a hundred boys from technical schools who took part in the pre-enquiry, only 8·5% mentioned moral difficulties. Among Italian working-class women interviewed there was an almost complete absence of the feeling of guilt.

The enquiry itself, covering 1,800 subjects, confirmed the difference already observed between students of humanities and technical students (averages respectively 41·7% and 45·7% with a significant variation of the order of 1%). This difference lessened with age (from 16–19 years). In the two streams, representative of different cultural environments, the factor 'moral help' was more prevalent than all other factors—material help, fear, God as Creator, etc. A detailed analysis of the replies also allowed a comparison between boys and girls. Boys were more taken up with the fight for good and the effort to avoid evil. They had a greater desire for God's help, and were more readily grateful for effectual help in temptation. But, also, they were more easily discouraged, and found God's help less efficacious. The girls, on the other hand, suffered more from a feeling of loneliness in which they sought more for the comfort of an understanding and consoling God. Among the boys, the presence of God was less felt.

It is easy to recognize here the elementary facts of differential psychology: subject to erotic and aggressive drives, the boy is more preoccupied with the moral struggle than is the girl. She, however, feels much more strongly the personal presence of the Other, and experiences longing in his absence. It is difficult to understand Argyle[32] when he says that it is obvious that grown women suffer more than men from the feeling of guilt, which explains, so he says, why, among Catholics, they go to confession more often than the men. As far as we can see this is rather the effect of three characteristics of male psychology. First, men are less inclined to show their inner feelings in public; secondly, they are less active in religious practice because they find religion more of an embarrassing dependence than do women—and confession is certainly the religious act in which dependence is most clearly expressed; a third cause, which is usually less remarked upon, is that grown men have experienced their powerlessness in avoiding moral faults, and they more frequently resign themselves to this. As psychological guilt lessens, the sense of sin often becomes less acute and consequently confession no longer seems so urgent. Our enquiry showed that there is progression, in this respect, with advancing age. The nineteen-year-olds turn less frequently to God for help because they feel it to be ineffectual. They give up supernatural support since experience has taught them that it does nothing to change the human condition.

In every one of the examples we have quoted, the functional role of religion is undeniable. Bowed down under the weight of wrong-doing, suffering from consequent moral isolation, the young people studied by Gilen expect pardon from the Church and rehabilitation in the ethical society. The adolescents whom we questioned turned to God chiefly in order to obtain from him help in the moral struggle or consolation in affective solitude. The older subjects who have acquired greater self-confidence, who are more realistic as to their moral capacities and, probably, a little freer from erotic anguish, have recourse to God less often. It will be objected that other factors may have repressed living faith in them, leading them to conduct the moral struggle with less confidence. Examination of the replies we received leads us to think that it is the contrary which happens. It is because they wish to realize their personal ethical ideal which is, of course, understood in reference to divine law, that the younger subjects cherish a special hope of God's help. But belief in moral help from God decreases in the measure that self-assurance and realism grows. There is, moreover, confirmation of this in an experience which worries many a religious educationalist but from which few draw the obvious conclusions: for many young people, religious practice, which is essentially bound up with their moral efforts, follows a curve in inverse relation to their emotional stability. Educationalists who take advantage of the moral situation of young people would do well to reflect upon the future they are thus preparing. True, a functional religion is not completely devoid of religious value; we cannot fail to remark, however, that the link between moral miseries and religious practice reveals the effects of an almost magical belief in divine almightiness; this belief is analogous to the one we have observed also in the appeal for divine help in distressing material circumstances or matters of life and death.

Death and Immortality

Death is the most painful wound which nature inflicts on man. In the nineteenth century, scientists could still harbour the illusion that one day they would be able to overcome death. These were vain hopes: every man knows that he has an appointment with death. Man's existence is rooted in the biological, and therefore draws its sexual and parental density from its insertion in the life and death cycle. But man, a personal being, conscious, self-concerned, refuses to find his end in nothingness; he aims at breaking down the barrier of death, and he draws energy for his revolt from the vital drive of self-preservation, as powerful as it is blind.

We may ask whether the profound hope which refers to 'eternal life' is one of the springs of religious belief. Is religion the cry for help which man, in a movement of passionate and unreasoning trust, addresses to an all-powerful Father to save him from nothingness? Freud was convinced that it is. Man, absolutely helpless in face of death, rediscovers the attitudes and fanciful beliefs of a child or of the primitives. He ascribes a kindly intention to fate and hopes for eternal protection and happiness. The anthropologist Malinowski[33] also attributed to religion the role of adjusting man to his mortal condition.

It is a fact that people having once passed the halfway house of their life, *in medio vitae*, discover with horror that they are on the edge of the abyss, and that one day, wearied by an overlong trek, they will finish by collapsing and tumbling into the void. Many enquiries have shown that from this moment they become more religious. The first of these enquiries, made by Starbuck, bears witness to this.[34] Among the motives which the subjects themselves have alleged, Kingsburg[35] mentions the 'certitude of immortality' which comes to have more importance with advancing age. Even those subjects who were hostile to religion and to any form of religious practice, gradually came to affirm their certitude of some immortality: 100 per cent of the subjects over ninety did so.[36] Taking another line of approach, clinical experience has convinced C. G. Jung that an adult can become ill for quite other reasons than a young person. What worries the older people is no longer conflicts arising from drives, but the significance of life and the question of death. The man without religion receives no reply. The therapy practised by Jung aims at restoring a certain religious sense (as Jung thinks of it) to the patient; this is the only remedy for anxiety about death.

However, in general, the rate of belief in immortality is lower than that of belief in God.[37] The difference is as much as 39% in Australia, 35% in Great Britain, 31% in Sweden; it is lowest in France, 8%, where belief in God is also lowest, 66%.

The history of religions gives us considerable supporting evidence of this. Belief in immortality has assumed many faces, but two tendencies gradually emerge as stronger than the rest. The mystery religions where the initiate was given a guarantee of immortality, were wide-spread through the Hellenic and the Graeco-Roman world. In other places the bond between religion and ethics tended to become stronger; where there was belief in re-incarnation or in metempsychosis (Greece and India), as well as where there was belief in resurrection (Judaism just before the Christian era, and then Christianity itself), what happened in the next world depended on fidelity to the moral code here below. It should be noticed that in the religion of Israel belief in resurrection was a late development and there were two elements which certainly helped it. Political and cultural circumstances favoured a keener awareness of individual existence, while integration within the community no longer sufficed as an answer to the persistent quest for personal happiness. At the same time belief in a personal and faithful God revealed the lasting nature of the pact which God had made with his people; here, belief in Providence preceded belief in immortality and gave it its theological foundation. The metaphor of the resurrection of Israel after the Exile (*Ezek.* 37) led on to the new doctrine of the individual resurrection of the just.

9

All things considered, anxiety in face of death, and the desire for immortality, are much less powerful motives for religious behaviour than Freud believed. What could be more different than the call to God for help made by an adolescent and that made by an old person? There remains, however, an undeniable common basic element: divine Providence appears the best resort in actual felt distress. In the measure that man becomes aware of being on the way to death, as much in the history of civilization as in the course of his individual life, the desire for immortality becomes more urgent, it gives a fresh foundation and a new content to belief in God. In support of the truth of this statement, we have only to consider the questions asked by unbelievers. For them, to renounce God very often means the agonizing perspective of a void at the end of life's journey.[38] Their resignation, stoic or revolted, gives us the counter-proof of the motivational bond between anxiety in face of death and religious belief.

Even here we could say much about the value of a religion which draws its strength from a very human desire for immortality; but we will keep our critical reflections for the end of this chapter. We merely give here the criticisms which many believers have themselves brought forward. They are perfectly aware that a desire for immortality anchored in vital drives has no guarantee of effective realization. Philosophical arguments that insist on the dualism of soul and body, are not any more convincing. A new philosophy of immortality, setting out from more existential considerations on the nature of the person, will and love, seems even less conclusive from a logical point of view. In the long run, their purely human convictions would lead these believers to share the clear-sighted resignation of unbelievers. But it is in this human wilderness that the proclamation of the gospel message re-acquires its strictly religious significance. It offers a promise of which the sole guarantee lies in faith in the God of Jesus Christ. Thus the movement is in reverse: God is no longer the instrument of some hope aroused by human passions. He is the word of the promise, spoken to the man who goes forward into the light. Those psychologists of religion who wish to reduce such a belief in immortality to nothing more than something originating in human drives err by over-simplification.

RELIGION: WARDEN OF ETHICS AND SOCIETY

In 1958,[39] French citizens aged between 18 and 30 years old were asked this question: 'Do you, or will you, give your children a religious up-bringing?' The answers received were: yes, 75%; no, 11%; no reply, 13%. Those who gave positive answers proferred a variety of motives. The most frequently given was the weight of tradition: 30%—'because it is customary'; 'because it is a family custom'; 'because it is part of family education'. Then there were the ethical reasons: 28%—'because it gives a moral code'; 'it helps a better up-bringing'; 'it is a guide, a help in life'; 'it makes them respect their fellow beings'; 'it is a way of showing them certain humanly social values'. Religious conviction only inspired 12%—'so that my children will be believers'; 'to assure their salvation and their eternal life' . . .

These statistics must be considered in relation to other facts furnished by the same enquiry. The majority of subjects, 73% in fact, believed in God, 62% believed in the divinity of Christ; 10% stated that they prayed very frequently; 19%, frequently. The religion of these subjects was not an expression of hypocrisy, nor a planned reckoning. Nevertheless, the very poor interest in an authentically religious education of children showed more clearly than anything else the highly functional nature of this religion—that it was motivated by purely human needs and interests. The subjects had recourse to religion in order to solve social problems though they would probably not have accepted so crude a statement. It may be, too, that many of the subjects, faced with our motivational interpretation, would have pulled themselves up and made an attempt at purifying their religion. But as long as religion for God was not separated from religion for man, we would have no right to speak of the latent authenticity of this religion. A man is recognized in his acts and his self-expression, in the complexity of his effective intentions. This leads us to think that we are not minimizing the subjects' intention as expressed in their replies. In their particular situation as educators, responsible before a family and society, the majority of these young people make use of religion as an educational service. We may justly suspect, then, the at least partly functional role which they assign to religion in the other expressions which we have cited.

Dostoievski's words, 'If God does not exist, anything is permissible', are well known, as also are the use and misuse to which they have been put by educators and apologists. The conviction that ethics is a purely human affair has long since been established. Obviously, man cannot set up a relationship with the most holy God if he does not humanize his existence by his ethical practice, but he carries within himself, as the principle of his humanity, an exigence for justice and respect for others. Moreover, these values are such autonomous human realities that more than one moralist has seen in them the clearest proof of the existence of God.

This appeal to a divine foundation of ethics is not the pursuit of an ultimate metaphysic or of religious finality. It springs from a human desire for some insurance against the risks of ethical practice. We may see in it the effect of the permanent tension between the individual and society described by Freud as one of the mainsprings of religion. According to him, society, necessarily frustrating, has three means at its disposal for recompensing the individual for the sacrifices it demands of him: the promise of a reward in another world; on earth, the setting up of a moral ideal with which the subject may identify himself and thus satisfy his narcissism raised to a social plane; finally, also on earth, the consecration of moral laws by the prestige of some divine authority. For Freud the calling upon divine authority is a narcissistic compensation. We do not doubt that there is here a powerful motive helping man to pass from ethics to religion, but we think that it is much more a question of an unconscious motive. As to the lived intention, man tries to guarantee his ethic. The bond between ethics and religion is, then, predetermined: it obeys two distinct psychological motives: the need for security and narcissism.

The ethical motivation of religion is probably not totally

unrelated to the preference of certain societies for certain religions. M. Weber, in a well-known study on religious sociology, *The Protestant Ethic and the Spirit of Capitalism*, has tried to show that capitalism results from the humanized, 'worldly' faith of puritanism. But, to our way of thinking, new technical and economic situations do not simply find the possibility of development in a certain type of religion, they also condition religion and give it a style and orientation which furthers and justifies them. The American sociologist Yinger[40] states that the liberal Protestantism of the American Churches reflects the political conservatism, the nationalism and the spirit of progress of the upper classes. In our opinion, the mentality of these conservative social classes which put their confidence in the promises made by technology is such that they are not satisfied with the self-expression possible in liberal Protestantism without giving it principles of justification. It is for this reason that in these societies the atheist is looked on with suspicion.

In *The Two Sources of Morality and Religion* Bergson has well described this link between ethics and religion. He sees nature as creative of a closed or static religion for biological ends. Spontaneous religion is 'a defensive reaction of nature against the dissociating power of the intellect'. It assures the cohesion of the group by restraining the individual. To this closed, static religion Bergson opposes the quite different, open and dynamic religion of the mystics.

RELIGION: ANSWER TO INTELLECTUAL CURIOSITY

We have never met a religious faith manifestly motivated by purely intellectual research. It is probable that man is astonished at the universe in which he lives and has his being. But if philosophy is the child of wonder, religion is scarcely so. When man asks himself vital questions about his existence, it is in order to orientate himself: he is not content to be merely a meaningless passing apparition. He tries to find his bearings on the map and to know where he is going. The intellectual quest feeds on the desire for immortality; there is a need to know what man must do. In our opinion intellectual curiosity can find three satisfactions in religion. In the beginning, the desire for immortality was predominant in gnosticism, the religious movement prevalent in the Graeco-Roman world of the first Christian centuries. It purported to liberate its followers from the weight of matter and to lead them to immortality. The knowledge which it spread abroad was a mixture of theologico-philosophical speculation and initiation into mysteries. It was believed that the knowledge of true human nature, veiled by matter, was liberating in itself. Man was supposed to find salvation in complete inner liberty, by his speculative initiation and its accompanying asceticism. Gnosticism was a closed system. The initiate, unaided by any divine grace surging up *in history*, unveiled and conquered the mystery of the world by his own power seconded by some revealing force. From time to time there is a revival of gnosticism in religious movements which favour a certain aloofness from the culture of their times, and isolate their followers by grouping them into conventicles of mystery initiates. Christian Science and all theosophical movements are part of these gnostic trends. It is extremely difficult to distinguish the presence of gnostic tendencies in religious belief. It would seem that, generally speaking, it is barely perceptible. The desire for initiation and participation in the veiled mystery of the world probably belongs more to a specific psychological type, the mystic type which will be discussed in the next chapter. The present orientation of civilization hardly favours its development but such tendencies continue to be among the possibilities permanently open to man.

The intellectual quest for an ethical design seems to have a greater part in religious adhesion. As we have already shown, man often turns to religion for the answers to two ethical questions which can be posed in Kantian terms: What must I do? What may I hope?

But religion satisfies yet a third intellectual motive: it offers man a reference-point by which to orientate his existence. For Freud the catechism is a sort of traveller's guide for the journey through life. Doubtless, believers themselves are hardly aware of this influence of psychology on religion. But clinical experience teaches us that man feels an imperious need to orientate himself in an organized and restricted world.[41] A world without guide-lines for the beings and functions in it is a mad world in which no personality can exist. Formerly it was the function of myths and symbols to organize the world and to designate man's place in it. The cosmos and society seemed to be an ordered and reasonable whole in the heart of which man was appointed a well-determined role. This meant that he could identify himself, recognize his personality and his specific functions from the simple fact of his being integrated with a significant whole. He had his own function, and by that he felt linked up with the whole. To orientate oneself demands a definition of role and of one's link with the organized whole. There is no doubt that religion, even today, can still offer man this organizing interpretation of existence. Of course, this sort of motivation for the religious attitude very rarely comes to the subject's notice: it is too deeply ingrained to appear on the surface of consciousness. But it is the underlying inspiration of many a partial motive, such as the desire for immortality, the search for absolute ethical assurance, the appeal to Providence. We do, however, believe that a strictly intellectual element unites and overlaps all these particular motives. It is the desire to find functional stability in the universe and a significant link with the hierarchical whole. Intellectual curiosity is sustained in this matter by a vital desire. In his theory of the world, man seeks a relationship of natural and necessary conformity with existence.

The intellectual quest at work in religion is not, in the first place, purely speculative reason; the history of myths, of phil-osophy or of theology is there to prove it. In the beginning the myth was nothing more than a naïve, pre-scientific propædeutic to philosophy or scientific theory. The ætiological preoccupation with the explanation of natural events, such as the rhythm of the seasons or the origin of the world, is secondary in relation to the function of orientation and revelation. Paul Ricoeur says, 'The first function of the myths of evil is to encompass humanity as a whole in an archetypal story . . . Through the figure of the hero, the ancestor, the titan, primordial man, the demigod—the lived reality is set on the path of existential structures . . .'.[42]

The real intellectual quest comes into relief against this existential background to which it is heir. But, built up into an autonomous theorizing function, it no longer has the same power as the original myths and living religions. The history of metaphysics does not give us the impression that it interprets a properly religious aspiration. It takes up living religious traditions and sets out to purify them. Such was the case with Plato, Plotinus, St Thomas, Hegel, and later with Heidegger. Philosophy, even religious, often takes the place of religion. There is a reason for this: by its intention, its own laws of reflection upon the essential structures and the conditions of the necessity of phenomena, it is led quite naturally to eliminate the lived relationship with the Other. Metaphysics thinks, or criticizes, the totality. Of itself it does not bring in the infinitely Other who bursts totality asunder in a non-reciprocal relationship. Religion, on the contrary, sets up a unique relationship between man and the Other. Pascal's opposition between the God of philosophers and the God of religion is still very significant, even if we do not judge Descartes to be 'useless and uncertain'.[43] Religion and philosophical research belong to two entirely different orders and intentions.

ANXIETY AND RELIGIOUS SECURITY

Anxiety is the fundamental distress of mankind. It is the night companion of all his major difficulties, material troubles, morbid sufferings, fear of death. It is all the more disturbing in that it is anonymous, silent, unaccounted for by reason. Faced with his troubles, man can put up a fight against the enemy who comes to him in open warfare. But when no known circumstance can be found to warrant anxiety, the defence movement gropes about in the void. It is then that anxiety becomes subtly all-pervading. Kierkegaard remarks that this anxiety differentiates man from the quadruped far more than does the upright position. Heidegger finds in it the experience of void from which springs the ontological questioning about the being of beings. This implies that anxiety is not necessarily pathological. Certain well-meaning psychologists may be led by a rather sublime ideal of the perfectly balanced and adapted man to identify anxiety with pathological disorder. Certainly, every pathological symptom covers and reveals a latent anxiety; anxiety underlies every neurosis and psychosis.

We would be the very last to dispute the disastrous effects which anxiety may have on religion. But we feel justified in asking whether anxiety, of itself, is necessarily morbid. One may as well identify sexuality with a pathological condition since, in the long run, all mental sickness arises from some disturbance in the sphere of the libido.

These preliminary considerations give us a setting for the question which we are now going to tackle: is it the function of religion to protect man from anxiety?

This is a most complex problem because it is practically impossible to measure anxiety as such. All one can do is to pick out individual manifestations of it. Practical psychology only grasps it in single and limited forms which it defines and investigates: timidity, guilt, fear of accidents, anxiety in face of death, etc. . . . Psychoanalysts know from experience that true anxiety can loom up unexpectedly; like a ghost, of unknown origin and having unknown designs, it is suddenly there in front of the horrified and fascinated subject. And, absurd as it may seem to phenomenologists and to non-analysing psychologists, there exists a truly unconscious anxiety; not only is it not seized upon reflectively as a conscious state, but it bears on no quality of the world. It is revealed solely by the secondary movements which it causes; a kind of stupor, withdrawal, phobia . . . All these processes can only be interpreted as defence movements against a nameless and repressed anxiety. The measure of the repression determines the pathological nature of the anxiety.

Scales and psychological tests have been elaborated for measuring anxiety intensity. But, from what has just been said it is clear they can only be applied to a more or less manifest anxiety. We are not quite happy about the way in which these methods detail the concepts of disquiet, fear, free-floating anxiety, covert anxiety; they are all unattached concepts, and it is not easy to appreciate just what these tests claim to discover.

In fact, the psychological reality of anxiety is too multiform and fugitive to be captured in a single static form.

To take another point, it is surely not enough to say that anxiety provides a motivation for religion. Anxiety as such leads nowhere. It is neither drive nor desire. It bursts in when the subject is bowled over by the force of his inclinations; or when their forbidden nature threatens him with mortal danger. It is the alert sounding in the very heart of the subject when he is on the verge of fainting, or when he feels menaced with destruction or with falling into the void. According to Freud's final theory,[44] anxiety precedes repression: the vital danger which his drives may represent leads the menaced subject to repress them.

We can understand that religion may appear as a solution for man at bay. The rites which it proposes can help him to ward off the anxiety of psychological guilt; it may even offer him the means of consciously redeeming himself, if he is conscious of having sinned before God. In times of distress, the religious man turns to his prayers in order to implore protection from the Almighty. By its moral code religion authenticates sexuality and consecrates the nobility of an act which otherwise may be seen as a transgression of taboo. The hierarchical ordering which religion introduces into life gives man the measures and standards which he needs for his subsistence. When death comes, religion offers the promise of a blessed eternity.

There is no human tendency which is free from the possibility of anxiety. And every one of them can find its fulfilment, the principle of its stabilization and of its justification in religion.

Thus we may ask whether, finally, to set religion in relation to anxiety is to do nothing else than to study it in its connection with the human drama. Who has ever doubted art simply because, according to A. Malraux, it is supposed to be a challenge to death? or love because it is supposed to vanquish fear of death?

To state that religion is a refuge against anxiety involves a real ambiguity. There is in this formula a suggestion of escape, of forgetting. But anxiety can also lead man to trace himself back to his origin. Through anxiety man can find rebirth: in guilt, in face of death, in loneliness he can take himself in hand and open out to the transcendental dimension of his being. The gift of confidence only shows up against a background of solitude. The hope of pardon can only arise where there is experience of wrong-doing. If there is escape into God, it is none the less true that the authentically religious attitude is only possible as a victory over fear, distrust, and the fascination of the void.

Anxiety can, moreover, just as easily cause escape from God. We shall meet with this when we discuss certain forms of atheism. In order to believe, do we not have to accept and overcome the anxiety awoken by the absence of every tangible guarantee? And do we not also have to confidently recognize that this most holy God is also most merciful towards man. Man is not disgusting in God's eyes—but faced with God's holiness, man cannot fail to see that he is always unworthy of him. Between man and God there is an ontological gulf.

In thus drawing up a table of complex, intermediate and changing states, we can sift out two essential forms of anxiety: pathological anxiety and existential anxiety. Likewise, there are two possible reactions with regard to the anxiety connatural to man: he can react by escape or he can react by taking things in hand. If he runs away, there are two possible escape-routes: religion, or else distraction which is a forgetting both of God and of the human condition.

If we consider the various psychological enquiries in the light of the principles which we have just set out, it would seem very difficult to interpret them. Let us deal first of all with the results of R. A. Funk's study on the religious attitudes and anxieties in a college population.[45] For measuring the degrees of anxiety, the author used a Taylor scale. More than 50% of the subjects state that religion brings them peace of soul and gives them a feeling of security. More than 50% also consider religion as being the only reality upon which they can rely. 64% say that if they lost their faith in God life would scarcely hold any comfort for them. It is worth noting, however, that 79% feel guilty about the poor showing of their religious practice; thus it would appear that security and guilt, far from excluding each other, may be seen as the two poles of the religious attitude. In comparing the religious attitude of the group showing greatest anxiety with that of the group showing least anxiety, we see that religion is not satisfied with an assurance of security; it also affords protection against insecurity. We notice that the group with the highest anxiety score is also the one which most clearly confirms (at a significant level of 5%) the items expressing correlation between religion and security, whereas religious practice drops noticeably in the least anxious group. Furthermore, the anxious subjects are more easily affected by doubt. They will, for example, be more concerned about conflicts between faith and science. The group which has the highest score for the 'religious conflicts' scale, has an average of 22·2% for anxiety against the 12·9% of the other group. Contrary to the results obtained by other psychologists, Funk finds no significant correlation between anxiety and religious orthodoxy. What counts most is the way in which religious faith is felt. There is, moreover, a positive correlation between anxiety and the theory of life—'philosophy of life'—which sometimes stands stead for religion. Neither the sex nor the intelligence of the subjects seems to have any particular bearing on their anxiety. The author concludes that there is a link between anxiety and religion: the most anxious seek security in religion. But, the positive correlation between anxiety and religious conflicts can be interpreted in two ways. The author puts forth the hypothesis of a circular relationship: a 'neurotic' anxiety might well be at the source of religious conflicts which, in their turn, reinforce anxiety. We dispute neither the results nor the conclusions of this enquiry. We merely disagree with the description 'neurotic' which the author gives to manifest anxiety as characterized by his method. This term seems all the more debatable in that the subjects studied are young men and women in open quest of an orientation for life and emotive stability.

In a study of subjects of over 65 years of age, Moberg[46] remarked that the most religious were the best adjusted. Likewise the thorough clinical examination of 39 cases led French to arrive at the conclusion that there was a positive correlation between the structuration of a more stable ego, characterized by an absence of projections and repressions, and a better defined theory, religious or otherwise, of life. In line with this, we can quote the observations made by Oates[47] on 173 psychotic subjects. Before their illness, 74 were not interested in religion, 89 had some interest, 10 great interest. During their psychotic crisis, especially in moments of great anxiety, a good many of them showed pronounced religious concern. Does this confirm James's idea that religion is an extreme state, even a pathological one? But may we not just as well draw the conclusion that an extreme situation, which throws man back on himself, his solitude and his finitude, makes him discover, in those very realities, his transcendental situation?

In order to delve more deeply into the problem set by anxiety and its relationship with religion, we should have to make a depth study of personality, and bring out the structuration of the different elements discovered by analysis: drives, conflicts, interpersonal relations, identification, sublimation. The following chapters will make soundings along these lines. But the foregoing analysis has already shown religion to be a focal point for man when he is shaken in the depths of his affectivity. Religion reaches the light of day from out of the deepest of his natural impulsions, from the effort which he makes to overcome existential insecurity. Religion is the answer to an anxiety-causing situation. Finally, the study of anxiety teaches us nothing new; merely that all our reflections on motivation lead to it. An exhaustive study of the relationship between anxiety and religion should be worked out on the basis of differentiated enquiries into the motives for interest in religion. Anxiety is only the felt signal; it warns man that the foundations of his existence are getting out of hand. Wherever he may seek a place which restores him to himself, giving him a calm hold over his existence, he finds that there is a danger of the ground giving way to open up beneath him on the abyss of his nothingness. That is why man, and man alone, questions his very being. Does it mean illusory consolation to answer this question by following a path which fulfils man's desires and expectations? Is there really no other attitude than the refusal of every hope. There is certainly a real greatness of soul in submitting to existence without complacency, and in drawing greater moral purity from an accepted certitude of one's final nothingness. But psychological criticism will discover another kind of impurity in this attitude: the turning in on oneself. The refusal to give oneself up to hope is a movement proceeding from vital drives. Inversely this abandonment of self, this self-surrender can unleash anxiety, no less than loneliness and distress. These two kinds of existence carry the same risks of inauthenticity. Far be it from us to conclude that every a-religious attitude is necessarily tainted with unconscious psychological motives. But we do think that the two modes of existence in question are deeply implicated in the network of man's psychological processes. Man is something quite other than pure, transparent, clear-sighted consciousness free of the vital drives which feed it. And so it is that man's religion or his atheism will always be embodied in the human.

The problem of anxiety has led us to the threshold of the metaphysical question of man and his religion. We shall not cross it. Our task is to examine to what extent and in what sense religion can be explained by motivation. By progressive stages we have arrived at the question of truth. The study of anxiety has gathered up all the preceding studies. It forces us with our backs to the wall to ask the crucial question set by contemporary psychology: can religion be completely explained? Or, in the words of Freud, is religion an illusion because it is motivated? Intellectual probity has obliged us to untangle the thread of an explanation which in aiming to be exhaustive has proved restricting. Having come to the end of this analysis let us sum up in order to draw clearer conclusions.

CONCLUSIONS

The many frustrations of man show themselves as so many powerful springs of religious behaviour. The need for providential aid in material difficulties, the expectation of supernatural help in the moral struggle and in times of emotional stress, anxiety about death in the thick of war or in declining years are all strong stimulants of religious activity. We must not, however, forget the ambivalence of these motives: they carry within themselves seeds of unbelief or of scepticism. Adolescents experience at one and the same time the test of greater self-control and the vanity of their religious search; this leads to a progressive decrease in their religious activity.

Men who find themselves on the fringe of society react against their social alienation by joining a community sect where they can enjoy the communication which is refused them elsewhere. The grudge which they bear against a hostile society is their justification for isolating themselves from it and allows them to live henceforth in the hope of another world which seems to them imminent. The particular form of their religious faith is motivated by social frustration; it appears as the antitype of the society which has rejected them. Their opposition to the Churches, however, weakens the Marxist theory, and modifies one of the Freudian theories on the origin of religion. Furthermore, the Marxist interpretation of religion is not confirmed by sociological observations.

Guilt is incontestably at the source of many religious acts and in this matter we have been able to point out the linking of cause and effect: religion liberates the subjects and reintegrates them morally. On the other hand, the witness of truly religious people gives us proof that another sort of guilt, the sense of sin, finds its motivation in religious faith itself. Inverse relationships devalue the generalization of Freud's thesis. It remains a fact that a lessening of psychological guilt very often reduces religious activities.

The necessity to give a foundation to ethics and to assure social stability is certainly an important factor in religious belief and practice. The need for security is observed in the seeking for a guarantee of life with God. Forced by the very dynamic of his personality, man looks for a law and an aim: who would supply this better than the Creator and supreme Judge? And where find a more constraining authority, a more powerful guarantee against the disorder which threatens all men and every society?

Intellectual curiosity does not appear to us to be a well-defined motive of the religious attitude. Nevertheless, inasmuch as it presents a structured vision of the universe, knowledge of the world opens out to religion which does, indeed, make it possible for man to discover the fundamental principles of a world able to save him from chaos and non-existence. We may then accept such a motive of religion as valid. But the fact that it hardly appears in the explicit faith of believers shows us that it is too ambiguous really to justify being called a motive of religion. Either this motive tells us nothing more than what we have learnt from the motives already mentioned—need for assured ethical practice, desire for immortality—or it uncovers a more basic desire, such as desire for the absolute. But in this case we are beyond the limits of psychology of motivation because desire for the absolute is of another psychological order as we shall see in the next chapter.

The study of anxiety has led us to the same conclusion: polymorphous in its origins and its manifestations, anxiety can only be put into a motivational relationship with religion if we carefully distinguish the different processes in it.

The religious need which is sometimes found in the categories of motivation psychology may thus be broken down into various dynamisms. These are so many efforts to overcome the necessities inherent in existential situations. Religion retains a differentiated structure which forbids us to postulate what the psychologists of motivation usually call the 'religious need'.

How many obscurities there are, then, in the apparently very clear concept of psychological motivation of religion. Each of the motives analysed is only human desire directed to a human end; immortality, moral support, protection. What is it, then, which gives them their strictly religious coefficient? The majority of psychologists content themselves with establishing a correlation between the motives we have just mentioned and religious behaviour. Their point of view has some justification: a good account can thus be given of religious behaviour with its fluctuations of intensity and intention, by putting it in correlation with the different situations where it occurs. But, for all that, it is not explained for what it is in its properly religious tenor. The psychologist has every right to circumscribe the object of his study. But we must understand what this means. We cannot speak of a psychological explanation of religion without abuse of words. In fact, when writers speak of the 'sources of religion', they only account for its special forms, and, to a certain extent, for the curve of its activities; but in no way do they account for the fact of religion itself.

In our opinion, many psychologists stop at an examination of religious forms and activities because of an implicit working-hypothesis: and they imagine that the sources of religion are revealed by this kind of study. What they do in fact is persuade themselves that every human aspiration has an adequate object. Hence it suffices to show that religion offers an answer adjusted to the various human needs. For example, if a man in distress longs for protection, and religion can promise it to him, this correspondence between demand and object will be a source of religion and a guarantee of its worth. And it is, moreover, very possible that believers are accustomed to this sort of reasoning which can be found in all apologetic writings. The theory is fascinating and man feels he recognizes himself in it; he willingly believes in the objectivity of his needs and desires.

After the study of the human motives for religion, the psychological enigma of religion remains unsolved. Freud claims to solve it. Conscious though he is of the extreme complexity of the religious phenomenon and of the multiplicity of the psychological dynamisms at work, he does not despair of sorting it out. He restricts himself to an exclusively psychological field and believes that, step by step, he can solve the mystery contained in the only really religious question: why does man believe in God? The motivational analyses to which he devotes himself in *The Future of an Illusion* have no other aim than to bring forward as evidence a very simple and fundamental reality: religion is man's appeal to a God envisaged as a providential and rewarding Father. For Freud God's distinctive mark is his paternity and every form of religion tends to this belief. Having arrived at this conclusion Freud sets out two facts of his own experience and his psycho-analytical theory. In the first place, every human desire is a form of belief. In the hidden depths of his being, adult man believes in the effective realization of his desires in just the same way as does a child or a primitive. From his primal narcissism man retains a belief in the all-powerful nature of his desires. This is attested to by magic and religion. In distress man continues to trust in the intention of his desires even when there is no reasonable basis left. And, again like the child, as soon as he finds the way barred by a fate stronger than himself, man transfers to another person the all-powerfulness which he sees he is lacking. In this transference, he is guided by the traces left in his consciousness or rather, his unconsciousness, of a childhood experience. He bestows on a supernatural father figure the all-powerfulness which he sees is wanting to his humanity. Thus religion arises from the blend of several psychological factors: confidence in the all-powerful nature of desire, failure in face of reality, transference to a father figure, idealistic and mythical fulfilment of the longing for a father. Freud sees in the anxious refusal to submit religious questions to a general examination (dogmatism), and in the gradual shrinking of the religious field before the progress of reason a double confirmation of his theory of the essentially affective conditioning of religion.

We must admit that the Freudian theory constitutes the only synthesis at our disposal for explaining psychologically the fact that man, be he child, adolescent or adult, spontaneously believes in a providential Father when he is in distress. This theory alone helps us to understand the lessening of religious activities once they have ceased to have any real motive. A theory which economically unites and gives a foundation to all these factors merits some presumption of truth; and all the more so in that no one has ever proposed another. But we do find fault with its abusive generalizations and its puritan excess. We also dispute the absolute and almost metaphysical claim on which it prides itself. We think that it expresses only a particular moment in the genesis of the religious personality.

Let us notice in the first instance that the theory of *The Future of an Illusion* does not cover all religious phenomena. Many religious witnesses can be brought in against it. Furthermore, the Freudian criticisms of the almost magical nature of religious beliefs can be read in many of the writings of the great mystics.

And by how many believers, heirs to our reflexive culture, are they not admitted? In the interviews of adult believers quoted in the chapter on religious experience, we met with none of the motives alleged above. Freud admitted[48] to never having met a case of purified religious belief and it is surprising that there should be such a lack in his information. Furthermore, he later admitted that Judaeo-Christianity presents a nobler appearance than do the religious forms on which his early criticisms had dwelt. It is probable that, in accordance with his usual method, he pushed to an extreme a certain line of thought which only accounts for a certain number of partial phenomena.

The second fault we have to find is bound up with the first. We are quite ready to allow that Freud's theory holds good, broadly speaking, if it is limited to the moment of the emergence of the religious impulsion. In the forms in which this presents itself concretely to the observer, it can only be understood in the light of the processes postulated by Freud. They cast considerable light on the almost magical beliefs of the religious impulsion which all converge towards a father figure whose all-powerfulness goes to make up the deficiencies of the human world. But, even so, we must ask ourselves whether this religious intention is necessarily an illusion devoid of any truth. Leaving to philosophers and theologians the question of ultimate truth, a question which Freud disposes of very much too glibly, we would ask a few questions of philosophical interpretation: they arise from the facts observed and are suggested by psychological theories. That religion is functional, there is no doubt. That it is largely illusory, the subjects themselves gradually realize with a resulting falling-off in religious practice. But do we have to conclude from this that this functional religion leaves no room for any real relationship with the Other? Flower[49] thought he could answer Freud by pointing out that religious subjects are very well aware of the real situation, humanly frustrating as it is; that they turn to religion for help in dealing with the situation which is recognized for what it is; and that, consequently, these subjects are not mentally unbalanced. But this reply is beside the point. No one has ever made the accusation that the recourse to religion is a delirious transformation of reality. And Freud did not call religion a neurosis, but an illusion. The real question is concerned with whether religion is not, perhaps, the substitutive, almost delirious creation of an unreal world overlaid on the real world. We can be helped at this point by a comparison which will serve as a general criticism of all the puritan theories which condemn imperfect religion for being no more than human. A child has no true knowledge of either himself or others. His laughter is satisfaction and happiness to be alive. His tenderness is the expression of his bond of vital dependence. And yet, he reaches others, even if only across transitional objects and in interested, utilitarian requests. His relationship with others already sets going a certain form of love. Likewise we may say that religious consciousness which takes its origin and finds its motivation in needs of every kind, is already a certain mode of communication with the Other. Martin Buber puts it beautifully in these words: 'When man says: Thou, the Other is present.'

What is more, the effective presence of God at the core of religious intentions, even primary, functional and imaginary ones, constitutes the light which shines on the successive stages of the religious journey and which allows them slowly to come to fruition. Were the God of psychological motives to be a mere idol, man could never move on to a more authentic communication. If, one day, he is able to turn to the true God, it is because he already holds this God, not indeed, in his understanding, but in an existential relationship.

The ideas which we have put forward find their confirmation in our study of religious experience. In it we meet the intellectual's conscious refusal of a religious experience which would reduce the presence of God to the level of human needs. But over and beyond any psychological motivation there is some confidence that human activity does not end in absurdity. The mystery enfolding existence, imbuing it with a certain hope, leads to a suggestion of an Other. By faith in the religious message the subjects are led to recognize the features of the living God. By psychological self-criticism these subjects have uncovered the face

of God who, at one and the same time, hid himself and prefigured himself in the God of their needs and motives.

In this way then, by urging the concept of motivation we come
up against a dilemma: either motivated religion is a false solution,
or it transcends its own motivation. When the observed religious
phenomena are restored to their temporal dynamic they also
appear to be in movement, in a state of tension between these
two poles. According to age, situation and education, as well as
personal fidelity, the subjects can be placed at stated points on
this dynamic line stretched between the motive and the presence
of the Other. The fact that religion emerges from human motives,
and that leaving horizontal tendencies it can find the vertical is
something which forces us to make a critical revision. All
conscious religion contains, of itself, the seeds of atheism. The
presence of the Other can be dimmed and crumble away in
criticism. Or else, by the silence with which he meets the requests
of frustrated subjects, God can slowly impose himself in the
otherness of his presence by dragging the subject out of his self-
centredness. As we shall see, the religious attitude is structured
in conversion.

Maslow[50] has elaborated a perfectly valid criticism of the
concept of motivation. To need-satisfaction conduct he opposes
that of growth and being. Subjects are rigorously selected according to the criterion of self-fulfilment. These subjects, whom we
may take as being psychologically adult, carry on intense activities
in the spheres of love, art, science or religion, even when they
are no longer driven by needs or motives. As Maslow says, they
love and they know according to the mode of being. But, if we
accept his criticism of motivation, his concept of being does not
appear sufficient for expressing the intentional relationship which
moves the subject towards the other, be he man or God. The
analysis of the state of being proposed by Maslow has one big
fault: the knowledge and love of being do away with true otherness in the relationship to the other. The subjects live their union
with the other as an experience of fusion. The presence is then
engulfed in an indifferentiation which is truly narcissistic. A
prisoner to some extent to this concept of motivation which he

criticizes, Maslow tries to deal with its deficiencies by an excessively spatialized style of thought: to the movement which implies lack, he opposes achievement which is rest in possession.

We have come now at the end of a long journey to the crucial problem of all religious thought: Is God the answer to human needs? Does his presence do away with want and distance? Or is God only silence and absence? Or, again, is there a mode of presence which respects otherness and union?

The various religious trends are divided by two diametrically opposed tendencies: Jung and Freud have given these their psychological foundations. In order to understand what is at issue we shall have to examine the two basic symbols of religion: the mother symbol and the father symbol. This will be the subject of our next chapter.

1 For the theory set out here we are greatly indebted to the excellent article by Hans Thomae, 'Einführung' in *Die Motivation menschlichen Handelns, herausgegeben von H. Thomae*, Cologne-Berlin 1965, 13-34.
2 See J. Nuttin, 'Origine et développement des motifs', *La motivation*, Paris 1959, 95-6.
3 *Pattern and Growth in Personality*, London-New York 1964, 201.
4 *Ibid.*, 206-18.
5 See A. Gehlen, *Der Mensch, Seine Natur und seine Stellung in der Welt*, Frankfurt a.M. 1962, 338 ff.
6 See A. De Waelhens, 'Nature humaine et compréhension de l'être', *Revue philosophique de Louvain*, 1961, 672-82.
7 C. R. Rogers, *On Becoming a Person*, Boston 1961: see also J. J. Dijkhuis, *De processtheorie van C. R. Rogers*, Hilversum-Antwerp 1963, 60-71.
8 See Dijkhuis, *op. cit.*, 25-6.
9 See K. Lewin, *Psychologie dynamique*, Paris 1959, 57-64.
10 The Standard Edition has 'Where id was, there ego shall be' *New Introductory Lectures on Psycho-analysis*, XXII, 80 (translator's note).
11 E. Jones, 'Religionpsychologie', *Zur Psychoanalyse der christlichen Religion*, Leipzig-Vienna 1928, 7-13; J. C. Flugel, *Man, Morals and Society, A Psycho-analytic Study*, London 1945, ch. 13 and 17.
12 *Moses and Monotheism, Gesammelte Werke*, XVI, 236-7.
13 See *The Future of an Illusion*.
14 S. A. Stouffer, *The American Soldier, II. Combat and its Aftermath*, Princeton 1949.
15 *The Individual and his Religion*, 46-51; see also G. W. Allport, J. M. Gillespie, J. Young, 'The Religion of the Post-War College Student', *Journal of Psychology*, 1948, 3-33.

16 See Chapter 1, note 49.

17 'Is Religious Behaviour Dependent upon Affect or Frustration?', *Journal of Abnormal and Social Psychology*, July 1947, 310–19. The enquiry which we quote here was carried out by H. Bustamante, and presented at the University of Louvain as a thesis for the Licentiate in Psychology, in 1965, under the title of *L'attitude religieuse dans les états de frustration et d'émotion*.

18 See Chapter 1, note 49.

19 M. Argyle, *Religious Behaviour*, London 1958, 131.

20 See A. Descamps, *op. cit.* (Chapter 1, note 36).

21 *Religion, Society and the Individual: an Introduction to the Sociology of Religion*, New York 1957, 133–42.

22 See J. Gillin, 'A Contribution to the Sociology of Sects', *American Journal of Sociology*, 1910, 236–52; and J. Wach, 'Sociologie Religieuse', *La sociologie du XXe, siècle, I*, edited by G. Gurvitch, Paris 1947, 417–47.

23 M. Yinger, *op. cit.*, 171–73; see also A. T. Boisen, *Religion in Crisis and Custom: a Sociological and Psychological Study*, New York 1955, 71 ff.

24 R. Poblete, *Puerto Rican Sectarianism and the Quest for Community*, New York 1959 (unpublished thesis of Fordham University).

25 W. C. Cohn, 'Jehovah's Witnesses as a Proletarian Movement', *The American Scholar*, 1955, 288–98.

26 J. Delay, P. Pichot, J. F. Buisson, R. Sadoul, 'Étude d'un groupe d'adeptes d'une secte religieuse', *Encéphale*, 1955, 138–54, 254–65.

27 See H. Carrier, *Psycho-sociologie de l'appartenance religieuse*, Rome 1960, 85–7.

28 Freud has greatly developed this theme in *Das Unbehagen in der Kultur* (*Civilization and its Discontents*), 1930; see: *Gesammelte Werke*; XIV, especially 482–506.

29 L. Gilen, *Das Gewissen bei Jungendlichen*, Göttingen 1956.

30 See A. Snoeck, *De psychologie van het Schuldbewustzijn*, Antwerp-Utrecht 1948.

31 We have developed these ideas in 'L'accès à Dieu par la conscience morale', in *Foi et réflexion philosophique. Mélanges Franz Grégoire*, Louvain 1961, 481–502.

32 *Religious Behaviour*, 79.

33 *Science, Religion and Reality*, New York 1925.

34 *The Psychology of Religion*, London 1899.

35 'Why do People go to Church?', *Religious Education*, 1937, 50–4.

36 R. S. Cavan, 'Personal Adjustment in Old Age', *Science Research Associates*, Chicago 1949.

37 See *Sondages III*, Paris 1959, 21.

38 See for example the writings of A. Camus and S. de Beauvoir.

39 *Sondages III*, 13.

40 *Religion, Society and the Individual*.

41 See for example R. Kuhn 'Daseinsanalytische Studie über die Bedeutung von Grenzen im Wahn', *Monatschrift für Psychiatrie und Neurologie*, 1952, 354–83.

42 *Finitude et culpabilité, II. La symbolique du mal*, Paris 1960, 154. See also M. Eliade, *Traité d'histoire des religions*, 384–5; *Le sacré et le profane*, 82 ff.

43 Pascal, Pensée 195.

44 *Hemmung, Symptom und Angst*, 1926; *Gesammelte Werke*, XIV.

45 *A Survey of Religious Attitudes and Manifest Anxiety in a College Population*, Perdue University 1955 (microfilm).

46 'The Christian Religion and Personal Adjustment in Old Age', *American Sociological Review*, 1953, 87–90.

47 'The Role of Religion in the Psychoses', *Journal of Pastoral Care*, 1949, 21–30; and *Religious Factors in Mental Illness*, New York 1957.

48 *Freud-Pfister, Briefe*, 1909–39, Frankfurt a.M. 1963, 12.

49 *An Approach to Psychology of Religion*, London 1927.

50 *Motivation and Personality*, New York 1954. Maslow has taken up the criticism of the conceptions of motivation and has elaborated it in the sense that we have sketched in 'Cognition of Being in the Peak Experiences', *Journal of Genetic Psychology*, 1959.

CHAPTER 3

THE TWO AXES OF RELIGION

In extreme situations man spontaneously strikes the note of religious appeal. Face to face with his powerlessness, he conjures up an image of an almighty Father, who benevolently supports society. Deceived (or, perhaps, more enlightened) believers suspect that their God is only a figment of their imagination. Many break away from a Father who is too readily acquiescent to their demands. In this case they tend to take up an attitude of reserve and they are brought up against the mystery of a silence which they hardly dare to name 'God'.

Nevertheless, in the long lineage of the Judaeo-Christian tradition, this same word 'Father' is the supreme name given to a God who has revealed himself in transcendent majesty; a God who refutes tirelessly all religious anthropomorphisms and idolatries. It is for this reason that theology finds it unbecoming to identify such a noble term with the mascot of narrowly human demands. Is there then no connection between the two uses of the name of father? We must admit that at first sight there does not seem to be any connection at all. However, if the separation were radical, there would be nothing left of any natural religious honesty in man. The god he had shaped according to his human tendencies would be nothing more than an idol. It is thus that Meister Eckhart, following in the steps of the prophets of Israel, has not hesitated to condemn many a religious attitude: what men call God is often but an idol.

It is not our intention here to go into the niceties of the theological meaning of the name 'Father'. We shall refer to theology only in so far as it gives expression to original and living religious traditions. Our aim in this chapter is to bring into relief the psychological implications of the name, Father. We shall carry out our research in two dimensions. We shall probe the depths of psychology, and we shall consider, also, religious belief as it appears once it has been purified of spontaneous anthropomorphic factors. We shall in no way try to make these two lines of thought converge but we shall endeavour to see beyond human needs in order to discover how the name, Father, is deep-rooted in man's elementary psychological make-up and how, once religious evolution has arrived at its term, this word signifies the divine being and expresses the attitude of the believer.

In this way we shall move on to the important question of the 'demythologization' of God. Psychological studies of religious needs have brought to the fore the connaturality between man and his God. This would seem to indicate that the name, Father, is nothing more than a mirror reflecting man's illusory aspirations. The figure of the Father which answers so deeply to human distress, is it anything more than the supreme myth of unhappy man? It is easy to understand that Plato[1] makes the advent of an enlightened humanity coincide with the disappearance of the putative father: 'They are . . . in the situation of a putative child, fed at the breast of riches, who, having arrived at adulthood, perceives that he is not the son of those who say they are his parents and finds that it is quite impossible to discover his true parents.' When they know their true state, Socrates goes on to say, they will free themselves from the authority of the presumed parents in order to follow the advice of others; they will set out along the way of dialectic questioning. If the father is only the cipher of man's unlimited aspirations, then man is bound to seek his principle of emancipation in agnosticism or in atheism, unless he follows along another religious pathway, the one which classical typology designates by the term of mysticism as opposed to prophetic religion. By means of mysticism man reintegrates the divine principle which is buried within the depths of his being and is also disguised in the phenomena of the world.

Mysticism

Mysticism is a complex phenomenon. It can only be defined in its actual forms. And these forms themselves are determined by the cultural and religious setting in which they have taken shape. Mysticism can be either theist or pantheist, rational or irrational, Christian or anti-dogmatic. But whatever form mysticism may take, every school has something in common with the others; they all aspire to an intuitive experience of God, or the divine. Mysticism arises from the painful experience of separation. It seeks to bridge the abyss between man and the world, between man and God. From the depths of his soul the mystic desires to touch God or the divine. Turning aside from the deceptive appearances of things he retires into himself by an introspective movement in order to discover the divine spark buried in the most intimate depths of his soul. Or else he longs to rend the veil which prevents him from seeing the basic unity of the universe; prevents him from seeing how all things are one in God. For the mystic, the multiple configurations of human passions are also so many deceptive disguises of the only true desire, the desire for God or the divine.

Traditionally, mysticism is the opposite of prophetic religion which turns towards action, builds up the community and carries God's message to the world. Presented in this radical way, however, such an opposition between the two religious types is entirely false. The proof of this lies in the presence of so many prophetic characteristics in certain mystics. In the first place Christian mystics always emphasize the distance separating man from God. Ruysbroeck is explicit: 'Even in union, we remain forever creatures.' Eckhart and Tauler emphasize the ethical service of humanity. And what more enterprising prophets and organizers could there be than Bernard of Clairvaux or Teresa of Avila?

It is useless then to attempt to define mysticism as opposed to prophetism, either from a doctrinal point of view, or even from the point of view of an experience, strictly religious in nature, such as that of the majesty or the holiness of God. The redoubtable asceticism which mystics like St John of the Cross practised is not a mere human technique for spiritual ascension. For St John of the Cross, for example, it presented itself primarily as a wish for the absolute purity required for approach to God.

Numerous though the forms and doctrines of mysticism may be, it is not by any means an extravagance of language to class them all under a single term. The word mysticism always designates man's intimate union with divine infinity, the foundation and the unifying force of all that exists.

The desire for union which underlies the mystic's search aims at the immediate presence of the absolute and suppression of every limitation. Of itself this desire leads to a communion in which the ego coincides with the infinite. Christian mystics need constant vigilance and an experienced theological conscience in order to arrive without illusion at union with the personal God of Jesus Christ. By the fact that it is rooted in the religious desire, the natural movement of mysticism may appear to support the theories of those psychologists and philosophers who all too easily confuse religious eros and theologically-proven mystic trends. It is this erroneous view which is at the source of the mistrust aroused by mystic phenomena in certain theologians, especially Protestant ones. They have an almost unconquerable suspicion that mysticism is a new manifestation of pantheism or religious naturalism. Karl Barth, for example, considers that mysticism, in ever new forms and degrees, is essentially a negation of faith.[2]

Our purpose here is not to undertake a study of the psychology of mystics.[3] We merely propose to determine the psychological movement that provokes desire for union, which is the stimulus of every kind of mystical experience. Mysticism, union, interiority, are all so many terms which frequently recur in psychology, especially in the analysis of religious phenomena. They represent a certain type of experience and desire, and it must be our concern to bring out the psychological incidence of this type.

I. Religious Desire and Maternal Symbolism

Plato tells us in his *Symposium* that Eros is the son of Riches and Poverty. He is the fruit of union between Poros, abundance, and Penia, penury. He is a mingling of finite and infinite: an intermediary being who dwells in the hearts of men and gives them a link with the gods. In this way our sublunary world is at once toilsome and capable of aspiring to divine plenitude. In *Phaedrus*, Plato takes up the same theme and gives another definition of Eros as belonging to both the human and the divine sphere. Eros is divine grace, but also the soul's longing. This 'gift from the gods', like some delirium, becomes in man 'a divine impulse jerking him out of his regular habits'. The final goal of Eros is contemplation which brings about a spiritual union of intelligence with Ideas.[4] In this unifying contemplation man brings to life the seeds of immortality latent within him. From that moment on he has effectual participation in divine life.

We may, then, define the desire for immortality and divine union which seems to motivate the mystic's search as a religious eros. This term expresses perfectly the deep aspiration to go beyond every contingency and every appearance; it testifies to the longing for plenitude in which every human anxiety will be reabsorbed.

THE DESIRE FOR GOD IN CHRISTIAN TRADITION

The researches of practical psychology into the motivation underlying the religious attitude record only rare and passing cases of religious eros. Nevertheless there is a whole line of mystical tradition to give us proof of its extraordinary power in souls. We might wonder whether it is not a thing of the past? Personally we are convinced that in our own times religious eros is the seed bed of many contemplative vocations, the point from which man sets off on the long road of religious purification. Dom Jean Leclercq, writing in his very fine study *The Love of Learning and the Desire for God*,[5] states that for the spiritual of the Middle Ages, the monastic life had no other aim than to 'seek God'. This life was conceived of solely as a means to the monk's salvation and his search after God. Separation from the

world, silence and asceticism stimulate desire for God. In studying literature and theology the monk has no other aim than to be
taught by God. His spirituality is that of the Canticle of Canticles.
'This is at one and the same time the expression of both desire
and possession. It is a song, and a song of Love. A song to which
one listens, to which one attunes one's whole being, which one
sings oneself. In this case it accompanies and sustains progress
in faith passing from grace to grace from the first calling, through
the conversion to the monastic life, up to the very entry into the
blessed life.'[6] 'The masters follow one upon the other elaborating
the doctrine of desire for God. St Gregory is the doctor of desire:
constantly he uses words like *anhelare, aspirare, suspirare*.'[7] If
we believe St Bernard, the monk does not so much seek God as
desire him; he does not have knowledge of God, but experience.
'. . . Desire, unless it is questioning, is satisfied by a certain
possession of God, and this gives further increase to desire.
From desire results peace refound in God, because desire is
already possession in which fear and love are reconciled. Here
below desire is the form of love itself and in it the Christian finds
God's joy, union with the glorified Lord.'[8] The Old Testament
had a special value for medieval monasticism. This value derived
from the prophetic nature of the inspired texts looking forward
to future salvation and in which desire is the prevailing sentiment.[9]

Religious desire was the objective of masters of the monastic
life. In it we find an interpretation of the theme of the hidden
God which springs from the psychology of love. St Gregory[10]
tells us that God hides himself so that the bride may seek him
and not finding, seek with renewed ardour. This is a great mystic
theme which St John of the Cross takes up in his turn.

This Christian tradition of desire is bound up with the ancient
Platonic Eros. History proves that this is so: 'In every age, and
in every milieu where there has been a monastic revival, there has
been revival of interest in Origen.'[11]

THE DESIRE FOR GOD TODAY

At the close of this impressive tradition of monastic mysticism
we must again ask whether the ancient fervour of religious desire

still nourishes truly contemplative vocations. We are sure that
it does, though we have as yet come across no practical enquiries
into this particular religious way. Among the adult intellectuals
whose witness we have examined, only two recalled a religious
experience which might be called 'mystical', in the broad sense
of this word. And even these were memories of adolescence, too
much permeated by emotion not to appear suspect to adult eyes.
It is probable that it is not a rare thing in adolescence, an age
when the first stirrings of warmth in friendship and existential
longing draw young people towards an experience of presence
and totality. According to an enquiry carried out by Allport,[12]
17% of the subjects who say they give a place in their lives to
the religious sentiment mention the occurrence of a 'mystical
experience'. The enquiry which we ourselves have made shows
that in face of suffering, solitude, loneliness, many adolescents,
mainly girls, have some experience of the friendship of God.
That this experience shows a sharp decline between the ages of
16 and 19, and that there is very little trace of it among adults,
indicates the emotional nature of such a desire for God felt
during adolescence. We may suppose that in certain subjects of
the 'religious type', the desire for God deepens and becomes an
abiding characteristic as they progress along their contemplative
way. But it is a fact that contemporary civilization is far from
favouring the birth and growth of such a type. An attitude of
deliberate realism towards passion-inspired love,[13] a marked
emphasis on personal independence, a will to dominate the world,
these are some of the most pronounced characteristics of the
contemporary cultural climate; it is hardly surprising that they
lead man away from the profound experience and the long
tradition of religious eros.

THE 'RELIGIOUS TYPE' ACCORDING TO SPRANGER

E. Spranger[14] has attempted to make an analysis of a 'religious
type' in perfect harmony with the mystical tendency as we have
just outlined it. He sets out, in the manner of Dilthey's 'human
sciences' to elaborate a phenomenology of human types, of
'forms of existence'. He strives to grasp the structures which give

meaning to the concrete activities of mankind. This leads him to distinguish six forms of existence which he describes as being characteristic of thinking man, economic man, aesthetic man, social man, political man, religious man. In each type there is a major value polarizing existence. According to Spranger, the religious sense is defined by 'the relationship to the totality of values which culminates in a supreme value.'[15] 'The world, as the totality of the connections of being and meaning which act upon the individual, is already, of itself, a religious concept.' 'The religious language gives the name of "God" to the ultimate reality which constitutes the world.'[16] 'The heart of religiosity consists in the seeking for what constitutes the supreme value for man's spiritual being. This seeking is restlessness and dissatisfaction . . .' 'The possession of what religion considers as good is always characterized as a redemption (*Erlöstsein*).' 'The religious man is the one whose whole mental structure (*Geistesstruktur*) is constantly directed towards the realization of an experience of the supreme and completely pacifying value.'[17] Within the category of the religious type, Spranger distinguishes three principal forms: the type of the immanent mystic characterized by enthusiastic approval of all fundamental values recognized in relation to a centre where they are all united (example: Goethe); the type of the transcendental mystic who, by total renunciation of the world seeks to discover the supreme value in a transcendental sphere (example: Plotinus); and lastly, the type most frequently met, the mixed mystic who at one and the same time accepts and renounces the various fundamental values.

Thus, Spranger identifies the religious man with the 'mystical' type. The typically religious man is seized by a unique, supreme value quite outside the limited spheres to which the existence of others is restricted. In this perspective the distinction of two extreme types and a mixed form seems inevitable. Religiosity consists, indeed, in a real experience of the final harmonization of all the values. The diversity of the forms results solely from the individuality of natures. The immanent, terrestrial mystic is content with the basic acknowledgement that our hidden drives have a quality of truth and can link us with the heart of the world.

The transcendental type is the result of a distrust of nature and life.[18] The mixed type is the product of a prudent estimation of personal motivations.

Let us notice in the first instance that, for Spranger, religion consists in unrest and dissatisfaction, in the attraction towards some ultimate value. Normally, restless seeking is directed to the terrestrial life in all its manifestations; even the atheist can have a religious participation in it.

But, is it not to confuse the issue to style a man religious when he follows up a Faustian experience of a totally terrestrial participation? This inordinate broadening of the word 'religious', as well as the attempt to explain transcendental mysticism by distrust, springs from a radical psychologism. But is belief in an absolutely transcendent God really nothing more than the result of a kind of perversity which turns man away from natural mysticism?

When we think over Spranger's position we cannot help remarking that his religious psychology is tainted with a serious confusion which reflects, on the level of his psychological theory, the troubled, ambiguous nature of desire. When eros first comes to the surface it is longing for fulfilment, for satisfaction. It is hunger. It desires to suppress distance and otherness. On the natural level this desire is felt as a need, even a fundamental need, the source and end of every other need. Is this need religious? In agreement with Spranger we believe that desire is the point where the religious movement comes to the surface. On the other hand there are two major points upon which we disagree with him: the assimilation of desire for the infinite with the religious attitude, and the identification of the 'mystical' type with the religious man.

First, we dispute the connection established between the term 'religious' and that of desire for the infinite or for unity. We ourselves use the term 'religious eros' to signify the religious dynamic which desire can arouse. But we prefer to make a distinction between the inner momentum of desire and religion. Natural mysticism may be held to be the richer; but here we are concerned only with distinguishing two fundamentally different

11

attitudes. Remaining faithful to traditional usage then, we reserve the word 'religious' for the attitude which acknowledges God as Other and approaches him with respect, admiration, hope and gratitude. It must be emphasized that, for us, there is religion only if the Other, the foundation and source of my being, is not the world taken in its totality, but the transcendent Other with whom I am united, and from whom I am at the same time separated. This is not a mere quibble; it often happens in psychology that on the very level of experience under consideration, a confusion in the use of terms corresponds to a disregard for radically differentiated structures.

Spranger sets up the mystical type as a religious type in opposition to profane types. It is certainly true that the religious man is defined by a relationship with the absolute. But is there no other relationship with the absolute than 'mystical' unrest? For our part, we have already had the occasion of describing other types of religious attitude. The conviction of having been given a human task to carry out, of being responsible for it before God, while counting on him to see it through successfully, is a religious attitude which is distinctly different from the mystic's search. But is it therefore necessarily of less value? Can it be said to be, as it were, a-typical? We do not deny that in religion there is always some mental perception of the ultimate value which ties together all the regions of being. But this perception does not necessarily inspire longing for union. Religious asceticism does not always serve to maintain desire for God in its vertical soaring. Its intention often is different; it can aim at giving expression to some ethical demand implied by a vision of the world.

All things considered, religious eros, though it is undifferentiated in its beginnings, can take various forms. It may turn in on itself in a longing for pantheistic union with the Great All. It may also be transformed and rise to be systematic quest of personal union with God. Finally, it may be the decisive factor in favour of a religious commitment in the midst of a human world to be built up with the hope of finding fulfilment in God. It is precisely because eros can be transmuted into the presence of the Other, over and beyond every need and every spontaneous aspiration, that there is room for very different religious attitudes: there is the contemplative mystical type; there is also a humanism built up before God. Thus, the transformation of desire by the presence of God may well be expressed by two very distinct, but equally religious attitudes. A sustained desire for union with God is the basic axis of the contemplative mode of existence.

Human labour and ethical practice carried out with confident awareness of the presence of God constitute the active religious type. Do these two distinct types depend upon the human differences revealed by the psychology of personality? We think that they do; though in the absence of sufficient data, we cannot prove this statement.

DANGER OF INDISCRIMINATE MYSTICISM

The confusions which surround the theme of religious desire have serious consequences. We shall say nothing about the theological problem which may arise from any assimilation of monasticism and Christianity in general with concrete forms inherited from neo-Platonism. We merely wish to draw attention to two effects which are the direct concern of the psychologist of religion.

The desire for the absolute may be seen as fatal to man: every desire can be regarded as dangerous. And, as we shall see, atheism can be a form of defence against desire. But if the absolute is nothing but the escape point for all human forces, man no longer has at his disposal any adequate means for maintaining himself in his own, temporal, contingent existence. If the otherness of the absolute in relation to the finite is not really safeguarded and justified; if, in union, all distance is completely obliterated, then man enters a limitless and bottomless abyss. Holderlin became mad because he could not maintain this distance. If we identify religion and an absolute mystical union, we do away with the specific human status and mankind is thrown into an atheism of defence. Confusion of this kind has no answer to the haunting fear of annihilation by which so many of our contemporaries are pursued in their religious seeking. Philosophical thought, too, has at its own level made a theme of the fear of destruction which many believers feel in certain moments of groping uncertainty. Merleau-Ponty, for example, says: 'When it is not useless, the recourse to an absolute foundation destroys the very thing it ought to support.' 'Metaphysical and moral consciousness perishes at the touch of the absolute because it is itself, over and beyond the flat world of everyday or sleeping consciousness, the living link between self and self, and between self and others.'[19] The mystical trend of medieval Christianity, modelling itself on the monastic ideal of the time, often tarred with a certain *contemptus mundi*, is partly responsible for the atheist revolt of the modern era.

PEAK EXPERIENCES

We have already had occasion to deal with the thesis of Maslow's study; he aims at bringing into relief the meaning of modes of behaviour and experiences which because they do not originate in a lack cannot be placed within the field of motivations.[20] As the term suggests, a peak experience is an experience of the fullness of being. And it is striking to see in what terms different subjects describe a peak experience. In it the object is discovered as complete unity free from any relationship and outside any finality: the experience is concerned exclusively with the object at rest within itself; in this experience the ego is forgotten and transcended; it is an experience of value and is self-justifying; space and time no longer exist; the object is wholly good and desirable, and the question of will loses any *raison d'être*; the experience is absolute; it is passive and receptive; it is fusion, identification of the perceiver with the perceived; the individual is absorbed in the object contemplated; conflicts and dichotomies, anguish and contrariety give way before worshipping love. Maslow considers that the term 'oceanic experience' adequately expresses this peak state. He distinguishes, however, two separate forms. Certain of his subjects, those who speak of philosophical, religious or mystical experience, see the totality of the world as one and absolute. Others, describing an experience of beauty or love, perceive a particular object as if it were momentarily the whole of the universe.

We cannot surmise what would be Maslow's position with regard to the state of our problem. We have the impression that he adopts the interpretation which the subjects give of their own experiences. They bear witness to the fact that among normal people, there is an invasion of an eros which is affective inebriation. In some mysterious way eros makes every object the centre of the world, and confuses subject with the admired object raised to the dignity of an absolute value. The experiences of love or beauty divinize a fragment of the universe; mysticism divinizes the world in its totality. Judgement, will, and moral law are suspended under the spell of emotion. All distance, every lack is done away with. And the Other as such likewise disappears. Illusion or truth? In this magical metamorphosis of the world, brought about by indiscriminate eros, the true and the real lose their distinctive marks. When these are lost, then religion in the strictest sense of the word is lost too.

The imaginative power of eros is not, then, religious of itself. It requires that the reality principle introduce a cleavage which restores lack to desire and opens a way to the Other. The father symbol contains this force of rupture; it snatches desire from its imaginary immersion in the false infinite of fusion and propels it towards the meeting with the Other.

PSYCHOANALYSIS OF MYSTICISM

Freudian psychoanalysis will help us to penetrate more deeply into the mystery of eros and its troubled origins. Maslow has already prepared the way. The peak experience, he tells us, is a healthy regression below the level of the dissociation of the reality principle from the pleasure principle. The secondary processes which relate to the real world are raised. Maslow even goes so far as to speak of the fusion of the ego, the id, the superego and the ideal ego, of the conscious and the unconscious, of the pleasure principle and the reality principle. Truth to say, these combinations appear to us to result more from confusion in theory than mystical fusion. If there is regression, it consists in the subject descending again beneath the reality principle. No doubt regression can be beneficial and in the erotic experience the regressive moment can even symbolize plenitude of life. It is none the less true that such an experience of affective fusion in itself is nothing but a moment of indistinction that is narcissic in the technical sense of the word. Personally, we prefer to adopt Freud's explanation of this 'mystical' experience, and the judgement which he brings to bear.

After the publication of *The Future of an Illusion* Freud received a letter from an eminent writer [21] (Romain Rolland) who expressed his astonishment that Freud should have lost sight of the true source of religion, so very far removed from the childish and vulgar motivations analysed in his book. Roland recalled a unique experience, known to thousands of people: the experience of eternity, of something limitless, something oceanic which, so he reminds Freud, is at the source of every religious need. Freud replied that he thought he understood this experience: was it not the interior breaking-down of the frontiers between the ego and the id (the primary drive sphere)? He went on to state more precisely that psychoanalysis of the genesis of the ego teaches us that the ego only becomes a subsistent demand in the course of its psychical history. The experience of eternal reality has to correct the ego's absorption in primitive pleasure by the reality principle. Originally, pleasure means everything to the ego; then, by entering into reality, the ego dissociates itself from the eternal world. Nevertheless, the primary ego sentiment is somehow maintained in many people, and its representative contents are precisely the images of the limitless and the bond with the all: that is, images of the oceanic experience. All stages in the psychical formation are preserved 'like the successive strata of the eternal city'. Man may still reactualize the memory of this – but Freud does not see it as being in any way the source of religion. This, as he sees it, is a relationship with a personal and fatherly God, and in his judgement religion has its origin in childish distress and longing for a father. What is more, Freud admits the difficulty he has in conceiving of such an oceanic experience; he never had anything like it. But he must have given some thought to it, as is witnessed by the last note he wrote, found on his desk after his death: 'Mysticism: the obscure autoperception of the reign which stretches beyond the ego: the id.'[22]

Certain psychoanalysts, such as Westerman-Holstijn, acknowledge the mystical virtue of religion. Together with art and love it is the symbolic expression of the affective experience of immediate union with the All from which man has drawn his substance. It can be salutary because, from time to time, every man needs to feel himself rooted and unified.[23]

MATERNAL SYMBOLISM

Close to the narcissic stage, to blessed indistinction and limitlessness, is dual union with the mother. Psychoanalysts have pointed out many symptoms of morbid disintegration which suggest the active permanence of the primordial mother-child bond. In view of the nature of our study we must try to discover traces of this early bond in certain religious forms. Every human psyche has been permanently marked by it, and it remains as a kind of active sediment in everyone. But let there be no mistake: the stamp of the mother image in the human psyche, and the affective values which it arouses, should in no way be regarded as a sign of immaturity, or a mere regrettable carry-over from infancy. Nevertheless, though not necessarily pathological, an exclusive and predominant seeking after the mother-image may lead to an affective, cultural and religious state which is harmful to the development of the personality.

Let us explain this. The primordial mother-child bond reproduces previous psychical experiences in a union of affective fusion: experiences of happiness in a diffused totality, of security in a single pulsation, of expansion of being to the limits of the existent. The affective connotations which go to make up the mother-image, even in an adult, contain values which the subject has experienced in the past and for which at the deepest level of his affective nature, he continues to yearn. Maternal values are, then, woven into existence as essential to the proper development of the affective. We shall not be surprised to find them reproduced in the divine image.

If we wished to build up the mother image without having

recourse to psychology or psychoanalysis, we should only have to gather together the vivid descriptions to be found in the literature of every time and country. The intimate bond between mother and child is constantly mentioned. The mother is described in all her aspects: a being who gives the child every care; she nurtures and caresses; she protects and shelters, she helps, she knows how to wait silently. The mother is affective depth. The mother image is connected with the womanly qualities: receptive fertility, veiled gift, warm tenderness, source and bearer of life. These affective qualities are portrayed in the female symbols: earth, nature, centre, water, sea, home, hearth, cave . . .

We have already shown in the chapter on religious experience that religions celebrate union with nature and with the vital mystery of the cosmos in a spirit of participation. Mother images abound in their rites and religious songs.[24] May we not say that the divine mystery, the fertile centre of nature, is generally regarded as the earliest symbol of the mother bond? The almost universal myth of a lost paradise symbolizes the pacifying harmony of which the mother remains the supreme image.

Thus, we see, the mother is a symbol with very deep religious significance. By symbol we mean an image which, because of its affective connotations, re-presents for us a reality whose depth of meaning will never be completely fathomed by the mind. The mother symbol is polyvalent. It contains threats and promises. In our discussion we have so far pointed out only the positive values of the mother symbol. The mother is a symbol of primordial totality, universal harmony, vital replenishment and happiness which satisfies every longing.[25] Sublimated, the mother image symbolizes the homeland to which the religious desire aspires.[26] And yet, of itself, the mother symbol is not enough to open out religious desire to a truly religious attitude. It is not by chance that the history of civilizations transmits God to us in the father symbol.

JUNG: A PSYCHOLOGY OF THE MOTHER SYMBOL

In our opinion the psychology of Jung may be defined as a psychology of the mother symbol. Within the limits of this book, we can only make very brief reference to Jungian psychology, as also to our critical reflections on it. This psychology is, we may say, a closed world, a kind of nebulous esotericism. In order to understand it we should have to undertake a critical comparison of each of its basic concepts with the facts of psychology and human sciences in general. To have recourse to concepts such as archetype, participation, inflation, self (*Selbst*), teleological libido and so forth, is of no help to us if we are unable to distinguish the real from the imaginary in those terms. Similar to some form of gnosis, the psychology of Jung demands that we give ourselves up to it entirely and that we adopt the language of the initiated. The little faith which we have in the intelligibility of the Jungian concepts discourages us from taking this step. Though we shall not call upon Jung's psychology, we do not deny that it has some real value: it has given rise to a widespread study of religious symbolism of which the *Eranos* circle is, of course, the well known centre.

If we wish to attempt an interpretation of Jung's work, we must look for the key to this system in the mother symbol; it is there too, probably, that it takes its origins. We have only to remark the great number of studies which Jung devoted to the mother symbol in order to realize that his whole theory gravitates round the mother. The father symbol is not entirely absent, but, in comparison with the importance which it is given by Freud, it has a very restricted place in Jung's theory. In particular, it would seem that Jung does not appear to have really grasped the dialectic which sets in opposition and unites the two symbols. Unlike Freud, he has not elaborated a psychology of conflict. His psychology is static. But could it be otherwise? By its very nature, the mother symbol evokes the first paradise which existed before rupture and conflicts.

Many psychologists, especially the disciples of Jung, are fascinated by the idea of a synthesis between Freud and Jung. But this is the mirage of a psychology which seeks to be complete. There is no doubt that this has never been realized by anyone. And it can only be usefully envisaged if we are ready to make a rather radical reinterpretation of Jungian concepts along the lines of the attempt which Szondi has made, not without some success.

The material element is, for Jung, the original foundation and the fertile source of all psychical life.[27] He sees the relationship between mother and child as being more fundamental than the bond with the father, and he therefore considers the mother to be at the heart of every neurosis.[28] The libido yearns to return to the womb in order to be born again to a new life.[29] The desire for incest which, in Freud's theory, is a dynamic conflictual moment, is regarded by Jung as signifying the desire to fertilize the mother in order to beget one's identical self. This fact leads us to three defining characteristics of the mother symbol: its fertile and nurturing warmth; its emotional character leading to the awakening to conscious life; its dark and hidden mystery, uniquely symbolic. The mother is essentially an archetype; under a multiplicity of expressions she belongs to the collective unconscious to be found in every man.

According to Jung, the mother symbol is also part of the concept of God.[30] The mother symbolizes God just as much as does the father. Religion, indeed, is latent in the desire to be born again and thus to rediscover one's entire integrity. But the rebirth of man to a new self-awareness comes about in and by the mother.

These few references to Jung are intended for those readers who are already familiar with his work and they prepare the way for our interpretation. We think that the emphasis given by Jung to rebirth to self, to the necessity of discovering one's inner integrity, to the surmounting of conflicts by assimilation of opposites (good and evil, father and mother, etc.) depends on a mystique of integrity in which we can discern the psychological effects of the mother symbol. Furthermore, the mother is regarded as being the one by whom this rebirth is brought about. We are, then, faced with a psychology which, making use of a very specialized language borrowed from the different branches of human knowledge, gives a new interpretation of all religions as so many symbolic attempts to fulfil the desire for union and original integrity.

If we are right, then we have accounted very satisfactorily for the fact that Jung's psychology leaves no room for a personal God. When he has accomplished the movement of his perfect reintegration, the subject has found his centre within his own self. And there he takes possession of the totality of the universe. In this phase of fulfilment and inward sufficiency, could there be any meaning in a lived relationship with the transcendent Other? As in the peak experience described by Maslow, time and history are abolished; otherness is reabsorbed in an imaginary inner affective plenitude.

The mystical tendency in search of immediate and experiential union with the All is innate in man, because of the affective power of the libido. The phases of narcissism and dual union with the mother strengthen the original aspiration of the eros; they permeate the ancient fund of active images and profound memories which man has retained from his origins. Religions have often drawn upon the affective and imaginative power of eros: we need only recall the mystery religions, the cosmo-vitalist symbolisms, the mysticism of fusion. Jung's religious psychology marks a stage in the mystical and mystery movement: it is an attempt to complete it by a strictly psychological technique. For this reason we regard Jung's psychology, in spite of the appearance it may assume, as little religious, to say the least, as atheist Freudianism, because it seals up any opening on the Other. Nevertheless, Jung has had the merit of restoring both the mother symbol and mystical eros to the domain of depth psychology whereas Freud paid too little attention to them.

EXPERIENCE OF HAPPINESS: PRE-RELIGIOUS CONDITION OF RELIGION

Though desire for God may completely transform original eros, it nevertheless arises from it, as we have already seen. Is there any religious man who does not hope that God will satisfy his desires? And how can fulfilment in God be expressed otherwise than by the symbol of paradise? The end reintegrates the origins. But between the two, the rupture in affective totality obliges the subject to leave his immanence, to change his original desire into a faith in things unseen and thus it opens out for him a way of access to the Other.

In the absence of material values, human desire would gradually die out. In order to hope, man needs to experience security, happiness and original integrity. The future only acquires some sense in relation to a basic primitive experience by which it is prefigured. The spells woven by esoteric mysticism, when they do not fascinate, easily provoke a rational refusal and a nihilist withdrawal.

That Freud showed himself so adamant in his refusal of all religion, we think was partly due to his puritan determination to purify the libido of its mirages, and to dominate its primitive hopes. In every desire for union, Freud saw, and rebuked, a regression towards the confused period when man's psyche was still plunged in undifferentiated libido. Freud was not able to see the symbolic power of human eros in the great mystical themes of paradise, integrity, completeness. Nor was he able to distinguish the symbolical moments graven into man's deep affectivity.

Religion, openness to the Other, can only come about by the dialectic force of the two constitutive elements of the human: harmonious and blessed plenitude in man's early life, and the reality principle, of which the father is the figure. In their reciprocal relationship, these two moments produce the time which moves towards a new type of union with the Other, recognized as utterly transcendent.

It is not only Freud's evident atheism which shows us the necessity of some primary symbolic experience. Clinical psychology also reveals that the indispensable conditions for the awakening of the religious attitude are to be found in a certain experience of happiness and a feeling of integration. In an excellent little study, the well-known psychiatrist, Rumke, has very cleverly analysed the aberrations of 'character and affective disposition' which can be an obstacle to the development of the religious attitude.[31] It is not our business to summarize this study here, but it is our source of inspiration when we bring to notice the primary affective conditions which seem to be necessary for religious development. We shall see that they are linked up with the dynamic process of desire.

In order that man may become religious, he must feel that he fits adequately into the whole of existence. According to Rumke, this sentiment emerges into consciousness at the moment of puberty. For this reason the author is wary of the idea of a personal religious life before that age. We believe that man is familiar with such a sentiment from his earliest years: he lives it in a faith which is perceptive, not explicit. In joy and trust, he experiences the well-being of the universe. And it is in this sense that some have been able to speak of the child's natural religiosity. Genetic psychology reminds us constantly of this paradox: a child's sentiments are at an affective level, but he is only aware of them laterally. The affective troubles of puberty which disorganize the psyche bring these sentiments to the level of explicit consciousness and the religious aspiration emerges as soon as the adolescent becomes aware of his place in a meaningful whole. If he has not had the early experience of happiness, the subject will be cut off from the source of religious desire. If eros has not been able to blossom out, man is deprived of this imaginative and affective power which makes him capable of the symbolic perception of the world. But the religious vision of the world implies, precisely, that in life, in nature, in the starry sky, or at least in existence, the subject recognizes the epiphany of an Other whose presence transcends all else and who is waiting for man in the future. The symbolic perception presupposes a fundamental and dynamic link between man and the universe; a link which is established by eros, the principle of happiness and union. If vital happiness is marred in early days, the dimension of the infinite may be definitively severed.

The negative side of this necessity for early affective satisfaction as a condition of religion is shown up in Sartre's work: 'I lived in terror . . . And when I look for the reason of this I find that being a spoilt child, a gift from Providence, my absolute futility was all the more evident to me as the rites of family life constantly appeared as forged necessity and nothing else. I felt I was too much, so had to disappear; I was a washed-out blossom threatened with perpetual extinction . . . God might well have dragged me out of trouble: I might have been a signed masterpiece; assured of holding my part in the universal concert, I might have waited patiently till he showed me his plans and my need. I had a presentiment of religion. I hoped for it, it was the remedy . . . But following on that, in the fashionable God I learnt about, I did not recognize whom my soul awaited: I needed a Creator, they gave me a Big Boss; the two were only one but I did not know that; I served without warmth the pharisaical Idol, and the official doctrine disgusted me in the search after my own faith.'[32] This admirable text bears witness to the absence of any pre-religious experience of happiness; it shows the anguished search for some answer from above which would fit the child into the world's harmony. Experience has convinced us that, in the absence of some previous experience of happiness, the religious message cannot be grasped: it responds to no natural and vital hope. For the child, the sacred is discovered in the continuation of vital and affective growth.

Several tendencies which show up during the upheaval of puberty may also impede the development of a feeling of having a place in the world, and thus close the religious perspective to the subject; such are rationalist intellectualism, voluntarism. On the other hand the absence of the phenomena of puberty may stunt religious growth forever, just as it stunts any authentic relationship with others.

The pre-religious sentiment is characterized and structured progressively. Rumke distinguishes in its evolution a second phase: the moment when being as a whole is felt as the original foundation of everything. Thus, reason already gives articulate meaning to the whole. In a third phase, the whole is experienced as being the 'foundation of my foundation'. At this stage a rupture is brought about in the insertion in the heart of totality; this is the beginning of a personal relationship between me and my foundation. It is then that religious doubt first appears. But we shall not deal with that here as it goes beyond the scope of this chapter, being a matter of genetic religious psychology.

A Pathological Case of Mother-Religion

We have remarked earlier that we have rarely, if at all, been able to discover religious desire as a religious experience or as the motivation of religion. It is only among adolescents that we have been able to observe a few ambiguous indications of this phenomenon. Nevertheless, taking into consideration clinical experience and historical evidence, which have some bearing on the desire for God, we feel certain that religion has its origin in eros, the principle of happiness and of union. This principle works underground, so to speak, and builds up the underlying arc and the symbolic power which connects man with the All, propelling him towards the promise of an infinite. When this affective and vital power is damaged by the vicissitudes of personal history, man discovers that he is a misfit, a stranger in the world, an absurd phenomenon faced with a meaningless destiny. The mother symbol, figure of harmony and happiness, recalls the primitive memory of full union and the hope of a future paradise. It is part of the divine image, but does not oust the father symbol.

In their exchange of ideas on the oceanic experience, Freud and his correspondent were both right, and both wrong. The oceanic experience is largely unconscious; it is the primitive symbol of a recognized infinity. It appears to be the source of religion because of the openness to happiness and love with which it colours affectivity. But it only flowers out into religion after a series of deep transformations which are brought about by the father symbol.

Other illustrations of religious desire are to be seen in the phenomenon which it causes in certain pathological cases. By way of example, we give here a summary of the clinical study of a case treated in psychoanalysis by H. Schjelderup.[33] The subject was a young woman, an unbeliever, but one who had received a religious education. The most striking features of her psychological make-up were attempts at suicide, glossolalia and mystical experiences. She sometimes had a very strong feeling of no longer existing; an experience which was accompanied by a feeling of complete happiness. She described it in these terms: 'not anguish: absolute harmony. I no longer think—I am not an individualized ego . . . No more wishes or desires . . . only a real feeling of being united to something else. In this state I am just everything; I am the light, the snow; I am what I hear.' The anamnesis showed the presence of violent opposition to an irascible father whom she thought mad. As a result she had the feeling of being guilty, hateful and loathsome; deprived of any sort of help, she took refuge in anguish which greatly strengthened the bond with her mother. Refusal of her femininity and fear of life made her fly to her mother. During the treatment she made an intense mother transference on to the analyst; she desired to enter his inner space and to live in him, in security, in fulfilled contact, sheltered from every responsibility. Little by little death fantasies gave rise to attempts at suicide: death was seen as a return to the mother, welcome and rest, warmth on her breast. Death seemed to be that union with the earth by which one becomes earth; that is to say, absolute all in all. Death signified, then, the permanence of a mystic experience of Nirvana. Death solved, once and for all, the basic problem of the impossibility of absolute communication with another person. Sometimes the subject expressed the return to mother-earth by means of Christian symbolism: the figure of Christ fused with that of the mother. In this mystical regression, the patient had regular attacks of a tendency to utter unintelligible sounds. She was unable to control the sounds which lived in her. In those moments she became a tiny child, in the euphoria of a wonderful intimacy with herself. She felt herself become bigger and bigger and seemed alone in the whole world.

Even the uninformed reader will easily recognize in these pathological experiences the regressive effects of narcissism and the reciprocal bond between mother and child. We have here a vivid example of the way in which morbid mystical eros shows up: complete union, harmony in plenitude, abolition of finitude and responsibility. The 'mystical' experiences pervade the entire psyche to the point of becoming mortal. This pathological case allows us to measure the basic naturalism, the destructive force, of a desire for union and harmony which is not validated by the acceptance of reality, of rupture, by the law of the father.

II. Father-Religion

Lessons of Religious History

As a result of our study of religious experience we discovered the paradoxical truth that the primitive peoples, such as the food-gatherers who belong to the most elementary forms of civilization with no economic technique, have a very simple and very direct notion of a Father-God. The pygmies of Central Africa, again, see the Creator as a personal being who has neither wife nor brothers, but who begot two sons and a daughter. These were the first men; the girl was forbidden to look upon her father.

The idea of the paternity of God arises both from an experience of existence as a free gift, and from the symbolism of the family. We have seen that this immediate intuition opens out into a mentality of cultural childhood, constantly renewed in times of deep distress, and that this mentality is in conflict with theoretical speculations and with the development of a cosmo-vitalist idea of the sacred. From the history of religions we learn, then, that the primitive religious intention contains a whole network of possibilities and that different types of civilization stress one or other aspect. In a historical perspective, monotheism appears as the reconquest of the primitive theist intuition which had been darkened by the development of such human powers as technical domination of the world, participation in the mystery of life, cosmological speculations, etc.

It is not the business of the psychologist to evaluate the different religious forms he meets. But if he wishes to understand the religious man, he cannot content himself with a mere description of religious phenomena. From their connection with the civilizations in which they were born and the meaning of their historical evolution, he should be able to establish certain correlations and laws. However this may be, the history of religions obliges us to set aside old attempts at an over-simple interpretation in which the history of both culture and religion was regarded as a continuous progress from the lowest upwards. On the contrary, everything seems to show that the primitive religious intuitions were made up of a set of very different elements which, in the course of

12

events, have broken up into the many forms of religion which we know today: magical, mystery, transcendental, polytheist religions. The psychologist is bound to be particularly interested in the intermittent appearance of a Father-God and the very varied meanings which he can assume. The history of religion gives us proof of the existence of three distinct theories of the divine paternity: the first is that of the food-gatherers and it corresponds to a naïve intuition; the second appears in moments of calamity in more developed milieux; the third form is found in highly evolved systems of religious thought, such as neo-Platonism. Then again, the Judaeo-Christian tradition has its own concept of the Father-God. The fact of these extremely different ideas of divine paternity during the course of religious history seems to prove that we have here something more than a symbol connatural to all men. And we wonder how it could be otherwise, for anything connected with the family depends on a structure with which the individual has to integrate himself, and on work resulting from the personal commitment of the subject.

Daring to propose a psychological interpretation of the religious history of the father symbol, we suggest that if the father is a primitive symbol of God, then it only begins to have some real meaning when it has ceased to be self-evident, intuitive. The father symbol is thought-provoking. In order to grasp it in all its symbolic power, man had to think about it, question it, exploit other religious possibilities. Furthermore in his rebellion against the father symbol, man had to assert his autonomy. To a certain extent we can say that the rupture of the 'Fall' was necessary to enable man to achieve adult self-possession, and thus restore its original greatness to the divine symbol, setting it free from his own too human projections.

But could man do this without help; was man self-sufficient? Has he need of any other help than that of divine grace at work in humanity? The Judaeo-Christian tradition believes in the irreplaceable part played by the word of God. Revelation has burst in upon history and set up a dialogue of questioning and acceptance which alone is able to show the divine paternity for what it really is. The psychologist has not to pronounce on the truth of this belief, but he cannot underestimate its religious effects. He must try to pinpoint the specific psychological structures which these beliefs assume and give rise to.

The Three Levels of a Psychological Study of the Father Symbol

The foregoing considerations lead us to think that the study of the father symbol should be carried out at three different levels. We shall have to go into the deep psychological structure of the father symbol. Then we must see how it is presented in theological tradition, for this is of no less importance for the psychologist than the many religious attitudes which can be observed in everyday life. Finally we shall have to examine the symbol of divine paternity as it is felt by those believers by whom it is accepted.

In the major works which Freud has devoted to this question, *Totem and Taboo* (1913), *Civilization and its Discontents* (1930) and *Moses and Monotheism* (1938), he attempts to reconstitute the sequence of the decisive moments in history which have led to the father religion. He is no longer dealing here with the popular and debased forms of religion shown up by clinical experience and which he has denounced in *The Future of an Illusion*. He attempts the psychoanalysis of the great religion of totemism and the Judaeo-Christian tradition. In order to get to the heart of the matter Freud makes a thorough examination of historical documents; it is there that he comes across the father symbol at its deepest and in all its dramatic power.

Many a psychologist has wished to test the Freudian theory of the father symbol of God. They have therefore questioned believers, using the methods of practical enquiry. But we have a strong impression that these attempts are vitiated by a double error in the point of view adopted. First, it is impossible for a practical study alone to verify a psychoanalytical thesis: the practical method does not achieve the same psychological depth as does psychoanalysis. Secondly, in his work Freud based himself on historical evidence. But we cannot state *a priori* that even Christians who believe in divine paternity, actually reflect their faith in their religious attitude. We have to distinguish between the image of God as it is presented by religious tradition and that effectively experienced by the faithful. There is in certain studies a confusion between the two which we condemn and which we regard as a result of the psychologistic mentality. The starting point in this case is the postulate that all ideal and affective terms are the natural outcome of the needs and tendencies of the average man. The study of the divine image among believers requires even greater prudence: the facts revealed by analysis are to be measured against the well-defined possibilities of the method employed: different methods reveal different and complementary components of the image of God.

In order to avoid any misunderstanding, we propose to distinguish three types of research: practical research into the image of God among believers: a clinical examination of the Freudian thesis; and finally a reflection on the experience and the attitude of Jesus Christ by whom the divine paternity is fully revealed. In religious history, Jesus Christ stands out as the most convincing witness, the one who is most explicitly aware of the fatherhood of God and this sense of the divine paternity is manifested in every one of his actions. For the psychologist this is an exceptional religious phenomenon of great interest.

PARENTAL IMAGES AND DEITY IMAGE

The image of God arises from the experience of the world and is therefore necessarily mediated by the two figures which are the source of each human existence: the father and the mother. Quite naturally the concept of God comes to us through the symbolic evocation of the father and the mother. But we must examine to what degree the idea of God does in fact correspond to the parental images.

The question has a double aspect. We might first ask in what measure the two images contribute to the formation of the deity image and what relationship there exists between them in their religious reference. The second aspect of this question is to know in what this religious reference actually consists: is it simply a continuation, a transference, an idealization, a projection? Often enough these technical terms are used without necessarily

signifying a specific psychological process. But this looseness in
the use of terms leads to a great deal of misunderstanding. The
process described easily leads us to infer some judgement. Thus
the thesis according to which God is the projection of the father
image sometimes leads to the conclusion that, being nothing but
projection, it is necessarily illusion.

The Symbol

We cannot give here the complete justification of the position
which we adopt in this matter, but we distinguish two dimensions
in the symbol. In the first place, resulting as it does from experience, the symbol is a mental and affective schema which has
impressed itself on the memory and in the affectivity. The subject
looks beyond this schema to a reality beyond the limits of his
human experience. Concretely, the real presence of the father
produces a certain father image in the consciousness of the child
which results from every affective relationship which he has had
with the father. We can say that a certain imaginary and con-
ceptual *Gestalt* has been formed. Let us call this the memory-
image. However, the father image is by no means exhausted by
the memory-image. It is also made up of all those meanings
conferred on it by the subject's cultural milieu. Language, custom
and law, no less than personal experience, each contributes some
connotation of its own to the sign-word 'father'. What is more,
the subject's experience is not limited to a passive reception of
visual images and affective impressions. The family constellation
itself gives a special position to the father and this in itself makes
him significant, a pole of meaning; an objective structuration is
imposed on the child, even if he is hardly conscious of this, at
least explicitly. Nor is the child merely receptive; he goes out to
the father with his requests and his desires, and he reacts according to the answers which he receives. He interprets the behaviour
of the real father in a relationship of active exchange of requests
and replies. Conflicts and disappointments strongly influence the
father image in him.

It is not possible to unravel all the factors which contribute to
the structuring of the father image. But we think that we can

distinguish two levels: the memory-image, which represents the real father as the subject sees him; and the symbol-image which represents the father according to the subject's desires. This distinction corresponds with the one which exists between fact and what would be 'right'. The image of the right is what we call symbol, preferring this word 'right' to many others. The expression 'ideal father' is sometimes used. But this is inadequate because the word 'ideal' suggests something of affective idealization, or some sort of extension in keeping with affective demands. Whereas the 'right' father implies, on the contrary, a note of reality which the subjects are often quite able to distinguish from their more or less unreal and deceptive idealization. The father 'concept' is another expression which is sometimes used, and it is not much more helpful because it suggests an intellectual schema. We also leave on one side the Jungian term 'archetype' which signifies an inborn, unconscious and collective symbol, whereas the father image is always tributary to cultural setting and the family constellation. The word symbol, on the contrary, well expresses the double reality which we mean here: a mental and affective schema resulting both from individual experiences and from the structural factors constituted by cultural environment and family. Beyond the applications which may be made to human reality, this schema envisages a deeper reality still, a law of the human being and the world, perhaps even an absolute Father who is the origin of every human fatherhood.

Researches into the Memory-Image

Several authors have interpreted Freud as though he saw in the image of God only a sublimated father able to fulfil human requests. We have already seen that many of Freud's texts support this position. A passage from his study on Leonardo da Vinci gives a good summary of this idea of the father as providence for all human needs: 'Thus we recognize that the roots of the need for religion are in the parental complex; the almighty and just God and kindly Nature appear to us as grand sublimations of father and mother, or rather as revivals and restorations of the young child's ideas of them. Biologically speaking, religiousness is to be traced to the small human child's long-drawn-out helplessness and need of help . . . The protection against neurotic illness, which religion vouchsafes to those who believe in it, is easily explained: it removes their parental complex, on which the sense of guilt in individuals as well as in the whole human race depends, and disposes of it, while the unbeliever has to grapple with the problem on his own.'[34]

A certain inconsistency is to be remarked in Freud's thought here : in the same text he passes imperceptibly from the longing for a father-protector to the ethical drama of guilt. Thus, he admits two sources of religion. Later he becomes more consciously aware of the radical difference between them. In the first sentences of this text the father and mother symbols are as yet but little differentiated. God, the father sublimated, and Nature, the mother sublimated, meet identical demands of forlorn man in search of security. God is nothing more than the immediate transposition of a childhood experience of the father.

If this is really so, then both parental images can signify God. The importance which will accrue to each one will depend upon the satisfactions the individual receives from either the father or the mother.

Several psychologists have examined affective preferences and related them to the deity image, that is the deity image as defined by these same affective preferences.

M. O. Nelson and E. M. Jones[35] have drawn up a series of sixty propositions expressing twenty sentiments which fit the parental images as well as the deity images: acceptance, unreserved acceptance, help, love, support, trust, understanding, easy to please, easy to satisfy, generosity, interest, forgiveness, patience, protection, nearness, easily accessible, significant relationship, respect, security, maintenance.[36] In the sixty propositions the subjects refer these sentiments to the father, the mother, and God, according to a scale designed to reflect their experience. For example, the item 'I feel protected by Mother' can be set under nine headings which range from total agreement to total disagreement. The results which Nelson and Jones obtained from the examination of twenty Protestants show that in all of them, men

and women, there was a closer resemblance between the sentiments evoked in connection with the mother and God, than
between those suggested by the relationship with the father and
God. The greatest resemblance was to be found in those subjects
who had a preference for their mothers. It was least in three
subjects who preferred their fathers. For those subjects who had
no marked preference for either, there was a significant correlation between the sentiments felt for the father and those felt for
God. But even here, it was lower than the correlation between
the feelings towards the mother and God.

O. Strunk[37] carried out this enquiry again on subjects of a
more uniform spiritual maturity. He obtained very different
results. The link between the mother image and the deity image
remains very pronounced, but the relationship established between
God and the father is not much less pronounced. With female
subjects, the correlation God-father is slightly higher than the
correlation God-mother. Strunk poses the hypothesis that a more
developed religious attitude influences the relationship between
the parental images and the deity image. His subjects 'project'
God according to the two parental images; with the more mature
subjects the father symbolizes God just as much as does the
mother.

Fr A. Godin, S.J. and Miss M. Hallez[38] applied the technique
of Nelson and Jones to seven homogeneous groups. They came
to some very carefully graded conclusions. As did the previously
mentioned authors, they remarked that the parental images
condition the deity image and, consequently, the attitude towards
God. With men there is a closer connection between the deity
image and the mother image; it is the other way round with the
women subjects. The connection between divine image and
parental image tends to disappear with age. The conditioning
of the deity image by the parental images is stronger if there is a
marked preference for one or other of the parents. In this case,
the deity image will be drawn towards the image of the preferred
parent, or else is associated with the least-liked parent to the
detriment of the deity image. Fr Godin has three hypotheses to
explain the separation of the parent images from the deity image

in older subjects: greater spiritual maturity purifies the deity image; or else the parental images become less differentiated through a process of idealization, after the death of the parents for example; or, again, there may be a combination of the two preceding phenomena.

Though these studies are very interesting, we cannot ignore the fact that the choice of the terms of the enquiry does set very definite limits. In our opinion they falsify both project and conclusions at the level at which the authors have chosen to remain: that is to say at the level of the comparative study of subjects taken individually, of parental images and the evocation of the deity. In fact, the affective categories which the authors use for delimiting the parental and deity images, are defined almost exclusively by values set out in terms of intimacy (acceptance, help, trust, nearness . . .) Thus it seems natural that the affective preferences should go towards the parent of the opposite sex. Or again, among older subjects, or among those who are separated from their parents by reason of the religious state, the affective preferences gradually diminish by process of retroactive idealization. Under these conditions it is impossible that the same categories applied to God should not incline the deity image towards the parental image of the opposite sex.

Whatever may be the outcome of all this, these enquiries cannot verify the Freudian theory of a deity concept formed according to parental images. Differing from the other psychologists we have mentioned, Fr Godin, a skilled psychoanalyst, is careful to warn us against any misunderstanding in this respect. Nevertheless, we think that these findings do complete and fill in the details of Freud's thesis of the relationship between God and the father-protector as he has set it out in *The Future of an Illusion*. And therein lies the interest that these studies have for us. For it is very striking to notice that the affective qualities of intimacy, understanding, consolation, which the subjects find in God are also especially remarked in the parent of the opposite sex.

It remains for us to ask if these qualities exhaust all that could be said of the parental and deity images. A subject may well love and admire other relationships with his father and with God.

Genetic psychology shows us the extraordinary influence of the father model with which the boy has to identify himself. But the efficacity of this dynamic relationship is no longer expressed in terms of affective preference. Love sets working very different affective vectors and they extend far beyond the limits of protective and trusting intimacy. Furthermore, as we have already explained, man may well seek God through a parental image which is not the replica of the real parent.

Study of the Parental Images as Symbols

In order to know the true correspondence between the parental images and the deity image we shall have to study them in their symbolism as we have it explained above. This is what we have attempted to do with the help of our collaborators.[39] We have tried to discover the specific qualities attributed to the father, to the mother and to God as revealed in profane and religious literature. The characteristics proper to the parental images were set out in two corresponding lists and these were submitted to the judgement of competent persons. This allowed us to draw up two scales, one of maternal qualities; the other of paternal. The father appears as: authority, law-maker, power, strength, norm, judge, ordering intelligence; he is distant, severe, immovable, dynamic; he enlightens, points the way to the future, directs, takes the initiative, shows up the child's littleness; he is the source of dignity. The mother seems to be interiority, depth, intensity, refuge; she is welcoming, affectionate, tender, attentive, patient; she shares the child's interests, surrounds him with care, knows how to wait, cares for, is always there, shows up what is delicate, allows the child to be child, welcomes and shelters. These two series of values were carefully worked out and established in such a way as to present the different functions and affective attributes which literature and psychology recognize in the two parents in their union and complementarity.

We asked 178 subjects, 82 girls and 96 boys, all Catholic university students aged between 20 and 24 years, to associate these different categories with the mother image, the father image and the deity image. For the reasons which we have already explained, we asked the subjects to consider not their real parents, but their parents as they should be; that is to say their 'right' father and mother image; this is the only image which has any symbolic value. The statistics give the following results: the paternal qualities are more apt for distinguishing the two parental images than are the maternal qualities. The father has, then, a more complex image; not only does it include a large number of the maternal qualities, but it is also made up of specific qualities which distinguish the father from the mother. The qualities of intimacy and tenderness are, however, peculiar to the mother. The attributes of judge, governor, strength are more exclusively characteristic of the father image. But in the application of these different characteristics to God, it appears that the deity image is even more complex than the father image: it includes in a still higher degree certain maternal characteristics such as: patience, depth, interiority, refuge, availability, welcome, care, sharing in man's interests, knowing how to wait. The paternal qualities attributed to God express above all firmness and directive action, such for example as the qualities of ordering intelligence, judge, power, strength, law-maker, authority, steadiness, concern with the future. The deity image results from the parental images; it is, then, nearer to the father image than to the mother image. But the maternal characteristics are attributed more emphatically to God than are the paternal characteristics. It should be observed that everything that has been said up to now concerning these two images is equally true of the attributions made by the boys and by the girls. Furthermore, it is also worth noting that certain parental qualities are very little connected with the deity image. The obvious reason for this would seem to be the too human character of these qualities. Two such characteristics are the maternal quality of attentiveness, and the paternal quality of distance, though in fact this is rarely attributed to the father. The calculation of the scores of these qualities taken as a whole, according to the degree of attribution to the three concepts, confirms our results: the distance between God and the father is noticeably less than that established between God and the mother. The totality of these qualities is attributed more normally to the father and to God than to the mother and God. A greater distance is remarked between the father and the mother than between the father and God.

We may conclude then that for the two sexes the maternal qualities and the paternal qualities evoke the divine being. This would seem to give good evidence that among Christian subjects, if not among others, the real idea of God is formed through the intermediary of the two parental images recognized in their differentiated functions. Both are truly symbolic: in their ideal content they are composed of elements which evoke God. But God transcends their human limitations; he appears as a synthesis of contrasts. The paternal symbol is more apt to be referred to the divine being because in itself it is already representative of a plenitude of qualities which point to God. In calling God 'Father' we in no way reduce the deity image to a single parental pole, exclusive of the second. Properly understood, the father image is more representative of the deity image than is the symmetrically inverse mother image. These conclusions are well expressed in the words of the young poet Francois d'Espiney: 'Father whose name is Father, and almost whose name is Mother . . .'[40] More-over this double invocation of God is met with in more than one religious text. We quote, for example, the prayer said by the Kekchis before the maize harvest: ' Thou O God, thou my Lord, Thou my Mother, Thou my Father, Lord of the mountain and the vales . . . Who knows when I shall be able to talk to thee again O my Father, O my Mother! Angel, Lord of the hills and the vales! But I will begin to pray to thee; why should I not, O my God?'[41]

To come to a valid conclusion we need a comparative study of subjects belonging to different cultures, matriarchal and patriarchal, in order to show in what measure the idea of God undergoes the influence of parental images when they are thought of in different terms than those of our western cultural milieu.[42]

THE FATHER SYMBOL IN PSYCHOANALYTIC THEORY

By means of depth analysis made possible by clinical experience, psychoanalysis has shown us how man becomes a really human subject, following the curve of his personal development through-out life by conflicts, renunciations, identifications, and the formation of his affective bonds. This dynamic becoming starts in the family constellation, where the father and the mother represent the two essential affective poles by means of which, and with regard to which, a child progressively structures himself until he becomes a man. It is in this sense that psychoanalysis shows itself to be a basic genetic study, a true anthropogenesis.[43] In this progressive humanization of man from childhood onwards, the father plays a specific role. Compared with the maternal function, the father assumes a unique role in humanization, not, in the first place, for what he is in himself, with his individual qualities, but on account of his position in the family. In his major works on religion, Freud shows us that it is in virtue of his specific function that the father awakens man to the deity image.

The Structuring Force of the Father Symbol

In order to have some psychological understanding of divine paternity we must, then, first consider the formation of the human father symbol. It would be rash to attempt to describe the father symbol in a few lines. We shall do nothing more than briefly recall the major facts of this theory and leave the reader to consult other works which deal with it more fully and provide examples.

Freud, and many psychoanalysts after him, have been able to show that the essential and definitive structuring of man is brought about by means of the Oedipus conflict which thus appears to be the origin of the whole of civilization and of its different dimensions: ethical, religious, political. Many people, including some psychologists who have been misled by popular writings on the subject, regard the Oedipus complex as a rather inconvenient hump which we carry with us through life from childhood onwards. But in reality, the Oedipus complex character-izes the psychological phase between the ages of three and six years when affective relations become more structured by differ-entiation and polarization. At the Oedipus age, the child, a being of pleasure and desire who has not yet acquired a true awareness either of himself or others, undergoes, in confrontation with the two family poles, an affective organization which gives him a lasting orientation in life and makes of him a being conscious of reality, of law, and thus capable of an ethical life. Up to that time, the child has lived in symbiosis with the mother. There has been no possibility of affective limitation because the libido cannot, of itself, say no; it is diffuse union, unlimited pleasure, though certainly language and family education have already imposed certain laws and limits. But these are only assumed in the deep affectivity from the moment the child really becomes aware, in his inner depths, that the father is set between him and the mother. In virtue of his function, irrespective of his personality, the father is the one who lays down the law. This is the Oedipean prohibition which often, and very wrongly, is limited to the sexual domain, as though the father were there merely to forbid the child any sexual commerce with the mother. The father is the person who, by the fact of his effectual presence, separates the child from the mother. He imposes a limit on the child's unlimited affective desires; he leads the child to renounce the affective paradise of diffuse union which is a mixture of pleasure, happiness, eroticism and security. The Oedipus complex is necessarily of the nature of a conflict: in the first instance, the law appears as an exterior violence, a purely negative prohibition. But, since he is bound to the father by an initial tenderness, the child has sufficient power to be able to identify himself with the father, to interiorize his law, and to recognize in him the model of a free existence directed to the future. From that moment the law is liberating; it refers to a future happiness yet to be conquered. The negative moment is necessary, for the father jerks the child out of his dream of indistinct harmony and passive pleasure. He separates the child from the mother and from this separation there results, in the child's psychology, a cleavage and a lack: these are the conditions of liberty, independent existence, true desire. Once the child has been separated from the mother, thrown back on himself and obliged to take notice of the real organized world, he will be able freely to dispose of himself. He will become conscious of his desires and accustomed to keep them under control. Thus he learns to become himself, a distinct and autonomous being. The desires which orientate him to a future in which his father is his model are no longer condemned to destruction in the artificial paradise of an imaginary satisfaction. Happiness lies ahead, no longer behind, in the past. Furthermore, the pursuit of personal happiness is now justified: having become an ideal figure with whom the child can identify himself, the father is the guarantee of happiness.

In spite of the limitations of this brief sketch, it helps us to discover the human elements which structure the father image. They fall into three basic categories: the law, the model, and the promise. In face of the demand for immediate union and unlimited pleasure, the father exacts separation, limitation and respect for others. But, by this fact, he introduces the reality principle as a basis for interpersonal relations. He is the law, with all its negative aspects, its limits, its prohibitions. He also represents a very positive function; the child can recognize the father as someone with whom he must identify himself. The father is the successful man, the happy man. And he is father because he recognizes the child as his equal in becoming. He gives the child a model with whom he can assimilate himself in order to bring about his own structuring. The encounter between law and model opens the dimension of the future: in the natural and diffuse bond with the mother the child has no real being; he has to become what he is in germ. The future is promised him, it is allowed and guaranteed.

All these paternal qualities can be summed up in one admirable expression: the father is the one who recognizes the son. To recognize means to accord someone his own personality by a word which is at once law, bond of spiritual kinship and promise. The recognition is made by the word. It assumes tender sentiments but goes beyond them. It is of quite another order. It is no longer an immediate fact welling up from a mere affective reciprocity. It is not natural; that is, it does not emerge from our nature, affectivity, desires, nor even from our reason. It has to be pronounced in all liberty. It is not a cry of either distress or desire. Recognition realizes the only fact which humanizes man: that is to say, recognition is the perfectly free assumption of one's own existence and the intentional creation of a conscious bond with another. When a man says to a woman, 'Now you are my wife' he changes both himself and the other.[44] They go beyond what is merely natural and set up a properly human bond which means commitment, and promise of a future. In the same way, the father, by his word, recognizes the child. This word is not necessarily spoken, it may be transmitted by the language of significant behaviour.

Freud has very strongly emphasized the decisive influence that the paternal function continues to have on the progressive spiritualization of both culture and religion. His clinical experience, joined to his knowledge of man, convinced him that, in the measure that men allow themselves to be transformed by the recognition of the ethical function of the father, they liberate themselves from immediate sensory satisfactions and come to devote themselves to the reign of the spirit, culture, language and intellect. Mastering their pleasure drives, they enter upon social institutions. Many psychologists and even some psychoanalysts, taken up with the maternal values, have reacted against this evaluation of the role played by the father and reproached Freud for exaggeration. But in fact, they have not been able to grasp the true significance of the father symbol. It will be recalled that in the studies we have quoted, no mention was made of the specific qualities of the father symbol. This led us to set out a scale of qualities which restored the father image to its original dimensions.

Freud and the Fatherhood of God

One of the most baffling and yet fascinating characteristics of the great Judaeo-Christian tradition is its claim to be essentially the religion of the Father and the Word. And even the convinced atheist, Freud, was capable of recognizing its greatness. Unfortunately, for want of a sufficient knowledge of Judaeo-Christian theology, he grasped in the word of the Father nothing but the moment of prohibition. Strangely enough, this man whose first book was his father's gift of a Bible, was never to discover that the Word of the Father is as much promise as prohibition, and even more so. Though the decalogue clearly conditions the Covenant between God and his people, Freud could only see the Law. He tried to elaborate an exhaustive explanation of the mysterious constitution of the symbol of divine paternity on the sole basis of a conflict between rebellious man and God. His view was that mankind felt guilty. It was for this reason that the sense of sin continued to be at the core of religion. Guilt was inevitable because man, urged by a libidinous nature, wanted to be, and to have, everything.[45] Repressing his guilt, which nevertheless continued to disquiet him, man came greatly to magnify the father image making it out to be an all-powerful, divine father who demanded respect and submission.

The Freudian interpretation of Judaeo-Christianity stops short, then, at the moment of conflict and ignores the word of recognition and promise uttered by the father. Freud believed that the Judaeo-Christian religion is explained by a single psychological fact: man's rebellion and consequent guilt. Though Freud was able to recognize, over and beyond the resolution of the conflict, a positive function of identification in the human father, in the religious relation he could see only sin. The moment of recognition and of reconciliation is entirely absent from his theory. Nevertheless Freud has insisted on the value of guilt from a spiritual point of view. For him the Jewish religion, purified by the Law, is characterized by an extraordinary progress in spirituality: the Mosaic prohibition of any representation of God, the obligation to adore an invisible God, the command not to take the name of God in vain are all factors which raise the Jewish religion far above any of the natural religions. Thus we may say that the father symbol makes all its demands for renunciation and promotes the reign of the spirit. The prophets are the outstanding figures of this religion which finds its full realization in the objection to, and the indictment of, the natural tendencies.

However, the father, understood as an external and law-making power, came to take on the aspect of a tyrant imposing a relation-

13

ship of subordination. Freud says that religion is enslaving, it makes man effeminate, and debases reason by obliging it to passive consent.[46] There is a curious ambivalence in the Freudian judgement of religion. This, however, is understandable for it is characteristically the judgement of an unresolved conflict. We find many traces of this in the conscience of those believers who still have this double attitude towards God, which is typical of the unresolved conflict: on the one hand they feel like subdued and fearful slaves, and on the other, they nurture sentiments of revolt and an ardent desire for pleasure and all-powerfulness.

The Judaeo-Christian religion, as Freud conceived it, is a neurosis of humanity; and yet it is not a personal illness. From it emerges the supreme figure of human spiritualization: the absolute, invisible Father, author of the highest ethical demand. But this father is only a cipher, a mere sign. For Freud he is non-existent and consequently there can be no dialogue with him. If, in actual fact, Freud has greatly distorted the face of Judaeo-Christianity, it is in the first instance because he refused, *a priori*, to see the truth of it. Hence, what other explanation can be given of belief in God except that of the laws of the unconscious, that is to say of unconscious guilt? Denying intelligence and experience any access to a transcendent world, Freud endeavoured to understand it through the effects of conflict and repression. He wanted to explain the Father religion by the genetic laws of the Oedipus complex. The theories on the history of religions which were then current helped him in his research: the Father religion, it was said, could only be the outcome of a long historical sequence of revolts and resultant guilt. And as the guilt increased, so the father image was magnified, exalted, divinized.

This review of the Freudian theory may seem overlong, especially as it was meant only as an allusion. It was, however, necessary in order to enable us to come to some conclusions. The completion of the father symbol in God, in whom it finds its highest expression, corresponds to the dynamic process which commands in depth the psychological genesis of man: that is to say, the Oedipus complex. But it is a great mistake to wish to deduce the idea of divine fatherhood from the psychological laws of man's becoming. It was this that led Freud to ignore several essential aspects of religion.

Correspondence between Human and Divine Fatherhood

Nowadays, no one disputes the fact of a certain correspondence between the family structure and the deity image. But the question is often too easily avoided by speaking of the projection of the father image on to God. And this very vague term of projection is padded with the more or less childish motivations which we have already spoken of and evaluated. But these explanations of the correspondence between the father image and the deity image do not take into account the structuring of the father image as found in the Oedipean constellation. We shall, then, have to restore to the father image its threefold function of law, model and promise. It will then be obvious that the Father-God of Judaeo-Christianity represents these structuring qualities to an even greater degree. The father, understood in his family function really does appear as the symbol of the Judaeo-Christian God.

Very interesting consequences arise from this correspondence. In the first place there are practical consequences: the effects of the affective personal history of the subject on his religious attitude must be very considerable, since the father image which mediates God is the result of a psychological becoming. The father image is not an inborn idea, nor the effect of a natural sentiment; it is elaborated in a family setting. And as, what is more, the idea of God is not a mere speculative representation, man sees God through his real father, but even more through the father image which has been formed in him in virtue of the Oedipus complex. In fact, the close relationship between these two images is witnessed to by the history of religions and by the many deformations which the deity image can undergo, even among Christians of sound intellectual formation.

Our thesis also brings in its wake a theoretical conclusion. Since the father image is essentially a function and a pole, it has value only in a dialectic relationship with the mother figure. The fatherhood of God must, then, also have a corresponding pole, otherwise it will be reduced to pure negativity: a mere demand for renunciation. God is only Father if he promises some maternal values. In his reference to God, Freud totally ignored this essential aspect of paternity, because he was entirely taken up with the opposition which he had emphasized between naturalistic enjoyment and the need for spiritualization. These considerations may seem strange, in which case we suggest that reference be made to the enquiry which we carried out on the paternal symbols of God: the deity image is there seen as the complex synthesis of the two parental figures. Moreover, it is an everyday occurrence in the life of a practising Catholic to distinguish between the functions attributed to God and those attributed to the Virgin Mary. The image of God is depicted in conformity with a law-making Father, a distant Judge, whereas the Virgin fulfils the role of a divinized mother, one who consoles, protects, is near, seeks forgiveness for her children. The unilateral accentuation of the paternity in its exclusive characteristics, such as law and judgement, leads to a doubling of two divine functions in the religious relationships to the detriment of a single relationship with God.

Can we go further than our first observations and attempt to explain the deity image by means of the human symbol; seeing in it something more than mere correspondence of structure? In other words, can we deduce the religious belief from the father-child relationship? We have already seen how, in attempting to give a psychological explanation of religion, Freud elaborated an impossible theory which is contradicted by the history of religions. If we have considered his theory at some length it was to forestall psychological over-simplification, which is so prevalent in our days, and which means passing from the symbolic correspondence between God and the father to an explanation of religion according to which God is seen to be nothing more than an expanded father image, the father image projected into infinity.

Let us say clearly that in its popular acceptance, the word projection is nothing more than a pseudo-scientific mirage covering no real psychological process. It is a learned word hiding the lack of any real thought. In reality psychology sets aside theological and philosophical convictions and only allows us to affirm that from his very beginnings man has shown belief in a God-Father, recognized in a direct and naïve experience. The image of a human father as author of life, has led man to suppose that the gift of existence and the disposition of the earth are the workings of a universal Father. Furthermore, we can easily conceive that man rebelled against this Father and wished to set himself up in his place. Moreover, the Bible begins the account of the history of mankind with the extraordinary episode of paradise; this is the story of a gift, recognition, revolt, guilt and reconciliation. Hence, the idea of the divine paternity, obliged to assert itself, made use of all the possibilities in the course of a dialogue consisting in a series of conflicts and successive pacts. Is this religious history, we ask, enough to establish the image of divine Fatherhood, as revealed to us in Judaeo-Christian history? We are not justified in saying so. On the contrary, it is rather astonishing that the only people which fully attested divine paternity is the very people which appeals to a personal revelation by the very word of God the Father. And nobody will ever dispute that the only man who ever claimed to manifest the divine Fatherhood in its properly interpersonal dimension also claimed a transcendent origin, that is to say, Jesus Christ. The psychologist can only give way before the evidence of the facts; he cannot pretend to clarify the mystery; this lies beyond the scope of his competence.

III. The Judaeo-Christian Fact

We shall now consider the Judaeo-Christian tradition in order to gain some light on its conception of divine paternity. But we shall not go into the theology of this tradition. It represents a unique and primal religious experience which practical psychology will never completely fathom. In making a return to the sources of this belief we are following in the steps of Freud himself.

God was called 'Father' by the people of Israel because he had begotten and adopted his people: on account of this act of creation and adoption he wished to be acknowledged in a religious cult of 'recognition' and in an ethical code of life.[47] But this relationship of father to son reached a peak in the relationship which united the eternal God with the man Jesus. It is this relationship of the Son to the Father which constitutes the essential originality and the fundamental paradox of the New Testament.

In Christ, the divine paternity is realized on a double plane. From the outset, the man Jesus never thinks of himself except in relation to the Father; he is Son and nothing more: his will is the will of his Father; his words are not his, but those he has received from his Father. He arrogates to himself no specific quality. But, though he refuses to take personal advantage of divine goodness and almightiness, he confesses that everything which belongs to the Father has been put into his hands. His life in public opens with the word of the Father who recognizes his Son; it closes with the word which commits him entirely into the hands of his Father, sure of being glorified by him. There is one fact which we must be careful not to let pass unnoticed under cover of words worn by frequent use; in the total recognition of the one who presents himself as being the Son *par excellence* is revealed the paternity of God who continues to be revered as unique in the holiness of his invisible transcendence, and who is able to renew human existence. It is here that the paradox of paternity assumes its true dimension: the Father as such is entirely present in a Word which establishes and recognizes the filiation. Absent yet present, invisible yet seen, more than ever absolutely transcending human nature, yet near in an unparalleled intimacy: these are henceforth the characteristics of divine paternity. The Father upon whom distressed man can call is only the distant reflection and the hazy foreshadowing of the Father who is revealed in the experience of Christ.

The Fatherhood of God is also realized on the plane of religious relationship with humanity. Two texts from St Paul will show us that this is so: 'God was in Christ reconciling the world to himself' (2 *Cor.* 5:19); and 'For all who are led by the Spirit of God are sons of God. For you did not receive the spirit of slavery to fall back into fear, but you have received the spirit of sonship which makes us cry, "Abba! Father!"' (*Rom.* 8:14-15).

The Word of the Father has a transforming effect on men, raising them to the rank of sons who participate in the divine dignity. There is a conjoining of the vertical relationship with the horizontal. The Father is not a supra-sensory idea, nor is he a model of spirituality, nor the all-powerful rival of any earthly Prometheus. He is not the internal principle of cosmo-vitalist expansion, any more than he is our other self wedded to our history. God becomes Father to all men by the Word which introduces a cleavage between the visible and the invisible, yet which nevertheless establishes a filiation transcending separation and revolt.

Religious history repeats, recapitulates and accomplishes the primal history of man's humanization. By his consent to the Word which establishes him as a son in the promise of a paternal heritage, man accedes to true sonship. On the human plane, the Word humanizes: on the religious plane it divinizes.[48] God as Father is no longer the mere correlate of human desires. The Word of the Father introduces rupture and distance into religious eros. Union with God is not brought about in fusion. 'Living in inaccessible light', God remains beyond the reach of a spontaneous affective grasp. God is the term of human aspirations, but satisfaction is something far beyond their power. Happiness is promised as the fulfilment of a progressive history; it does not lie in a return to immanent origins.

The paradox of divine paternity culminates in the fact that it condenses the entire scale of sublimated parental values. God is the author of the promise as well as its object. The Word which establishes the bond of sonship renders God even more invisible and yet he promises that he will be the object of ultimate contemplation. Thus, Word and vision seem to be two lines converging on the same divine centre.

The task of religious psychology is to examine religious experience, attitude, belief and behaviour; it would fail to attain its goal were it to neglect the lived relationship existing between believers and their God.

IV. Guilt

What we have said concerning the father symbol leads us quite naturally to the psychology of guilt, because in the genesis of human or religious experience the paternal function is defined by the word which is prohibition, reconciliation, and recognition.

Guilt operates on three psychological planes and three religious planes. We have already mentioned one, the taboo, in the first chapter. In the taboo guilt shows itself as an instinctive fear of something one feels to be a menace to vital values: the stranger, blood, death, sex, life. Whatever may seem to have an occult power (*mana*) is seen as an object of horror and fascination, and many examples of this are afforded by ethnology and clinical psychology. We have seen that the sacred can be incorporated in the taboo which explains that the psychological taboo may assume some religious value.[49] This is the psychological explanation of the surcharge of supposedly Christian guilt, which can accompany minor sexual faults. Sexual guilt becomes doubly strong as a result of another psychological process amply brought to light by clinical psychology and which spontaneously connects sexual impulses with the father's prohibition. Thus the sexual fault is particularly connected with God for two psychological reasons: sex belongs to the domain of the sacred-taboo and God represents the figure of the Oedipean father. There is little need to insist on the fact that such guilt has very little real religious value: it is nothing more than a pre-religious sentiment. Its reference to God is a troubled reference and needs to be purified, filtered of its hidden affective deposit which is still too often exploited in a misguided religious education.

A second level at which guilt operates is that of the narcissic wound inflicted when the subject commits a fault and feels himself to be diminished, lowered, rejected by society. In this instance, the fault is spontaneously measured against the ideal image which the subject unconsciously has of himself. We may speak here of sociological guilt because the ideal image always corresponds to the expectations of society. Basing ourselves on two enquiries, we have shown in Chapter 2 that among adolescents guilt is very largely narcissic and sociological. For them religion is a means of building up again the broken ideal image and of moral reintegration in society. Once again the strictly religious content of such guilt is low.

Repression may have the effect of fixing these natural and truly psychological forms of guilt. It is then that guilt begins to influence man in his unconscious and becomes psychic illness; but we shall say no more about this here.

Guilt only becomes religious if the fault is recognized as a personal fault before God. The religious fault, the sin, can only be judged in relation to the law of the Father. He alone is able to show up evil in its true dimension; that is to say revolt and rupture of the basic pact between man and God.

Though our definition may seem to be clear, it covers a number of very great psychological difficulties: we must consider these if we are to avoid misrepresenting the religious conscience. The repugnance which many unbelievers have for religious guilt and the embarrassment which believers so often feel at having to confess to repeated faults show well enough that there is often a discrepancy between human experience and religious formulas.

The typical experience of St Augustine offers a good starting point for the elaboration of a psychology of the religious fault.[50] St Augustine wrote his *Confessions* in order to sketch the history of his conversion. The title itself gives food for thought: the *Confessions* give expression to both trusting adherence to God, and a judgement made in the presence of God on his former sins of the passions and intellectual faults. Before being reconciled with God by baptism Augustine did not recognize the true significance of his faults. Thus we see that religious guilt is both a movement of consent to God and the acknowledgement of a past which the light of grace shows to be sinful. The present word of God calls the past up from oblivion, demystifying it in the very act of pardon and reconciliation. The religious consciousness of fault is, then, naturally directed to the future. The retrospective vision of the past is the means to a renewed attitude to existence. Religious guilt is the opposite of auto-punitive remembering, of flight, of psychological isolation. The religious conscience is delivered of the affective deposit left by psychological fault. This means that before the confession and the reconciliation there is no real religious fault recognized as such, and that it is overcome at the very instant that it presents itself to the subject's conscience.

Psychological study should preserve us from the tendency to harden and substantialize fault, for the religious fault can degenerate into hatred of self. It easily slips into this servile and unmanly attitude, so often denounced by Freud, Hesnard and others. In fact, once the subject puts himself in the presence of God, examining his passions and desires in his presence, he is tempted to impute to them retrospectively the evil which he has that very instant recognized in them. It thus happens that he sees desires and human passions only under the aspect of evil. He forgets that man is a being of desire and passion; that he is not moral or religious by nature, but that he has to become so. In the manichean judgement of past faults, the religious man is in agreement with certain psychologists who imagine that there exists an education and an existence free from faults and guilt.

In fact, a good conscience is never more than a bad conscience on the mend. Good results from the exclusion of a pre-moral evil, a passion which knows neither limits nor laws. From a psychological point of view it is not by chance that eight of the ten commandments are phrased in the negative—the two exceptions are the commandments which speak of respect for God and for parents. The fault is revealed in its religious significance at the instant of confession and of lucid and trusting acknowledgement of a hidden fault, for the greater part unconscious, which precedes assent to the divine word. By assent to God, man liberates himself from the lie by means of which he more or less voluntarily covered up his behaviour.

It is, then, in the order of human becoming that all religious faith should also be an avowal of fault. But an avowal, insistent and too often repeated, often rings false. It betrays a resentment against oneself and an unhealthy vexation. One often speaks of sin as if man had committed it clear-sightedly, out of deliberate ill-will; whereas, in fact, man has no clear consciousness of the religious significance of his sin. For those who are experienced, the insistence on sin is a sign of puritan pride, or to use a psychological expression, of moral narcissism. Fault is spoken of as though man were able to live faultlessly. But psychology confirms the wisdom of human experience: ethics and religion arise from desire and are necessarily dynamic: they wrest the pure from the impure, good from evil.

In *Civilization and its Discontents*, Freud gives a forceful description of the necessity of psychological guilt which is constantly present in the experience of a developing humanity. Freud says that man must renounce his longing for purity, which is not human. Impressed by the witness of saints who, more than others, feel the suffering of guilt, Freud comes to the conclusion that religion is unable to provide a remedy for it: but that, on the contrary, it confirms and increases it. We consider that this judgement is both true and false. There is no doubt that the saints are more conscious of religious fault than are other men. But their guilt is no longer psychological; it has become religious. Their sense of fault is no more than the reflection of a greater confidence in filial reconciliation with God. For them, the recognition of the law of the father, and the guilty conscience which results from it are merely the negative moments of a reconciliation which leads them to an assurance of pardon and peace.

The enquiry conducted among 1,800 Belgian adolescents which we have referred to several times already, offers us considerable information about guilt. The highest scores for fear of God are seen in subjects with the least spiritual religious attitude; that is to say among technical students and working-class subjects. But these same subjects have the lowest scores for the category 'a merciful God'. And it is also they who express to the greatest extent their revolt against God. On the other hand, the subjects from classical humanities and from the university have lower scores for fear of God and revolt, but higher scores for divine mercy. This leads us to conclude that a rudimentary religious and human formation, received, moreover, in a lower social setting, leads to the interpretation of divine judgement as an oppressive demand. Thus the split between prohibition and reconciliation enlists the dialectic of master and slave as demonstrated by Hegel and Marx.

CONCLUSION

The examination of religious facts has led us to discover that there are religious principles which cannot be explained by psychological motivations in the strict sense of this term. These two principles are desire for God and its opposite pole, the father image, as a symbolic representation of God. And it is worthy of note that these two principles take up the themes which we encountered during our enquiry into religious experience.

The desire for God opens man up to religious orientation which has been described as mysticism: that is to say, it is the quest for immediate, direct experience which will satisfy the aspirations for complete happiness. We have pointed out the very different forms which religious mysticism may assume: natural pantheist, theist, Christian. We have examined carefully the foundations and psychological structures of desire for God which, we saw, derives from eros, an affective and imaginative power directed to a happiness in union and harmony. Eros, in its turn, originates in an early stage of psychological development: the narcissic phase and the period of dual union with the mother which leaves in man a primitive memory of affective plenitude. The examination of a wide range of experiences has led us to see that they are all so many attempts to recover this initial happiness: the experience of fusion with the sacred, the longing for a lost paradise, so-called peak experiences. We dispute their right to be called religious experiences on account of their affective regression; they ebb below any personal relationship with the Other. Nevertheless, we have acknowledged that there exists a pre-religious experience in these unitive experiences. In representing the universe in terms of unity they can prepare the way for religious experience. But, neither the sentiment of the infinite, nor the union which satisfies desire, is God.

In a theist setting, religious desire can be a powerful incentive to the religious life: the history of the monastic tradition shows a cultivation and a deepening of the desire for God. Nevertheless, if desire for God still has some influence on strictly religious vocations, it is exceptional in an unfavourable cultural climate. We have emphasized the profound change which Christianity has wrought in the value of religious desire. Freud attacks Christian mysticism when he vigorously denounces the regressive nature of the oceanic experience which he identifies with it.

The mother, we showed, is the specific image of mystical desire: she symbolizes vital replenishment and pacifying union. In the cosmo-vitalist religions and the mystery religions which celebrate participation in the mystery of cosmic life, maternal symbolism is abundant. This religious trend, centred on the maternal symbol, was at the core of Jung's school of psychology which can be adequately defined as a kind of scientific mystique of the reintegration of self and the world.

Though we denied the term religion to the mystical trends, we emphasized the maternal qualities of religion: the primitive experience of happiness prefigures man's fulfilment in God. And the complete rejection of these values, or their defacement by a wound received early in life, throws man back on himself and destroys the profound affective vectors which can lead him to God. It was for these reasons that, following Rumke, we insisted upon the affective conditions necessary to religious development. We are convinced that such experiences are first made in the preconscious impressions of very early childhood. Long before puberty the child must feel himself bound up with the totality mediated by motherly love and fatherly protection. Family experience points the way to a realm of happiness, where he can take root and fulfil himself.

When desire is not transformed by contact with reality the maternal fixation does not merely establish man in regressive mysticism, but can even entail really pathological experiences. We were able to see that longing for the mother can prepare the way for a fascination with death.

The reality principle breaks affective union by setting up the relationship with others, and in this relationship the Other who is God can appear. The reality principle is introduced into affective depths through the agency of the father whose word dispels fascination. By means of the differentiated relationships which he sets up with the two poles of the family constellation, the man-in-becoming is progressively structured and humanized.

In the Oedipean conflict the father figure is seen in its true function. He is at once author of the proscribing law, the model with whom the child can identify himself, and the promise of future happiness. He introduces renunciation and dynamic orientation towards the future into the affective union between mother and child.

The father, in virtue of his specific function, evokes God under other aspects than those of a motherly protector of a distressed subject. God is seen to have the same qualities as the father. He is the author of the moral law, negatively formulated on account of the demand for spiritualization which it implies. He is the model of holiness to be imitated. He is also providence, in that he offers the gift of a promise which directs man, not to the archaic paradise of his desires, but to a final happiness where he will be completely spiritualized.

Freud taught us that the father has a symbolic value. On the other hand, the fact that he failed to explain the Judaeo-Christian faith confirms us in the opinion that psychology is powerless to deduce God from the simple image of a human father. Psychology can do nothing but point out the similitude in structure between the father-child relationship and the relationship between man and God. This correspondence moreover is not mere chance. Man, as he humanizes himself in the family relationships, becomes capable of acceding to the true religious dimension.

But the divine paternity is more complete than human paternity. it seems to be a harmony of contrasts: all the parental qualities are united in God. Thus desire for God can direct man to God by means of the transformation worked by the paternal symbolism; desire is now able to accede to union with God without endangering the real recognition of the Other.

Practical studies have shown us that the father image is seen by Christians as being more complex than the mother image and that it may well mediate the divine being. But the deity image is even more complex than the father image and thus realizes the dialectic synthesis of the two parental figures.

Christian theology has shown us the entire content of this divine paternity. The divine gift, the recognition conditioned by the law, the setting up of sonship, are all so many decisive signs of God. Thus a psychology of guilt must come to terms with the language of judgement and recognition. The religious fault is quite different from the taboo and the narcissic wound to which many believers accord too great importance in their assessment of guilt.

Psychological theories show their limitations when they try to explain belief in divine paternity on the basis of merely human aspirations; the term religious 'projection' used in this instance covers no psychological reality. The term 'transference' of the parental qualities onto God would be more appropriate as long as respect was maintained for the distance which separates the father image from the deity image. We have preferred to use the term 'symbolization': man can guess at the divine reality through human figures because human history and religious history are carried out effectively according to the same law.

We have done no more than consider the deity symbols as realized in a strictly religious setting. We have not covered all the counterfeits of religious symbolization and the extent of their influence though we have analysed one or two of them when dealing with motivation. We could also refer to Simone de Beauvoir when she describes how the girl, seeking virile support, develops an erotic attitude towards the father figure. It remains to be seen whether in all the masks which can be discerned there may not be some symbolic value. Wise in the lessons learnt from psychology, we believe that human modes of behaviour are very mixed: under cover of masks which hide his too human desires, man continues to seek, in one form or another, a certain image of the transcendent God. It is indeed a very complex task to untangle unerringly the human aspiration from the religious intention.

1 *Republic*, VII. We have taken inspiration for our commentary from J. Hyppolite, 'Le mythe et l'origine', in *Demittizzazione e Morale*, Rome 1965, 24–9.

2 *Dogmatik* I/2, 352.

3 There are two classical works on the psychology of the mystics which should be noted: J. Maréchal, *Études sur la psychologie des mystiques*, two volumes, Brussels-Paris 1937, 1938; and Evelyn Underhill, *Mysticism. A Study in the Nature and Development of Man's Spiritual Consciousness*, London 1960.

4 *Republic*, VI.

5 *Initiation aux auteurs monastiques du Moyen Age. L'amour des lettres et le desir de Dieu*, Paris 1957 (E. tr. *The love of learning and the desire for God*, New York 1961). The passages quoted here have been translated especially for this book. The references given are from the original French text.

6 *Op. cit.*, 13.

7 *Ibid.*, 36.

8 *Ibid.*, 37.

9 *Ibid.*, 82.

10 *Ibid.*, 85.

11 *Ibid.*, 93.

12 *The Individual and his Religion*, 39.

13 See the enquiry *Les 16–24 ans*, Paris 1963, 202 ff.

14 *Lebensformen. Geisteswissenschaftliche Psychologie und Ethik der Persönlickkeit*, Tubingen 1950.

15 *Ibid.*, 237.

16 *Ibid.*, 238.

17 *Ibid.*, 239.

18 *Ibid.*, 265.

19 *Sens et non-sens*, Paris 1948, 190–1.

20 'Cognition of Being in the Peak Experiences', *Journal of Genetic Psychology*, 1959.

21 *Civilization and its discontents, Gesammelte Werke* XIV, 421–31.

22 *Gesammelte Werke* XVII, 152, note written 22 August 1938.

23 *Hoofdstukken uit de Psychoanalyse*, Utrecht 1950, 155–67.

24 See M. Eliade, *Traité d'histoire des religions*, 211 ff.

25 See J. Lacan 'La famille' in *Encyclopédie Francaise*, VIII. *La vie mentale.*

26 M. Eliade, *op. cit.*, 327; see also G. van der Leeuw, *La Religion dans son essence et ses manifestations*, 312–31.

27 *Die Beziehungen zwischen dem Ich und dem Unbewussten*, Zürich 1939, 123.

28 *Von den Wurzeln des Bewusstseins*, 1954, 101.

29 *Symbole der Wandlung*, 1952, 357.

30 See R. Hostie, *Du mythe à la religion*, Bruges-Paris 1955, 198.

31 *Karakter en aanleg in verband met het ongeloof*, Amsterdam 1949 (E. tr. *The Psychology of Unbelief*, London 1957).

32 *Les Mots*, Paris 1964, 78–9.

33 H. and K. Schjelderup, *Uber drei Haupttypen der religiösen Erlebnisformen und ihre Psychologische Grundlage*, Berlin 1932, 4–25.

34 *Ein Kindheitserinnerung des Leonardo da Vinci*, 1910, *Gesammelte Werke*, VIII, 195 (E. tr. in vol XI of the Standard Edition, 123).

35 'An Application of the Q technique to the Study of Religious Concepts', *Psychological Reports*, 1957, 293–7; *Les concepts religieux dans leur relation aux images parentales*, Lumen Vitae, Brussels 1961, 105–10.

36 We have taken up the categories which A. Godin has used to synthesize the twenty sentiments expressed in the sixty items. See A. Godin and M. Hallez, *Images parentales et paternité divine*, Lumen Vitae, Brussels 1964, 248.

37 'Perceived Relationships between Parental and Deity Concepts', *Psychological Newsletter*, New York 1959, 222–6.

38 *Op. cit.*, 243–76.

39 We have made use here of two unpublished theses prepared for the Licentiate in Psychology under our direction: M. R. Pattijn, and A. Custers, *Het Vadersymbool en het moedersymbool in de Godsvoorstelling*, Louvain 1964.

40 Text found among his papers, and reproduced on his mortuary card.

41 See F. Heiler, *La Prière*, Paris 1931, 177–8.

42 In our study 'Le symbole paternel et sa signification religieuse', *Archiv fur Religionspsychologie*, IX, 1967, Gottingen, we have presented the statistical tables of our researches carried out with differential semantic scales; a strict analysis will be found there of the parental and deity images. We have also pointed out the influence of certain cultural factors on these images in different populations.

43 For the explanation of all that follows on psychoanalysis see W. Huber, H. Piron, A. Vergote, *La psychanalyse, science de l'homme*, Brussels 1964; see also P. Ricoeur, *De l'interprétation. Essai sur Freud*, Paris 1965.

44 See J. Lacan, 'Fonction et champ de la parole et du langage en psychanalyse', *La psychanalyse*, I, Paris 1956, 81–166, i.c., 138; see also A. De Waelhens, *La Philosophie et les expériences naturelles*, La Haye 1961, 122 ff.

45 In our interpretation of guilt we differ from that of A. Hesnard in *L'univers morbide de la faute*, Paris 1949 and *Morale sans péché*, Paris 1954.

46 See Appendix to *The Future of an Illusion*; *Gesammelte Werke*, VII, 132.

47 See the excellent exposé of J. Jeremias, *Paroles de Jesus. Le sermon sur la montagne*; *Le Notre-Père*, Paris 1963; for a more technical study, see W. Marchel, *Abba, Père*, Rome 1963.

48 Limiting ourselves to the examination of psychological structures, we shall say nothing of an element which is essential in Christian doctrine and in the experience of the mystics: the Spirit of God present within man. He makes man consent to the Word, and through this consent leads him to acknowledge the Father. This theme ought to be developed by a study of the Christian experience in itself; there should be some interesting points to show how God reveals himself at the very heart of man's consciousness, through his inner presence.

49 See J. Goetz, 'Le péché chez les primitifs, tabou et péché', in *Théologie du péché*, Paris-Tournai 1960, 125–88 and especially 172–4.

50 For a deeper analysis of all this see J. M. Le Blond, *Les conversions de saint Augustin*, Paris 1950.

CHAPTER 4

THE RELIGIOUS ATTITUDE, TENSIONS AND STRUCTURES

We devoted our first two chapters to the spontaneous forms of religion. In the first place we considered the perception of those signs in the world which refer to that 'Other' which religion calls God. We then dealt with the affective and passion-inspired motives which propel man towards his God in an insistent demand for help and satisfaction. In these analyses we contented ourselves with pointing out that religion, in the full meaning of this word, is a personal assent transcending spontaneous religious movements. Man's first mute intuitions are intentionally assumed and consecrated in religion which is a conscious and firm grasp of the beliefs transmitted by society. We give this personal religion the psychological term 'attitude'; we have distinguished it from primitive experience and from spontaneous and motivated religious movements.

In the third chapter we saw that this personal religious attitude does not result merely from the demystification of spontaneous religious motives. It is influenced by the father symbol. A new bond is thus established between man and God which, without lessening the distance and the otherness, creates an intimate unity. The bond of sonship leaves God free to affirm himself fully God, and it divinizes man without destroying his humanity. In sonship the desire for God becomes presence before him, and the vital demands which are made of him are converted into conscious responsibility with regard to the reign of the Spirit.

Thus, in the religious attitude, religion has ceased to be what it was in its first beginnings. Little by little the successive conflicts and tensions have been resolved leaving room for a highly differentiated and personal form of religion.

We are well aware that, in identifying true religiosity with the religious attitude as we understand it, we have chosen an interpretation to which many psychological studies of religion are opposed. We cannot entirely justify our standpoint merely on principles of psychology—but we have given the reasons for our choice. On the one hand the Judaeo-Christian tradition teaches us that true religion results from the purification of spontaneous idolatries. And on the other hand, dynamic psychology, broadening its scope, shows that there exists no pre-established harmony between man and his essential values. They have to be created through long personal efforts and by man's continual criticism of his illusions and alienations. These references to Judaeo-Christianity and to dynamic psychology authorize us, we believe, to identify the religious attitude as true religion.

We shall now try to explain the elements and inner tensions which compose this religious attitude. First, we shall define the word attitude in its psychological meaning and then examine how it fits in with the three essential dimensions of the human being: lived time, commitment to earthly realities, the relationships between the person and society. The religious attitude, indeed, links up the past in a relationship with the future. It differentiates present human values in order to unify them again on the religious plane; it realizes a synthesis between personal becoming and social solidarity.

In a third section we shall examine the psychological fact of religious conversion. From the point of view of religious psychology this is a privileged phenomenon in that it allows us to observe clearly how the religious attitude comes into being through experiences and resistances.

In the last part of this chapter we shall examine the deep tensions which bring human autonomy to grips with religious assent. All the preceding analyses converge on this paradox and this antinomy. There lies the kernel of the real problem of the religious attitude.

I. The Psychological Definition of the Attitude

The word 'attitude' speaks for itself: it is a mode of being with regard to someone or something; it is a favourable or unfavourable disposition expressed in words or behaviour. It is composed, we see, of three elements: it is a complete behaviour (a mode of *being*) in intentional relationship with a given object (with *regard to*), and it is observable (it is a *behaviour*).[1] We shall now study each of these elements in an attempt to define them.

In so far as it is a mode of being, a complete behaviour, the attitude has many functions. The affective, cognitive and volitional processes build up an organized, complex structure within the attitude. Each man's unique personality is determined by these concrete relationships of knowledge and affectivity which he has made with persons and things in the course of his own history.

The psychical processes do not operate in a closed circuit. Affectivity and intelligence, being in a relationship of continual exchange with the world, develop in a social context in such a way that the attitude is always both personal and social.[2]

Because the attitude results from the interaction of different psychical processes, and from the exchange between an individual and his socio-cultural environment, it is a dynamic structure, an evolving equilibrium. Thus, it is characterized by a certain stability and also by its readiness for relationship with the environment. This stability and integration vary from individual to individual. Normally adults reach a higher level of integration than children. But it can also happen that even an adult does not manage to achieve sufficient structuring. Whole regions of existence can remain unassimilated with personality. Religion, for instance, can remain on the fringe of personal existence; or, again, affective life may be stifled by a will for professional success. This lack of integration may occasion conflicts between the different regions of the personality. It even happens that, as a result of early and radical exclusion, certain dynamic elements form, as it were, nuclei which are alien to the person: this is the case with really pathological forms of existence.

Two processes in particular play an essential part in the structuring of attitude: the Oedipus complex and learning. The preceding chapter brought out the importance of the profound influence of the Oedipus complex. Even before the Oedipean phase, the child has his own character, but his personality is differentiated in and by the Oedipus complex and its recurrence during adolescence. Learning does not modify the person as profoundly as does Oedipus. But it nevertheless contributes very greatly to the formation of attitudes because personality is elaborated through learning about things, about others, and about the cultural environment. We have already mentioned the importance of the religious message: it alone, it would seem, enables us to decipher the religious signs to be found in the world. But learning only creates an attitude when it has really taken hold of the person. The person must appropriate the teaching received and not merely store it up as a list of ideas alien to life. A true attitude is one which has integrated the elements which have been learnt. It moulds them to its own form and in assimilating ideas it makes them bear fruit.

The intentional relationship to things and to persons is the second component element of an attitude specifically orientated towards objectives which man regards as belonging to his proper field of action. It differs in this from character which 'designates a more or less general mode of reaction of a person, without specifying the situations or objects to which it is applied'.[3] It is thus that aggressiveness towards religion can represent the deliberate attitude of a man who does not necessarily have an aggressive character. The opposite is equally possible. The term 'habit' is equally unsuitable for expressing the intentional relationship to the world; although every true attitude implies a certain number of habits.

Of itself, attitude is not yet behaviour, but in so far as it is a personal structure open to the world, it predisposes to a given mode of behaviour, either favourable or unfavourable, in relation to a given object. This is the third characteristic of attitude.

Because it represents a personal disposition, its beliefs are far from being neutral either emotionally or in practice. On the contrary, in the very measure that they are profoundly integrated by the subject, beliefs embody a practical orientation modifying the subject's environment.

Applying our definition of attitude to religion, we see immediately that certain distinctions must be introduced: this is not an easy thing to do. Attitude is more than opinion, belief, or religious behaviour, and differs from them. Religious beliefs do not necessarily make up an attitude. They may be nothing more than opinions inherited from society or intellectual opinions dissociated from the real personality of the subject and having no transforming effect on either himself or his environment. On the other hand, taken at the objective level of their mental content, beliefs may be charged with many personal connotations which determine their real significance.

In order to know the specifically religious tenor of a belief, we must know the reasons for which the subject has made it his own. We may simplify things by introducing the basic linguistic distinction between the signifying and signified. Let us take, by way of example, the belief in the paternity of God. We have seen the many and diverse elements which can enter into the father symbol. 'Father' has a fundamental significance, is a primordial symbol. But, for the different subjects who refer to this symbol, it may mean many very different things, corresponding with as many characteristic attitudes. It is not much use, then, simply to make a list of the subjects' beliefs. Such enquiries do nothing but collect opinions; they do not reveal the underlying attitudes. Many scales of religious attitudes, modelled on sociological enquiries, do nothing more than this. Nor is it any more helpful to observe religious modes of behaviour without interpreting their meaning: what attitude do they express? Regular religious practice may result from social influences, or morbid anxiety, as much as from personal conviction. The absence of regular religious practice, significant though it may be, does not necessarily denote a less firm religious attitude: it might well be accounted for by socio-cultural influences. Thus, if the attitude is always expressed by behaviour or words, it nevertheless remains subject to interpretation. Faced with the ambiguous nature of attitude, psychological techniques must determine the exact meanings which believers give to the symbols of their faith.

II. The Structure of the Religious Attitude

Many psychologists have remarked upon the fact of the characteristically all-encompassing nature of the religious attitude. Allport[4] even wonders whether there exists any sentiment other than religion which is sufficiently all-embracing to cover every human interest. According to him, mature religious sentiment seems to be the only psychic factor able to integrate all the components of personality. Further, according to French, the attitude of the believer tends to structure and unify every aspect of behaviour.

Certainly it is true that religion is not the dynamic factor which effectively integrates all the modes of behaviour in every believer. At the end of his enquiry into the structure of sentiment, French concludes that the religious sentiment is more highly organized in certain subjects and constitutes an integrating part of their ego, but with others religion is only slightly integrated with the ego and remains on the level of the superego. In the former, religion gives a positive orientation to life; with the latter it assumes a defence function and acts as a protective screen to the ego.

How could it be otherwise? If it is in the nature of religion to integrate the whole of life, it is not surprising that its real power over the person comes up against many obstacles and a profound resistance, and that, often enough, integration is not effected.

In the following section we shall go into the structuring power of religion considered from an *a priori* point of view. We shall examine how integration is ideally carried out by an open and dynamic religion. This will help us to understand better why the religious structuring of the person is often defective. Such a study will reveal the many dissociations which man must overcome in order to achieve effective integration of religion with his life.

Drawing inspiration from the schema set up by Allport[5] in his study on the formation of attitudes, we shall distinguish three stages in religious integration: the assimilation of the past, the differentiation caused by conflict, and the imitation of a model. These three stages coincide in fact with the three dimensions of the personality: lived time, being in the world, relationships with others and with society.

INTEGRATION OF THE PAST

Since the past is part and parcel of existence, it cannot be ignored with impunity. To forget the past does not save the future. Quite the contrary, it is precisely when it is excluded from the present that the past produces its disturbing effects.

One truth which classical psychology has established is that the past must be fully accepted in order to achieve redemption in a positive orientation towards the future. No one can efface every trace left by the past in the depths of affectivity. Denied, the past becomes fixed and acts on the subject in an autonomous way, obliging him to a constant effort of repression in which his vital forces wear themselves out in fruitless effort. If man cannot freely accept his past it is transformed into relatively autonomous behaviour[6] in a show of stereotyped attitudes, Neuroses are nothing more than thoughts, sentiments or behaviour which, as a result of early and repeated repressions, lead an independent life within the subject and wage constant war against him.

The same is true of the religious attitude. The evil done or submitted to, the failures which we undergo or bring about, every suffering endured or caused, asks to be recognized and assimilated under pain of harming or warping the religious attitude. How many people are unable to face the future with religious confidence simply because unhappy memories stand in the way? Opposition between past and present will often make man incapable of surrendering himself to an attitude of religious trust. We need only quote the example of Tchen the revolutionary hero depicted by André Malraux in his *La condition humaine*: in order to escape from the past which pursues him with horrifying memories,

Tchen, spurning the religious message proposed by a pastor, attempts to kill himself.

Conversion, on the contrary, is a re-reading of the past. In the past, recognized for what it is, the religious man is able to read the signs of a positive future. We have an example of this in the *Confessions* of St Augustine who recognizes the true facts of his past life in the light of faith, judges it for what it is worth and learns to accept it with confidence. The major themes of religion find their concrete application in this interpretation of individual history. Faith in the providence of God does not suddenly loom up as a magical and exasperated form of research; on the contrary, it is the art of deciphering the meaning of existence with realism. Faith in God's judgement is not the anguish of being hypnotized by the angry eye; it is both avowal of past fault and assent to present grace, which, the convert sees, has been at work throughout past experiences.

If religion is correctly understood it can bring about the integration of the past. Here is the application of St Paul's words 'how much more' (*Rom.* 5:9, 15, 17). To the eyes of faith nothing is lost, no suffering has been in vain. If, then, the assimilation of the past is the necessary condition for man's religious orientation, such assimilation is favoured by religion by reason of the principles of truth and confidence of which it assures man.

DIFFERENTIATIONS, CONFLICTS AND SYNTHESIS

Since the beginnings of our modern times, religion no longer has a relationship with the world based on a diffused and immanent presence such as characterized the cosmo-vitalist beliefs. Nor is it found in the perspective of a constitutive foundation and controlling unification which were characteristic of medieval Christianity. Every profane sphere has fought for and achieved its autonomy and thus set itself free from the sacred. And yet religion cannot remain a stranger to the world. Without seeking for the moment to define the point of insertion of religion into the world, we merely wish to point out that harmony between the world and religion is a crucial problem for many believers. The religious attitude is built up by meeting this problem.

The child's world is still largely undefined, but the adolescent and the adult inevitably take part in the process of humanization and desacralization of the world. The organization of society, philosophy and ethics depends on their autonomy with regard to religion. What is more, man has become aware of his creative faculties and, rather than live in a kingdom of supernatural mysteries, he has set up his centre of gravity in this human history which he himself has helped to make. Far from wishing to escape from this new orientation, a young man can only see his religion in the framework of this godless world. He will, then, have to differentiate the many forms of existence and also try to give them a new type of unity.

This means that religion will have to free itself from the primary solidarities to which it was first bound. Religion does indeed tend to associate itself with all the values which bind man to his origins: family tradition, national movements, class interests. Very often nationalist movements are based on religious movements. The principle of *cujus regio illius et religio* not only concerns a relationship which has come into being in the course of history, it also expresses a profound psychological law: religion is the basis of interpersonal relationships. Modern civilization wants to declare its principles without any intermediary and to take possession again of both itself and the world. Thus, from the fact that it no longer carries human values, religion risks finding itself separated from the world. The religious young man will have to make his own the different spheres of existence, recognizing their autonomy, and he will also have to embrace them in a religious attitude capable of animating them without becoming confused with them. He must learn to integrate human particularities into his religion, without identifying religion with what is human.

In theory, it is easy to admit that the liberation of the profane has restored human liberty to man, and universality and transcendence to religion. In practice, once they have seen religion and the temporal as separate entities, many believers wonder, 'Well, why God then?'[7] and, 'What's the use of religion?' Some apologists try to demonstrate the human efficacity of religion. But we think that in so doing they go against the evidence of history no less than against the becoming of religion. They hope to save religion by inserting it into the network of human solidarities. To speak the language we used in Chapter 2, we should say that they attempt to motivate religion. But, as far as we can see, man must, on the contrary, recognize that instead of helping to build up the human order, religion should open man out to the new dimension of his relationship with the Other.

In order that religion may effect the new integration of differentiated values recognized as autonomous, it must be orientated towards God for himself. On this condition only will religion be sufficiently universal to embrace all human interests without alienating them. As long as religion emanates from the dark depths of affectivity it will remain enclosed in the narrow confines which restrict its universality. A magic religion will always remain an enclave in the heart of an adult personality. Thus, it will make use of religious rites in order to remedy a situation of misery and guilt without ever being able to embrace man's existence. Likewise, a fearful dependence with regard to the Father-Protector only maintains a servile attitude of distrust with regard to human enterprises, incapable of assuming responsibilities and shy of all initiative.

We are again dealing with the father symbol and its structuring efficacity. The religion of the Father can be hostile to man's emancipation. And, in fact, it has often been so in the history of civilization as well as in the personal life of believers. By its very nature, however, the recognition of the Father should completely liberate man and religion, since the religion of the Father is essentially the liberty of the children of God. Even beyond the bounds of Christianity, the adoration of the Father should not fix men in the fear of an angry and jealous eye. Similarly, the recognition of an end and of a supreme accomplishment of the world does not kill temporal initiatives or make consciences unhappy. On the contrary, religion which is structured in the sense of a filial relationship becomes part of everything human.

Whatever belongs to man has some meaning for the Father, and in his light the sons see that everything that attacks and alienates man is an insult to the Father who is with mankind, making his history with them, being glorified by the dignity of his sons.

'A religious sentiment that has thus become largely independent of its origins, "functionally autonomous", cannot be regarded as a servant of other desires, even though its initial function may have been of this order.'[8] Once religion has ceased to be functional, in the sense defined in the chapter on human motivations, it becomes a source of dynamic power even for human values. In broadening the world's horizons, it helps to create a distance which favours liberation from human spheres. But this liberation with regard to the world will not be simply passive absence. The religion of the Father is a life-giving principle for all human enterprises. Thus, freed from too human solidarities, the religion of the Spirit will be a dynamic force integrating all the human interests which it has helped to liberate.

IDENTIFICATION WITH THE MODEL

No human attitude can be structured without reference to models. The particular importance of the Oedipus complex lies in the opportunity for identification which it gives the child. We prefer to use the word 'identification' rather than 'imitation' which tends to suggest interior assimilation of a social behaviour. The social sciences readily use the word 'role', but this also is unsatisfactory; it suggests a certain mimicry by means of which the child merely copies in his acts what he sees done by others. Identification goes further. It allows the subject to assume inwardly a system of behaviour and to reorganize himself in keeping with the assimilated schema. Rather than imitate the other, he in some way becomes the other. The other whom I recognize and love becomes a principle of behaviour in my most intimate depths. The identification does not, however, become an object of introspection within me; very much to the contrary: the more it becomes a principle of interior structuring, the more the model loses its character of my inner double and becomes the acting ego. Moreover, far from alienating me, identification develops within me certain powers which hitherto could not be either organized or expressed.

That the religious attitude is formed by means of identification with models is a fact amply proved by sociological studies. The majority of men adopt the religion of their parents: thus, from generation to generation, religious practice is perpetuated in more or less constant forms.[9] There are, of course, many properly psychological factors which account for this permanence of religious practice from generation to generation. Such factors are the psychological impact of childhood memories, education, the cultural and spiritual climate of the group, and even social pressure. But, in these sociological influences, we think that we can also recognize the effects of psychological identification which consist precisely in the interior assimilation of social models. Experience shows us, indeed, how difficult it is for a man to lead a form of religious life different from that of his parents. We feel sure that were we to go more deeply into the psychological study of the different social factors which contribute to the formation of the religious attitude, we should be led to emphasize the importance of identification.

Christian Identification

We notice, moreover, that every religion has its models in the persons of men, of divine or mythical figures which, by reason of their wonderful behaviour, are proposed for the attention of believers and held up to them as examples. In the Christian era, it is Christ who is the supreme model. Never, before him, did any man even think of linking his religious doctrine with his own person. The proposed criterion of true Christian religion is, finally, conformity to Christ's own way of life. And we know that Christian tradition has not turned a deaf ear to this teaching: the theme of the imitation of Christ is a bond of unity between different schools of spirituality. What is the situation of really lived Christian faith? In the enquiries which we carried out among intellectuals and adolescents, we rarely came across a reference to Christ. Of course, religion is always much richer and more complex than might be supposed from the conscious expression of it. It is nevertheless significant that, in reply to questions about religious experience and the foundation of faith in Providence, Catholics rarely think of quoting Christ's witness. We cannot help feeling that the incarnation of God in Jesus has scarcely had any direct influence on their religion; doubtless the gospel precepts do have some part to play in the ethical life of Christians, and the Church as an institution links man to God by her rites and her teaching. But it would seem that the Person of Christ is rarely recognized as the model of the Christian attitude and only to a relatively restricted number of people is he a really visible sign of God.

In his enquiry, *God and the adolescent*, Fr Babin points out the difference between the faith of Catholics and that of Protestants.[10] Catholic adolescents only occasionally mention the Person of Christ. The Protestant adolescents, however, relate their faith in God to Christ much more frequently.[11] 9 of the 106 replies even made explicit mention of God as 'Father of Jesus Christ' or 'Our Father in Jesus Christ'. On the whole, their religious language is more biblical and they insist on the soteriological aspect of faith: God is above all the Saviour. And this leads Fr Babin to ask 'Why do (Catholic) adolescents speak so little of God as he is revealed by Jesus Christ? Why do they still have such a primitive idea of God? What is the influence of teaching and what is the influence of psychology?'[12] We, too, asked these questions after our enquiry among 1,800 Belgian adolescents carried out at the same time as Fr Babin came to his conclusions. We are convinced that the unilateral presentation of the divinity of Christ is responsible for a certain failure of Christian education. Catechesis too frequently forgets the nature of Christ's own religious teaching. He spoke to men first of all on the level at which they could understand him: the level of evangelical wisdom and of the experience of God as Father. Christ is himself the model and teacher of this wisdom. It is in his visible humanity that we see his filial attitude towards God. There are few Christians, we think, who are conscious of the fact that Christ was really man. As a result of an insufficient theological formation they tend to interpret the humanity of Christ as a veil covering his divinity. Nevertheless it is in his very real humanity that Christ is the model of the religious attitude and that he shows himself to be the one who reveals the Father.

Religious Membership and Social Religion

We associate group membership with identification because society as such also offers ideals of behaviour and models to be imitated. We shall do no more than recall this social dimension and identification: we leave it to our readers to consult the numerous existing works on religious sociology.[13] Scherif and Courtrie[14] have shown that men's attitudes are related to the groups to which they belong. Thus the community is both the object of an attitude, inasmuch as one belongs to it by deliberate choice, and a source of attitude because it proposes models of behaviour and judgements of values.

Sociologists consider membership itself as being already an attitude. It is a more or less stable and dynamic organization of the affective and perceptive life of the members. But for us membership is only an element in the formation of the attitude.

Many studies of religious sociology have shown that this reciprocal relationship between the individual and the group is also true of the religious attitude. The believer chooses the religious group which represents and symbolizes his values and behaviour, and takes inspiration from it for his personal attitude. And it is even one of the special objectives of religious sociology to study specific forms of religious behaviour related to membership of different groups.

But not every membership has a structuring effect on the religious personality. As a general rule membership precedes personal attitude. Man is born into a certain religious culture; he is, therefore, a group member before he makes a personal choice. It is well-known that forced membership can greatly influence the attitude. It is in order to purify religion of this sociological anonymity that many sects wish to recruit members solely on the basis of voluntary adherence, that is to say on the basis of conversion. Some sociologists even regard this fact as a distinguishing characteristic of the sect. There are Christians who prefer not to give their children any religious education in order to leave them complete liberty to choose their own religion once they have become adult. It is often remarked that there are mass defections among Catholics who move to the cities. It may well be asked whether this is not an indication that their faith was too traditional, and had not been personally assumed. But we think this conclusion is open to doubt. It is true that a really personal attitude is more stable, open to adaptation and able to adopt new community forms. But the religious man must be able to fulfil himself in one way or another in a given community. If there is too great a difference between the previous group and the new setting he will not easily discover the necessary forms in which to express himself. Deprived of objective models, his religious attitude will almost inevitably wither.

We have previously reported the witness of intellectuals who insist upon the necessity of finding some guarantee of objective faith in the religious community. Wary of subjective impressions they try to turn away from themselves and to authenticate their faith by expressing it in a community. This desire to live faith in fellowship with others does not arise from the need of moral support or social approval. It is, on the contrary, the outcome of a critical judgement of truth according to which the only true human attitude is the one shown in objective and universal forms and lived in communion with others.

The religious defections observed among many believers uprooted from their groups and transplanted to alien settings give weight to the question which sociologists and psychologists so often ask as to whether there is not a profound difference between the personal attitude and the fact of being a member of an institution. It is tempting to regard the personal attitude as the only true one.

Furthermore, the results of enquiries among adolescents show that while they remain in Catholic circles they have not yet assimilated their institutional religion. Their credo and their practice do not seem to have become part of their personal attitude before God. And, indeed, what other explanation can we give for the almost complete absence from their replies of any

15

mention of Christ? The interviews and other personal contacts which we have had convince us that most Christians live on two planes: that of their individual personality and that of their institutional personality. But it would be a mistake to restrict their personalities to these individual convictions and practices. We should prefer to say that they have a double truth because their community membership results, more often than not, from deliberate conviction. And in this sense it is part of their personal attitude. In the community where they are, in a sense, more than themselves, they find a broadened personality which they can only maintain by immediate social identification. The community transforms them and momentarily raises them above themselves. In listening to the religious word, by becoming visibly one of their Church, they adopt a Christian attitude which they are unable to maintain in the midst of other human solidarities, be they professional, familial or intellectual. In such cases membership should be considered as truly religious, but we must also recognize that the cleavage between the individual personality and the institutional personality witnesses to a radical insufficiency in their religious attitude.

Sometimes it happens that, in certain psychological circles, the matter of institutional solidarity is falsified by a deliberately anti-dogmatic and anti-institutional outlook. There are some psychologists, indeed, who consider the dissatisfaction of adults with regard to the dogmas and institutions of their religion as marking progress in personal attitude. In our opinion, there may in fact be some progress in such cases, in the measure that believers liberate themselves from an institution to which they only adhere as a result of a non-assimilated education or under the influence of social pressure. But once believers consciously enter into solidarity with their religious community, it is obvious that their affiliation to the Church gives their religion a more personal and better structured character.

In connection with this we can quote Kelley's experiment.[15] Through the reading of religious texts adapted to different populations he tried to measure both the consciousness of religious membership and its effects. This led him to notice that attitudes were more stable in those subjects for whom the reading aroused an awareness of religious membership. He concluded that attitudes are dependent on the fact of consciousness of belonging to a group. This confirms our interpretation of the institutional personality. Kelley also remarked that older subjects were less easily influenced by his attempt at awakening them to a consciousness of their membership. Unfortunately Kelley's study tells us nothing about the quality of the personal attitude of the subjects. We do not know whether they show a more coherent synthesis of the double personality, or whether the search for a certain inner unity has meant the abandoning of institutional identification.

In the religious attitude, social identification has yet another significance, a very specific and strictly theological one. Religion, which is ecclesial by nature, binds men together in brotherly communion. Man can only truly encounter God if he is able to associate others with his personal undertaking. Man is never solitary in God's eyes. Filiation is essentially corporate. For this reason a person's community sense is a good criterion by which to judge his religious attitude.

From all that we have said it is evident that the religious attitude is most complex, and that it does not easily harmonize its two component poles. It implies great liberty and entire truth with regard to the past; it requires sufficient zeal and light for converting the past into a well-spring of faith and a pledge of hope. It requires a shaking off of the natural conditionings which tie down religion to its affective motivations and its human solidarities. And, at the same time, it must be able to animate and integrate all human values without reducing them to servitude. We may say finally that the right attitude must actualize the paradox of a religion which is at one and the same time highly personal and profoundly community-centred.

For the Christian, religious integration must be brought about by means of identification with the unique model, the Man-God. Our enquiries have shown how difficult it is to realize the synthesis of the various relevant elements; they have shown the imperfection of many religious forms. And if that is not sufficient evidence to convince us, we have only to think of the many ambiguities and misunderstandings for which different religious groups have been responsible all through history: repeated refusal of human emancipation; preference for group identities over human solidarity; certain stand-points adopted in social or political matters which betray an attachment to religious forms rather than true human sincerity. The difficulty of realizing complete integration is an indication that the religious attitude can only result from a conversion which overcomes many resistances.

III. Conversion and Resistance

We may go more deeply into the question of the religious attitude by considering the case of conversion, which shows up, with particular acuity, the tensions contained in a religious attitude and the sincere effort it demands.

To the psychologist,[16] religious conversion appears as the dissolution of one mental synthesis and its replacement by a new one; conversion is a restructuring of the personality. The word conversion is often used in psychology or in sociology to designate a change of opinion in political, aesthetic or social matters.[17] It is, however, rare that such conversions affect man profoundly, whereas a true religious conversion always goes to the roots, to the very principle where his personality is organized. We intend to show that it is in his soul that, by deciding to adhere to a religion, man commits himself to a new covenant with God, mankind and the world.

TYPOLOGY OF CONVERSION

The further we go from somatic structures, the more complicated typology grows, running the risk of becoming arbitrary. For this reason we do not intend to draw up a detailed structural table of the different types of conversion; we shall merely define five types easily distinguishable to phenomenological analysis and which bring into play distinct psychological processes. We shall leave on one side the conversion of pagan peoples to Christianity. Readers who are interested may consult the fine monograph by

Pastor Allier.[18] Nor shall we deal with the special problem set by conversion to a sect.[19]

Conversion in Religious Revivals

This was the object of the first systematic study in religious psychology. In 1899 Starbuck[20] devoted a book to this subject, in which he studied nothing but adolescent conversions in his own evangelical milieu. He even suggested that 'conversion is an adolescent phenomenon'. And although this is not such a universal law as he thought, it is true that in his study of evangelical adolescents, Starbuck discovered a particular type of conversion which is still very common in present-day revival movements—such, for example, as that stirred up by Billy Graham.

This type of conversion is brought about in three different stages. The preacher speaks to a subject who is indifferent or hostile to religion. Then he provokes within him feelings of moral distress. In this stage of depression Leuba[21] distinguishes a typical sequence of feelings which progressively intensify the candidate's depression: feelings of guilt, humility, powerlessness, absolute misery, despair. When the preacher has reached zero he urges his listener to surpass himself in religious dedication which, he tells him, will restore his peace of mind. Leuba breaks up this ascending phase into a series of simultaneous feelings: hope, trust, assurance of salvation, love, joy, a feeling of newness, peace, light.

This type of conversion seems to be characterized by the accentuation of moral misery. Hence the message of salvation assumes a very special subjective importance: the subject wants to be saved from his moral distress. It is obvious that the affective shock gives a dramatic intensity to such conversions, and therein lies its weakness. However, sociologists have tried to measure the relative importance of this kind of conversion in the very environments which favour it. We can quote Zetterberg's[22] enquiry carried out among 376 members of a Swedish sect of whom two thirds were listed as converts. Only 16% of these subjects correspond with the type analysed by Starbuck. The subjects spoke of an abrupt change of role, a sudden passage from a life of sin to a religious mode of living. For 55·8 % conversion consisted in the sudden identification with a new role: without having lived in a state of sin they nevertheless had, at a certain moment, made a crucial experience of confident trust in faith. The remaining 28·2 % saw conversion as a gradual assimilation of a religious role.

Religious Conversion a Solution to a Human Problem

The psychoanalyst De Sanctis[23] distinguished two types of conversion: conversion by rebirth and conversion by substitution of complexes. In the first case, according to De Sanctis, an infantile religious complex is aroused and imposed on the conscience by a highly charged emotional event. The second type results from a struggle between two very distinct psychological systems. With adolescents for example, sexual tendencies can suddenly become religious tendencies. De Sanctis, inspired by psychoanalytical theory, gives this transformation the name of sublimation.

We feel he was right in isolating the type of conversion 'by substitution'. It does happen, indeed, that men suddenly discover in religion an outlet from their human impasses. It may, for example, offer them a final assurance of a recognition for which they had vainly waited from their human milieu. Or again, religion may open up a haven of peace the lack of which was cruelly felt in the tumult of unsatisfied passions. We can quote the example of a young girl, suffering from depression and haunted by the idea of suicide. She felt herself to be abandoned by her family and, especially, disowned by her father. During a trip to Italy she heard a conference on the Church, Christ's mystical body. Suddenly light dawned within her; a sudden illumination made her discover that all that she had hitherto desired was offered her in a more wonderful manner in the Church, Christ's mystical body: a life-giving strength and communion with mankind. Here indeed was Christ's life, rendered sensibly present by the sacraments, communicated to all men and making them one big human family united in love. There is no doubt but that this was a real Christian experience, an authentic conversion. Very few Christians, we may say, have discovered the mystery of the Church to such an extent. The feelings of peace and joy which the convert felt lasted several weeks during which time she received instruction and was baptized. Her spiritual director, impressed by the depth of her theological intuition, advised her to enter a contemplative order. More expert in theology than in psychology, he does not seem to have realized that vocations arising in moments of crisis frequently give place to moments of crisis in vocations. The reality of the mystical body, so admirably lived for a few weeks, answered only too well to the convert's immense need for affection and vital energy. Depression gradually set in again, stifling her faith and undermining her joy. Furthermore, the bitter disappointment of a relapse into neurosis re-awakened all her former feelings of revolt. She kept her faith in God and in the Church, but religion became a heavy burden. She felt as though weighed down under the violence of an exacting God: 'I cannot get rid of him; I cannot very well kill God!' It was many a long year before she was able to link up again in some measure with the truths she had sensed on the heights of exalted affectivity.

In this type of conversion we come across an aggravated form of a process which we have already described in discussing the motives of religion: there is the same extreme situation of frustration, the same affective anticipation of a substitute value, the same deception following the religious call, and the same need to undergo a long phase of affective purification before finding the lost faith once glimpsed in an affective flash.

We might also mention another case of sudden conversion brought about during psychoanalytical treatment. The detailed report of this case has been published by C. Berg.[24] But in this case the conversion was only a fleeting moment, for it was too exclusively motivated by affective needs.

Progressive Conversion

But not every conversion is as dramatic as the examples we have given. It can happen that a principle of religious faith is progressively elaborated within the subject's intimate depths. At the term of a peaceful intellectual and spiritual maturation he suddenly realizes, not without some surprise, that he is a changed man. Newman, in *Loss and Gain*, a novel which is often taken to be autobiographical, describes a young Anglican whose religious opinions have undergone a complete evolution; he was hardly aware of this until the day when, during a discussion on religion, he suddenly realized that he was already a Catholic at heart. Going back to the schema of Pénido we may say that here the unstructuring and restructuring of the mental synthesis has been going on simultaneously; this double process was being activated by a single immanent principle.

Conversion Resulting from a Dramatic Experience

Sometimes it happens that man, deeply shaken by a dramatic situation and by the crumbling away of the values which gave life some meaning, turns to God as to the only value left after the upheaval has subsided. Such conversions bring into operation the psychical processes and the religious movements which we have already considered in connection with extreme situations. Doubtless converts have a clearer consciousness of the truth which these situations underline; that is, that man does not dispose of his life, and that all human values are as straw in face of fate and death. Human dramas, however, can never be reduced to a single explanation. By reason of their ambiguity they can just as easily harden man in his hostility to religion. Furthermore, the emotive shock does not often last long.

Having carried out an enquiry among 76 converts, the sociologist Iisager[25] comes to the conclusion that the dramatic or decisive experience is of less importance than personal reflection. The dramatic event only has an effect if a subject finds in it a personal application and investigates the truth of it.

Conversion Through Religious Experience

Every conversion implies some religious experience, but we believe that there is a kind of conversion in which the type of resulting adherence is determined by a specifically religious experience. Such is a conversion in which the reality of God suddenly becomes a self-evident fact presented as an absolutely new value. The signs of the divine presence may be of different kinds: human love, a gospel reading, ritual symbolism. Without there having been any preceding questioning or any dramatic happening, a sudden illumination reveals God beyond the crumbling away of existence. It is possible that these conversions are also pre-determined; but the religious polarization is so intense and so decisive that we may not legitimately speak of a substitute value. Claudel's conversion,[26] so admirably described in one of his autobiographical writings, offers a typical example of a conversion following on a religious experience.

RELIGIOUS EXPERIENCE, RESISTANCE AND DEPTH RESTRUCTURING

It is noticeable that a sudden conversion is very seldom assured. Only the gradual conversion in which questing faith seeks an ultimate truth seems to be complete in itself. Even converts who hold that their faith is beyond doubt are not dispensed from the effort of acquiring it against powerful inner resistance.

Directing our analysis along the lines suggested by the witness given by Claudel in the account of his conversion, we shall begin by quoting substantial extracts:

A very sweet emotion in which, however, there was mingled a sentiment of fear, almost of horror. For my philosophical convictions were complete. God had regardlessly left them where they were, and I saw nothing to change in them, the Catholic religion seemed to be just the same treasury of absurd anecdotes, its priests and faithful inspired me with the same aversion which even went as far as hate and disgust. The edifice of my opinions and my knowledge was still standing and I saw nothing wrong with it. It only happened that I had come out of it. A new and formidable being with terrible exactions for the young man and the artist which I was, had revealed itself and I did not know how to reconcile it with anything of all that surrounded me. The state of a man suddenly snatched out of his skin to be set down in an alien body in the midst of an unknown world is the only comparison which I can find to express this state of complete bewilderment. That which was the most repugnant, to my opinions and my tastes, was nevertheless that which was true, it was that to which, willy nilly, I had to accommodate myself. Ah! But not at least without my having tried every possible way of resisting.

This resistance lasted for years. I dare to say that I put up a good defence and that the struggle was loyal and complete. Nothing was omitted. I used every means of resistance and I had to abandon, one after the other, arms which were useless to me. It was the great crisis of my existence . . . young people who give up the faith so easily do not know what it costs to recover it and of what tortures it becomes the price. The thought of Hell, the thought also of all the beauties and all the joys, which, so it seemed, my return to truth would oblige me to sacrifice, were especially what held me back.

Nothing could illustrate better than this quotation how much the personality is unstructured by religious conversion. Religion justifies existence and must be essentially the subject's centre. Nevertheless, for the newly converted young Claudel, the sway of religion is only apparently complete. All that makes up the basis of his personality remains foreign to him. That is to say, his moral conduct, philosophical considerations, his instinctive judgements of values, his human solidarities. Torn from himself, doubled in his personality, he feels God's call as both a blinding evidence and a horrifying violence. Conversion is only achieved when his personality is organized in relation to his new outlook.

Incubation

Such a surprising disproportion between former certitudes and present adherence makes it impossible for us to follow James in interpreting this type of conversion as the irruption of subliminal tendencies in the heart of the ego.[27] It is certainly evident that in the case of sudden conversion there are unconscious memories and religious sentiments in the subject. But how can we reduce the sudden illumination to a phenomenon of psychic automatism or to a prolonged subconscious incubation? James refers to pathological cases where buried memories seem to be the cause of evident disturbances. But, in the light of clinical psychology, we are obliged to set in absolute opposition these two types of divided personality. The disturbed patient's personality is torn between the conscious subject and the ideas and strange behaviour which are forced upon him and which he can in no way relate to normal standards of experience and reason. On the contrary, in conversion, the conflict which splits the personality sets the religious truth to which the subject assents in opposition to all that rises from the affective strata of personality.

Pathological Belief and Religious Faith

A brief comparison between conversion and aberrant beliefs will clearly show the profound difference between the two phenomena. Pathological belief can be illustrated by the example of fetishist perversion which psychoanalysis explains as a form of belief. The fetishist subject, though he knows the anatomy of woman, refuses, in his unconscious imagination, to recognize that she does not possess the male organ. On the affective level, he disavows his knowledge by maintaining the image of the phallic woman. He perpetuates the attitude of the child who, having come to know female anatomy and remarked upon the absence of the phallus, rejects this fresh knowledge and keeps up the 'belief' in a feminine phallus.[28] As Freud says, from now onward he has a divided attitude with regard to this belief. In other words, what comes up from the subliminal, from the unconscious, are the beliefs belied by reality but to which the subject clings by denouncing known reality.

This analysis of the underlying processes of fetishism shows how different are the structures of religious faith and pathological belief. A certain analogy in the doubling of the personality may explain a wrong impression drawn from superficial observation, but in fact, the pure and simple transposing of a schema taken from pathology to the case of religious conversion merely serves to confuse the phenomena. Unlike morbid 'beliefs', the truth discovered in conversion imposes itself on the whole person as the true reality. Instead of being kept on the periphery as a blind belief, it is questioned by the subject and questions him too. If there is some doubt, it is because the truth which has burst in upon the subject obliges him to reconsider former certitudes, even those which appeared to be most unshakeable. In pathological beliefs, on the contrary, the subject suspects that they are not true but he unconsciously refuses to examine them. In conversion the relationship between consciousness and belief is the inverse of that seen in pathological cases and in cases of incubation. Only the psychological concept of resistance can offer some explanation of the division of the personality which accompanies conversion at the beginning.

Resistance to Conversion

Clinical experience allowed Freud to formulate the concept of resistance. Convinced that only the complete truth about himself can free man from his psychological shackles, Freud offered his patients only one remedy: to say quite freely whatever came into their minds. But at the same time he noted that hesitations, silences, avoidances, and veiled avowals troubled his patients in their talk and always at the crucial moment. In spite of their good will, the subjects were unable to conform to the fundamental rule of psychotherapy until they had been effectively set free by truthful statements. Thus, a resistance which does not come from the conscious ego opposes itself to the avowal of truth. Another subject gets in the way. There is a censor who makes a selection among all the things that would come to the light of consciousness, retaining only what is not too painful for the ego.

This phenomenon of resistance which Freud discovered in pathological cases can also be seen in other situations. We have only to notice the reactions of shame in order to recognize the same processes of defence and selection. Man hides from his own eyes, no less than from others, what risks diminishing him and causing him suffering. If he is naturally open to others he may quite well conceal himself in order to preserve a constantly threatened interiority. Resistance is as normal as is modesty, and considered in itself it is a healthy reaction.

In the same way the convert frequently defends himself against God whose intrusion into his life shatters a personality which has been built up at great cost in the course of preceding experiences and commitments. Here again, resistance represents an instinctive criticism arising from the very core of personality. It comes up from the deposit which over long years has been laid down in the preconscious by thoughts and vital choices. In itself reason is open to truth, but affective memories are opposed to it. The deeply affective force of resistance is shown in the spontaneous judgements which we find, for example, scattered here and there in Claudel's witness: 'It is too absurd', 'it is too stupid', 'it is shameful'. In the perspective gained by our study it would be useful to make a careful study of the sense of religious modesty. Clinical psychologists know from experience that it is even more intense and more profound than sexual modesty. One wonders what inner weakness it signifies?

Affective Shock and the Restructuring of the Person

The intrusion of God into human existence as a result of sudden conversion is an event of the order of an affective shock.[29] Through clinical psychology we have come to know the extraordinary effects of such shocks. During the first years of his existence every man has healthy resistances to inner dangers such as the feeling of guilt, or the longing for affective intimacy. But the sudden inroad of a strong emotion, loss by death, or a first love, can sweep away these resistances. The best established habits are unsettled, the strongest convictions are bowled over. In the same way, a sudden religious illumination can overcome the firmest resistances. But they will reorganize themselves and take up the fight again until the personality has been restructured in depth. If such a rending of the personality is to be overcome, the habitual judgements and the affective reactions must come to full consciousness and be patiently reorientated by the convert. To borrow a very neat expression from Freud we may say that conversion is only achieved when the person has been reorganized in depth as a result of 'working out' (*Durcharbeitung*)[30] his memories and his sentiments. Round this new centre of gravity the subject will have to weave a new network of significant relationships with the world and with men. By means of such an elaboration, after a certain period of interior division, the religious integration of the personality will be accomplished. This complete conversion may be helped on by certain psychological conditions, for example, greater adaptability, the absence of any too intense anxiety, or the intellectual capacity for objectivizing a situation. But a conversion is never achieved without the revelation and the restructuring of resistances.

Need for Certainty and its Dangers

In the religious sphere men rarely remain sceptical. This is the conclusion reached by Thouless after an enquiry among 138 university students.[31] The replies to the 26 religious items of his enquiry express a well-defined conviction, positive or negative. The subject takes up a position. The same is true, but to a lesser degree, for the items proposing a political tenet. This implies that political ideas also affect a man's whole behaviour and they, too, have practical consequences. But on the other hand, the other profane beliefs arouse only very weak agreement or rejection. Thouless thinks that the need to have some conviction in religious matters explains to some extent the suddenness of many conversions where subjects come to accept positions which only a short time before they had just as strongly refused.

We agree with the interpretation which Thouless gives of the facts observed during his enquiry: every time that ideas urge a man to commit himself he needs to feel convinced. This need is confirmed by other phenomena. There is in the first place the fact, rather surprising at first sight, that few men are really agnostic. Very often, even those who deny reason any possibility of justifying belief in God nevertheless make use of philosophical principles for proving that he does not exist. From an agnostic thesis they pass quite naturally to a philosophical criticism of religion, thus contradicting their agnostic position. In the same way, we sometimes notice among believers a radicalism and an intolerance which leads one to suspect a sudden passage from non-belief to belief. The rigidity of a religious position is to be explained by the psychological need to unify one's personality and to defend it against every doubt which might disorganize it.

The need for certainty may also be shown by the pursuit of ecstatic experiences. This phenomenon has been studied by Allier among uncivilized peoples converted to Christianity.[32] He shows how 'the systematic pursuit of emotion, regarded as the best means of provoking the crisis, almost inevitably leads to the conclusion that the only true conversions are those preceded by an affective shock'. The convert, wrongly directed by the preacher, seeks in affective experience a tangible sign of inner conversion.

We are now in a position to clarify this study on conversion. In the rending of the personality by which it is preceded and followed, we can put a finger on the integration which religion brings about in man. Resistances are negative signs of the profound restructuring which results in the religious attitude. And we must not be led astray by the apparent freedom, the joy or the generosity which animates the newly converted. We must remember here the psychological law according to which the most insidious resistance is to be found precisely where the discovered truths are most easily accepted, that is, where one does not commit one's whole personality. The ease with which a conviction is assumed is often the symptom of a dissociation between reason and deep affectivity.

IV. Human Autonomy and Religious Assent

FAITH, CERTAINTY WITHOUT GUARANTEE

Up to now, in our analysis of the religious attitude we have passed over in silence one of its essential elements; that is, the relational nature of the attitude. Our study of resistance was also very formal, restricted to the consideration of the seat of the resistance and, correlatively, the manner in which religion comes to reshape the person from within. But it is not a negligible fact that resistance puts the believer in opposition to a God who is presented as a person. It is this interpersonal relationship defining the religious attitude which we are now going to examine. We shall consider all that it implies in the way of ruptures, conflicts and appeasement.

The concepts of integration and structure could mislead us. They signify a mode of being, fixed and organized. The word 'structure' implies these two characteristics. A structure is a hierarchical organization integrating the different spheres of the personality by unification around a centre. In the case of the religious attitude, it is faith in God which enjoys the power of integration. The study of conversion has shown us this integration in process of realization, often at the price of a hard struggle. Once the person has been structured around religion, his faith will put up a resistance against any too contingent changes. But it would be a serious mistake to imagine that this stability of the religious attitude is accompanied by complete clarity of vision, or a good conscience able to rest in what it has acquired. The religious attitude is intentional, it therefore relates to God more by its aim than by possession. In faith, God gives himself only in answer to human assent.

If we wish to understand the conflicts inherent in religious assent, we shall have to go more deeply into this paradoxical truth of religious belief. Our method here will be that of a phenomenology of the act of faith. Using the empirical data of psychological studies, we shall try to grasp the meaning of faith as a relationship with the Other, attempting to bring into relief the different moments of faith and the connection between them. We shall begin with religious facts but we shall go beyond the purely empirical level and attempt to clarify the ideal type of religious belief to which, moreover, believers refer both in their efforts and in their difficulties.

God, Object and Foundation of Faith

It is evident that, being a relationship to God, the act of faith has God for object. God is the end and content of faith. Religion is not concerned with a concept, but with a reality, the divine person himself. The Christian who professes his belief in dogmatic truths still refers directly to God in person through the intermediary of dogmatic expression. If this is so, we can see at once the psychological difficulties entailed in the act of faith. How can one refer to an invisible person, to a person who is regarded as the centre of human existence, without engulfing all other human activities? And, again, how is it possible to make a personal reference to God through a system of dogmatics? These are the difficulties which we shall meet in the course of our discussion. But first we must endeavour to understand the act of faith in itself.

Faith, we have already said, has for its object the person and the manifestations of God. For the believer, God is both the goal of his intimate aspirations and the person in whom he trusts, on whom he counts for the ultimate fulfilment of his existence. Religious faith, then, is always indissociably an intellectual conviction, an obedience and a relationship of love.

The complex nature of the act of faith corresponds to that of divine paternity. The believer affirms that God has created the world, that he maintains it in existence, and that he is its ultimate end. God is the author of the law which will humanize and divinize man, therefore we obey his prohibiting and promising word. Lastly, faith is also an act of love because the presence of the God of grace is a source of happiness and a pledge of ultimate fulfilment.

This personal relationship with the living God is described by the word 'encounter', so often used in our times. But we must admit that we do not like this expression very much. Taken in its strict sense it denotes an immediate presence and a reciprocity, neither of which is the order of faith.

The man who believes in God, also believes *because of God*, on account of God who alone, in the long run, is the foundation for religious faith. Often the classical theme 'reasons for belief' misleads the judgement of both believers and unbelievers. We look for reasons on which to base our faith in God; we weigh them up and discuss them. Some people find them scarcely convincing, whereas others consider them so evident that faith is only a corollary of their rational convictions. This is to forget that faith in a person is an intellectual and loving adherence; it

16

goes far beyond the signs by which such a person is manifested to us.

It is interesting at this point to recall Pascal's question: What is the self? It is not a person's physical beauty, nor his intelligence, nor even his character. Self is the hub of all that, yet always something more. I shall never contact the man in himself, if, in each of his aspects, I do not reach directly to the heart of his being. And only words permit that. That is why faith is of the order of a word. Even apart from belief in an historical revelation, faith is always of the order of attentive listening. It is not for nothing that in many religious traditions, the prophets listened to the divine inspiration and transmitted it in the form of oracular pronouncements.

The word is the authentic means by which a person makes himself known and gives himself to another. The word makes the other present as a whole composed of meaning and consent. The content of what is said is even secondary to the saying; in the word, a person exists for someone else. At the deepest level, to welcome another means first to listen to him. As a source of qualities and initiatives, he is always something more than what he does and expresses. But in the word, he sets up a relationship in which he transmits the heart of his being. Similarly, religious belief is not based on any intermediary set up between God and man. It is, finally, not justifiable by any motive, either rational or affective. It goes directly to God himself, listening to him and responding with assent. It is, then, founded on God in person. There is coincidence between the object of faith and its motive.

Our phenomenology of faith as the welcome and the gift of a word does not mean that we reduce faith to the word alone. The word, isolated, would express the absence of the Other and the impossibility of entering into any true communication with him. The exchange of words is preceded and sustained by a living presence made manifest in many signs, which gives such an exchange existential reality. We must, then, reset our phenomenology of the word in the movement which animates our whole study; the movement which flows from experience to the attitude of faith. Our intention here is to underline the novelty which the word introduces into an experiential presence—the Other naming and revealing himself. After this, in faith, as it is mediated by the word, every sign of an anonymous presence can be given the coefficient of a personal presence. It is at this point that the attitude is formed and personalized; it is here that we may speak of a religious (or Christian) experience in the full sense of the word.

The intellectuals already mentioned observe very clearly this specific nature of the act of religious faith which is beyond every religious experience. They invoke the signs upon which their faith is founded; but they also recognize the rupture which separates these signs from the object of faith.

Unbelievers constantly accuse faith of being blind. And it is indeed true that to the eyes of scientific reason faith is not reasonable, that is, it is not based on reason even if there are signs which guarantee that it is reasonable. But is faith unreasonable simply because it is no longer of the order of reasoning reason? In this case the same applies to human love. But phenomenology has sufficiently shown that a certain faith is essential to every human judgement. Scientific reason itself supposes some preceding and sustaining perceptive faith.[33] We cannot, then, simply oppose faith and reason.

Certitude by Assent

A person never has any guarantee other than himself. In the relationship with others, certitude does not come before assent. It is concomitant: it is its fruit. And so it is with religious faith. When man addresses God, he would like to know first what it is that he is believing in. But that is something which he only knows the moment he has faith: 'scio cui credidi' (2 *Tim.* 1:12)—'I know whom I have believed'. Religious faith offers no familiar security to reasoning reason, neither that of deduction nor that of induction. And yet it is a certainty. We may compare it to the problem of motion as raised by Zeno at the dawn of philosophy. For discursive reason motion is impossible because the analysis of its elements never allow of the synthesis of the whole. Yet, in the act by which motion is brought about, it exists and can be observed. Zeno's reasoned negation becomes a certitude of another order. Similarly, when the believer renounces his need for a pre-established certainty and interprets the signs of God positively; when he gives his assent, another order of certitude is set up. This is not founded upon a pre-established guarantee, but it becomes its own guarantee as it is lived.

Nevertheless, the believer is never in possession of his faith as something assured to him once and for all. He can always cease to place his trust in God. If he does so, his former certitude dims and fades like the memory of a dream.

The act of faith, as we have described it, has nothing to do with a fideist attitude, a confidence supported solely by some vague affective attraction, or justified only by religious tradition. Faith is a conscious act accomplished by the whole person and its certitude is a light radiating on human existence, making it more reasonable.

Over and beyond any previously established guarantee, consent can only be effected in a deliberate personal commitment. The receptivity of religious listening no longer has the pathic character proper to experiences of the sacred. The believing man does not 'undergo' God in the same way that he may have undergone such experiences. The welcome extended to the Other results from a reasoned and willed disposition. It is the work of practical reason. It filters out human desire, it confines reasoning reason within its own bounds and it tunes in to God.

The act of faith is, then, an eminently free act, even though the attitude of obedience which it implies may often give both believers and non-believers the impression of a lack of liberty. In the first place, faith supposes inner freedom. It can only be lived if moral attitudes and psychological conditions have predisposed man to welcome another. A certain humanization and a certain psychological equilibrium are both necessary. But, in return, they set man free; they broaden his being in an interpersonal relationship. It is obvious that all external constraint, physical or sociological, does away with the conditions necessary to an act of faith.

Questioning Faith

Faith is certitude and questioning. One can understand why: the evidence of its object, though real, is never total. The realities of faith are not imposed on reason with absolute rigour; both affectivity and will remain free to resist them. Reason will always seek the satisfaction of guarantees; this means that faith will constantly have to tear itself away from its grasp. Faith can only be maintained at the cost of a continual struggle against reason—the leap into the unknown must ceaselessly be renewed. The methodical doubt of reason will then be as long-lived as faith. But far from diminishing it, it constitutes the very setting in which the certitude of faith is to be discovered.

On the other hand, assent to faith is never total. In common with every other human project, it is realized progressively, finding new perfection in each experience. There is, then, a doubt which is immanent to faith and of quite another order than the doubt of reason. Faith doubts by fidelity to itself. Like love, faith must prove itself, become true. The source of doubt by fidelity does not concern the exigencies of reason, but those of faith itself. It is the will for union with God which urges man methodically to question himself about both God and his own relationship with him. In belief, God appears to human questioning as both a new field to be explored and a fresh norm for faith.

Thus, doubts of faith are not necessarily of a guilty nature. They are inherent in faith, in keeping with the twin track we have just followed. Of course, since faith is never complete, it is never faultless. The act of faith is no less pre-determined than any other human behaviour. Doubts about faith are never pure; they are always tainted with motives of selfishness, servility and pride. But it is no use pretending to be able to distinguish positive from negative doubts. Man is a living mixture of passion, reason and moral conscience, and he never altogether innocently questions himself either about God or about himself. Here the precept 'Judge not' should be remembered.

In analysing the act of faith, we have ignored up to now any specific dogmatic belief. In the following section, we shall examine the particular problem set by the act of faith in God when this faith includes the acceptance of dogmatic truths.

DOGMATIC FAITH

In this section we shall deal more particularly with the psychological problems posed by dogmatic faith; we shall only consider its theological aspect in so far as a doctrinal point of view throws light on the psychological structures. Furthermore, we shall not deal with the criticisms which psychologists such as Freud and Jung have made of dogmatic religion. Such criticisms concern a form of dogmatic faith which is certainly aberrant and pathological.

Studies on the faith of adults have shown that they often abandon dogmatic faith. For example, an enquiry among 500 American university students[34] shows that though they remain religious, most have fallen away from the dogmatic faith in which they were brought up; 56 have left the Church to which they once belonged. In the chapter on motivation, we remarked a similar falling away among ex-service men. However, it should be noticed that the subjects of these enquiries come mainly from Protestant communions which leave a wide margin for freedom in assent to dogmatic beliefs and religious practice. We do not know to what extent the Catholic milieu is affected by this phenomenon of dogmatic disaffection. In the preceding pages we have already had occasion to interpret some cases of abandoning dogmatic faith as the rejection of certain religious representations still too full of sentimentality and infantile imagery. But this is by no means always the explanation. A psychological difficulty relating to dogmatic faith may also be the motive for abandoning it. In order to study this kind of motive we shall once again have recourse to the testimony of intellectuals from which we have already quoted.

The majority of them insist often on the discrepancy which they have remarked between religious knowledge and actual experience: between what they are taught by their Church and what they are able to put into their religious attitude in the world in which they live. They know what it is they must believe and they admit that these truths penetrate neither their concrete religious attitude nor their dealings with the world: in fact, they never become the regulating principles of a lived religion. They remain pure theoretical knowledge and thus assume a coefficient of unreality. They are nothing more than ideas. We could well say with Kant that they are empty ideas since they are filled with no intuitive data.

Among intellectuals, this impression of unreality is so intense that it even prevents them from rehabilitating dogmatic truths by means of systematic reflection; there are some who wonder whether the cause of the gap between dogmatic beliefs and effective religious life is not due to a lack of sustained attention and systematic studies. But they admit their reluctance to correct this state of affairs, fearing lest truly theological reflection should make them lose themselves in useless theorizing far removed from real life and, ultimately, stripped of any guarantee of truth.

There must be no mistake over the object of this scepticism. It is not concerned with minor theological theories, but touches on the very kernel of the Christian message: the atonement for sin by the death on the cross of Christ, God made man; the salvific power of the resurrection, the specific efficacy of the sacraments, the doctrine of original sin . . .

That this feeling of rupture between dogmatic truths and effective religion is, at the present time, a very widespread phenomenon, is proved by the enormous repercussions which the book by the Anglican Bishop Robinson has had. Robinson does not aim at substituting a vague humanistic religion for faith in God. As he sees it, the need is to overcome in Christianity the division of faith into purely speculative truths and to establish a living relationship with God as part of human reality.

It must be acknowledged that Robinson's observations come very near to the complaints of our subjects: 'You can hear as many theological lectures as you like, they do not catch on, they leave you cold, they do not concern you as you really are.' These are major facts, massive facts which religious psychology cannot avoid.

An honest appraisal, it seems to us, must have three stages.

We must first consider the observed fact itself; then we must compare it with the nature of religious faith as we have already analysed it. Finally this comparison will allow us to make a well-founded judgement.

We must take seriously the criticisms made by believers who suffer from the discordance between dogmatic faith and lived religion. Their scepticism is, indeed, doubly justified. Any theoretical idea must first find some practical application, under pain of being cut off from life and reduced to the realm of fanciful imagining. Without giving way to common empiricism, it must be admitted that if they are to be anything more than abstractions, any ideas which concern man personally must influence his mode of existence. They have to affect the judgements which we make of man and the world. Contemplation is nothing more than an escape into the imaginary if it does not sustain creative virtues for praxis. In religious matters, this necessity for linking the idea with effective behaviour is all the stronger in that, by its very nature, every authentic idea about God expresses an interpersonal link and is bound to commit the whole of existence. If it does not polarize the entire man, if it seems to be without any practical application, a dogmatic truth is nothing but a product of the brain, like the many mythological fables. Of course, when we speak of practical application we do not necessarily mean a specific moral praxis which would distinguish Christians from other men. But, since it purports to penetrate and structure the whole personality, the religious conviction should contain practical possibilities for a reinterpretation of human history and life's orientation. If dogma finds in the world no echo that can reveal its existential density, then it is nothing but a fruitless ideology.

Of itself, dogmatic faith sets up a dialogue in which man listens to what God says about himself and his designs for man and the world. If we take dogmatic faith for what it intends to be, what it is meant to be, it is evident that in listening to revelation, the believer wants to be in contact with God as he is, and not as man would like him to be. This turning away from self in order to approach the Other who speaks of himself, is quite the opposite of infantile religion. Dogmatic faith is opposed to any subjective motivation. The God of revelation is, in principle, the opposite of a God made in the image of human desires. We say 'in principle' because the man who listens to God, still interprets him according to his own ideas. That is why one of the constant tasks of religious thought is the effort of demythologization.

Therefore, in order to judge the discrepancy between dogmatic faith and lived religion, we must base ourselves on two principles: on the one hand, the word necessarily brings about a rupture in the natural bonds between man and God; and on the other hand, this word must effectively link up with the concrete religious attitude. There are two stumbling blocks to be avoided: religious subjectivism and the separating of truth from life.

We could, at this point, go into the meaning of Christian dogmas and show that the truth they express is not as abstract as it is absolute. These dogmas expound the history of God's plan of salvation in the world. Since it is history, revelation follows a certain sequence, that of the progressive manifestation of divine paternity in the gradual establishment of the kingdom of God. We should have to show also that religious history is really one with human history, that it is not superimposed, but that it completes it from within. It is not our business here to do the work of a theologian, but we should not be faithful to the task we have set ourselves if we did not develop the psychological consequences which dogmatic faith entails for the believer.

Let us notice in the first place that a conflict is unavoidable. It is not merely by widening the scope of his human enterprises, or even his initial religious intuition, that man will be able to arrive at a religious relationship structured by the word. Certainly, the word of God does answer in a sense to a certain desire of man. But God, in taking the initiative and in setting up his kingdom, forces man to rethink the ideas he has of the world, of his own personal mystery and even of God himself. God satisfies man but also in some way contradicts his desires. Far from religious projection, dogmatic faith means assent.

In our day, the quarrel between spontaneous religion and dogmatic faith is more acute because man is becoming more deeply rooted in the world of his making; unlike the man of ancient or medieval times he no longer lives naïvely and passively in the symbolic universe in which the visible world seemed to be suspended. The centre of gravity of existence is now the terrestrial. This revolution of contemporary man's mental universe makes great demands on religious thought. Theology must open up to a new dimension of existence—the dimension of history created by man's work in the world. Theology must assume this dimension and be renewed by it. Every truth, human or divine, can contribute to a better revelation of the full meaning of religious history. Every reality is part of the comprehensive network linking man and God.

Because of the conflict it involves, the truth of the relationship between man and God is necessarily discovered progressively. Man can only gain access to the fundamental mysteries of divine paternity by a progressive discovery of its true dimensions. We believe that, as a general rule, an attitude of life inspired by the ethical principles of the gospel is the first phase of a gradual preparation for the comprehension of dogmatic realities. An evangelical attitude is the normal basis for faith in the word. The man who listens to the word inevitably discovers God. And, as Pascal reminded us, God is only discovered by way of the gospel. Nor must it be forgotten that the way of the gospel has always been, and remains, very progressive.

Studies in religious sociology risk falsifying our outlook. Up till now they have been mainly devoted to studying religious practice and they thus reinforce the tendency to measure Christian faith by the sole standard of fulfilled Christian faith—at least in so far as it is expressed in practice.

In the dynamic perspective which is ours, fulfilled faith must be considered rather as the hearth which gives out warmth to a population more or less influenced by Christian preaching and which even sheds some radiance on the godless civilization of contemporary society. If it is useful to know the figures for religious practice, we must not take them as being the sole index of faith. Is the low figure of 20% to 30% for Sunday church-goers such a catastrophe as is made out? Who knows, indeed, the number of believers who already live according to the gospel and are advancing towards the God in whom they believe? Furthermore, no one can tell how much real atheism lies behind the religious practice of certain so-called believers.

Having come to the end of this discussion on dogmatic faith, we now wish to go back to the general problem of religious assent, taking into consideration in turn the two human tendencies which emphasize the conflict inherent in every kind of faith: human autonomy and the affirmation of terrestrial values.

THE LIBERTY CONFERRED BY GOD

The interviews which we have mentioned have brought out the fact that assent to faith contradicts secret tendencies in man. The conflict is crystallized in two main points: the concept of divine almightiness, and the fact of the Church as an institution.

The idea of divine almightiness suggests a kind of fatalist dependence and servile subordination. At first glance man does not see how to reconcile this with human liberty. Does it not seem to contradict one of the essential tenets of faith, namely that God has given man a human task to accomplish? The idea of divine almightiness is a difficulty even in the sphere of the religious relationship. Our subjects see this as something that may develop in different ways; even within the religious attitude there are still choices to be made.

The dogmatic truths which the Catholic Church so uncompromisingly proposes may increase the tension of belief. Certain believers feel that in order to answer God's call, the free man should be in a position to discover the truth of religion for himself. They find it difficult to conceive a freely given assent to a dogmatic system elaborated and imposed by authority.

The moral prescriptions of the Church sometimes conflict with the consciousness of liberty, even in believers who accept them in principle. It is the assertion of a moral authority as such which these intellectuals find most unacceptable. The disagreement which is to be noticed between their personal convictions and certain more or less official moral teaching (such, for example, as that on birth-control) only accentuates a more general problem.

One has the feeling that ethics is above all something which it is man's responsibility to assume personally as part of a dynamic concern to promote moral values. It is not a question of having a lower moral standard than that which the Church requires; but one has the impression that in asking for obedience to laws imposed from without, the Church robs man of something of his essential dignity as an ethical being. What motivates a profound spontaneous resistance to the Church as a moral authority is precisely that an elaborate moral code does not give man this impression of being appealed to as an ethical being. There seems to be a paradoxical inversion which weakens the ethical dynamic of the gospel.

We have reported the problems as they might well present themselves. We insist on the fact that we have given here the witness of believers who have no wish to leave their Church. And we can see, moreover, that they are anxious to overcome the conflicts we have defined.

Indeed, the will for liberty which kicks against dependence and obedience is only the first phase of a movement which tends to return to a harmony in which human tendencies and the truths of faith correct and reveal each other in their individual truth. It is in the name of liberty that the idea of divine almightiness is rejected. However, it has been pointed out that the idea of divine paternity, as Christ revealed it, gives back to man his true liberty within a religious bond. The Father is then recognized as the one who respects man's autonomy and upholds his responsibility. As to the conflict which sets a creative ethic in opposition to a morality of obedience to ecclesiastical laws, we have no evidence of explicit signs of a reconciliation. Therefore we prefer to restrict our reflections to the former point which is, moreover, by far the more essential to the act of faith.

For the theologian the almightiness of God does not exclude human liberty, but rather is its foundation. But for the believers we interviewed it seems to be a despotic power which leaves nothing for man to do. In the first phase, man conceives of the relationship as mutually exclusive. And it is significant that for our subjects, the idea of a creative God suggests something in the nature of a temporal sequence of several initiatives. God sets man in being, but after this initial act he then, so to speak, withdraws. He gives man the tasks to be done until he shall come again at the end of history to ask him to give an account of what he has done and to bring all things to an end.

One would be tempted to say that in order to develop, human creativity needs a sort of free field, away from the creative power of God, a sort of half-way house. It is useful to recall here the Freudian myth of the primitive father, all-powerful, owning everything, and from whom murder alone could set the son free. In this interpretation of the origins of religion, the mythical representation of the father is obviously that of the Oedipus conflict. But, for this very reason it is not just pure fantasy. In the actual problem of our witnesses, we can recognize a reflection of this same essential conflict. When man first encounters liberty he regards it as total liberty. He must, in a second phase, be willing to base it on the Other so that it can be something more than empty freedom. Already at the level of his temporal initiatives man must begin to select the actual situations which will orientate his choices: his liberty must be supported by the information which furthers the effective realization of his potentialities.

Similarly, religion expects man to accept the fact that even his liberty is willed by God. Man must establish his liberty in God and renounce any liberty which might tend to be exclusive. The idea of God's dynamic almightiness can be interpreted as the mythical correlative of a so-called sovereign freedom. It is natural that in the first moment of this confrontation, the concept of divine almightiness, taken in its radical abstraction, may seem to annihilate man's liberty.

Faith, going further than liberty which aspires to be absolute, is an assent structured on the pattern of the three sequences of time. Man consents to acknowledge his beginning in a God-Creator. He consents to commit his freedom to a future which beckons to him but which he does not possess. Finally, in the present exercise of his will, he recognizes that he is borne by an absolute will which maintains and furthers him in existence. The well-known Delphic motto, 'Know thyself', had originally, not a psychological meaning, but a religious one: 'Know thyself; and know that thou art man, not God.' Liberty in its upsurge is undivided, and therefore aspires to autodivinization. Religion is an act of humility, consent to the truth about self.

In psychology, liberty is in many ways a very problematic fact. In our foregoing considerations we have dealt with it at the level of actual awareness. But if we go a step further as some psychological theories do, we shall discover to what extent the conflict between autonomy and assent to faith is a fundamental and constituent element of religion.

We have in mind L. Szondi's psychological theory of the link between the 'paroxysmic' type and the religious type (*homo sacer*), a link which Dostoievsky so astonishingly illustrated. Szondi's theory follows Freud's in regarding religion as essentially the sublimation of the aggressive drive. Baffling as these psychological theories may be, we are convinced that they can throw light on the heart of the problem with which we are dealing.[35]

Liberty emerges from the passions. Plato was already aware of that; he distinguished in the soul an affective dynamic (*thumos*) which can join forces with desire, giving it an aggressive force, or with reason, endowing it with the virtue of force and the anger of moral indignation. Liberty rises from the foundation of the aggressive drive. If it were not so, it would not involve the whole man, and would never become a creative power. But, at the level of a drive, it can be just as much a destructive force as a constructive one. It is aroused in opposition, and takes the form of negation before being converted into creative consent. Szondi's theory explains why it is that the stronger the first savage and destructive drive, the more intense can be the sublimation in religious assent. The contrast between autonomy and consent is a constituent of religion and it has its roots in drives and in the process of sublimation.

THE ASYMMETRY OF THE TERRESTRIAL AND RELIGION

Liberty is not acosmic. It is one with the realities which it brings about and with the society which it helps to establish. In modern times, man has acquired a more acute consciousness of his liberty, not only by turning in on himself, but in the affirmation of the human world which he is actually building up. His technical mastery over nature, his consciousness of the historic dimension of the human world, have had the result of identifying man more than ever with his action, and have made it increasingly difficult to think of the fulfilment of the human condition on strictly religious lines. The integration of earthly values into the religious attitude has become a crucial problem for believers. For contemporary man, the evangelical invitation to lose one's life in order to keep it seems to mean that the divinization of man in his relationship with God can only be acquired at the cost of his renouncing his human condition. But at the same time, the believer still has the conviction that the maker of the world cannot be a wicked and jealous God who wants at all costs to destroy his own work.

It is against this background of asymmetry between earthly tasks and their religious integration that the conflict between the will for autonomy and assent assumes its full magnitude. Between the two there can be neither coincidence nor exclusiveness. Religion should penetrate terrestrial values without absorbing them. Human commitment must spark off the religious attitude without exhausting it.

In the next chapter we shall see that atheism is essentially the manifestation of this asymmetric polarity between the terrestrial and the religious.

CONCLUSIONS

The religious attitude, as the structuring of the whole personality in harmony with the relationship with God, supposes an inner liberty of which man is hardly capable before adulthood. For this he must have resolved the affective confusion which is betrayed in impassioned religious transports. The silence with which the Other meets his human demands seems to be the decisive trial in purifying religion. Furthermore, man must first know the experience, so often rebellious, of his autonomy and his creative powers, before being in a position to discover divine paternity and the meaning of filiation. The relationship to the

Other also demands that man should have freed himself from the indiscriminate and egocentric ties made in childhood with both men and God. Unless he has done this, the believer will look to God for a magnified substitute father, able to answer his selfish demands. It is certainly no easier to acknowledge God simply for his own sake than it is to love a man in truth.

As to religious sonship, though it may be legitimately called spiritual childhood, it is nevertheless quite the opposite to infantilism. It involves indeed a double requirement, psychological and religious. Man must first have acquired a certain degree of affective freedom, by his psychological development and by the use of his faculties in a human commitment. But these psychological conditions are not sufficient. The whole man is involved when he hears the word. To the eyes of faith, it is essential that man's psychological formation should end in assent. And, in view of this, everything which belongs to man must be reinterpreted in the light of faith: his past, his human projects, the autonomy he has acquired. This movement of consent and reinterpretation can only be made in deep conversion which overcomes many resistances. Faith is suffering, a passion. The word of God is a sword piercing to the roots of being. But freely assumed sonship restores to man a spiritual childhood, of which the first childhood, that of the lost paradise, of the incipient man, is only the primitive prefiguring. The religious integration of the person brings peace to the whole being against a background of accepted suffering. It is fullness answering need; union without confusion; divinization in humility.

Many of our contemporaries think that in the religious attitude there is something infantile, or perhaps even some unmanliness. What is more, sociology informs us that in the West religion has become mainly the concern of women, whereas everywhere else it is, in fact, the men who are charged with religion.

Very often, religious reserve reveals a secret fear that religion is not a manly attitude, not something free and adult. This fear is a sign similar to a symptomatic slip of the tongue. It witnesses to the fact that in these believers spiritual childhood is still very much the same thing as human infantilism. If they did not secretly feel religion to be some human weakness, they would live it without any reticence, entirely committed in the project of a free assent. In such instances it is evident that because of its immersion in archaic infantilism, spiritual childhood is still closely tied to such infantilism, and in support of this we should like to mention those believers who have told us that for them religion was something of which they felt both very ashamed and very afraid. This embarrassment was the obverse of a servile religious obedience and a profound anxiety at the thought of God's judgement.

The accusation of infantilism is all the stronger in that, in order to judge religion, the non-religious man sees himself in imagination at the moment of conflict. Often he refuses the gift in the name of his human dignity, understood in terms of an autonomy which, though contingent, is freely assumed.

A certain religious hypocrisy in human relationships and sentimentality in prayer have certainly not furthered the spiritual liberty of a sincerely acknowledged sonship. It has been often said that there is no other sphere in which the danger of infantilism is so great as in religion. Rooted from the beginning in the family constellation, the religious attitude, more than any other, risks keeping the form fashioned during childhood. Thus, for example, in the pseudo-mystical exaltation of the Virgin Mary we can detect the cracked sound of a false paradisiac childhood.

Another indication of religious infantilism is to be found in the excessive emphasis accorded in certain epochs to passive virtues such as humility, obedience, chastity, poverty. This has had a part in robbing Christianity of something of its virility. It has obscured the sense of true humility before God which is also courage before men. It has taken away the true nature of obedience which is also boldness in the truth. On the other hand a certain human masochism has too much concealed the suffering of faith, and respectful humility before God and men has too often taken on the aspect of infantile narcissism.

A free and integrated religious attitude will be quite the opposite of this unmanly religion. It is heuristic, never ceasing to invent new means for building up human society and the kingdom of the spirit. It is realistic and measures its truth against its ethical relationship with men. The rite unifies the whole man for it is the total and free expression of reconciled man. It expresses the body recognized in its force and beauty. It gives man his place in human society and contributes to the building up of the religious community. By its symbolic reading of the whole cosmos, it connects the terrestrial with the religious.

The true religious attitude is a dynamic equilibrium which is difficult to attain and maintain. It has to integrate many apparent opposites. It supposes an effective contact with humanity in the making, and a clear assent to a God who is holy, transcendent, and, at the same time, present at the core of human history. In Part Two, devoted to genetic religious psychology, we shall see how the religious attitude can be progressively built up, in the course of the discoveries which man makes of his humanity and of God. But before dealing with that, we must consider, in the next chapter, how the germs of atheism are contained within the interior tensions of the religious attitude.

1 See *Les attitudes, Symposium de l'association de psychologie scientifique de langue francaise*, Paris 1961.

2 See H. C. J. Duyker, 'Les attitudes et les relations interpersonnelles' *Les attitudes*, 86.

3 R. Meili, 'Les attitudes dans les reactions affectives', *Les attitudes*, 79.

4 *The Individual and his Religion*, 73; see also V. French, 'The Structure of Sentiments, A Study of Philosophico-Religious Sentiments', *Journal of Personality*, 1947, 209–44.

5 'Attitudes', in *A Handbook of Social Psychology*, edited by C. Murchison, Worcester Mass. 1935, 798–844.

6 On this subject see K. Goldstein, *Structure de l'organisme*, Paris 1951, 31 ff.

7 This was, in fact, the title of one issue of *Jeunesse de l'église*, Paris 1951.

8 G. W. Allport, *The Individual and his Religion*, 64.

9 See, for example, the enquiry conducted by J. van Houtte, *De Mispraktijk in de Gentse agglomeratie*, St Niklaas-Waas 1963, 146.

10 *Dieu et l'adolescent*, Lyon 1963, 71 ff.

11 *Ibid.*, 181.

12 *Ibid.*, 72.

13 See M. Argyle, *Religious Behaviour*, London 1965; and H. Carrier, S.J., *Psycho-sociologie de l'appartenance religieuse*, Rome 1960.

14 *The Psychology of Ego-Involvments: Social Attitudes and Identification*, New York 1947.

15 *Salience of Membership and Resistance to Change of Group-Anchored Attitudes, Human Relations*, 1955, 275–89.

16 See M. T. L. Penido, *La conscience religieuse*, Paris 1935, 41 ff.

17 J. Stoetzel, *Théorie des opinions*, Paris 1943, 307.

18 *La psychologie de la conversion chez les peuples non-civilisés*, two vols., Paris 1925.

19 See H. Carrier, *op. cit.*, 71–84.

20 *The Psychology of Religion*, New York 1899.

21 'Studies in the Psychology of Religion', *American Journal of Psychology*, 1896, 309–85.

22 'The Religious Conversion as a Change of Social Roles', *Sociology and Social Research*, 1952, 159–66.

23 *La Conversione Religiosa*, Bologna 1924, 101 ff.

24 *Deep Analysis, The Clinical Study of an Individual Case*, London 1947, especially Chapter 7.

25 'Factors Influencing the Formation and Change of Political and Religious Attitudes', *Journal of Social Psychology* 1949, 253–65.

26 See 'Ma conversion', *Pages de prose recueillies et présentées par A. Blanchet*, Paris 1944, 275–80.

27 See *The Varieties of Religious Experience*.

28 See O. Mannoni, 'Je sais bien, mais quand même', *Les temps Modernes*, 1964, 1262–84; and S. Freud, *Fetischismus*, 1927, *Gesammelte Werke*, XIV, 311–22.

29 See W. H. Clark, *The Psychology of Religion*, New York 1958, 215–6.

30 See S. Freud, *Erinnern, Wiederholen und Durcharbeiten, Gesammelte Werke*, X, 125–36.

31 'The Tendency to Certainty in Religious Belief', *British Journal of Psychology*, 1935, 16–31.

32 *La Psychologie de la conversion chez les peuples non civilisés*, I, 302.

33 See M. Merleau-Ponty, *Le Visible et l'Invisible*, Paris 1964, 17 ff.

34 G. W. Allport, J. M. Gillespie, J. Young, 'The Religion of the Post-War College Student', *Journal of Psychology*, 1948, 3–33.

35 See *Trieb-pathologie, II. Ich-Analyse*, Berne 1956, 361 ff. We have gone more deeply into this information in our study 'Tiefenpsychologie und Ethik. Der Oedipus und der Kaniskomplex', *Szondiana*, VI, Zurich 1967.

CHAPTER 5

ATHEISM

Atheism concerns the psychologist of religion in so far as it is observed to be an existential issue and a choice against religion. It must not be forgotten, however, that doctrinal positions do not really belong to his domain. Some thinkers, agnostics and neo-positivists, say that it is not possible to form a valid concept of God. Others share Sartre's ontological conclusion and consider that such a concept would be self-contradictory. Still others, Merleau-Ponty, for example, think that the affirmation of God is metaphysically incompatible with that of human liberty.

These theoretical objections are all part of philosophical thinking and the psychologist cannot justly refuse a man the right to elaborate, lucidly and honestly, an atheistic vision of the world. Nor may he presume that such a vision has a hidden psychological motivation.

However, metaphysics is not just a set of non-temporal ideas. It concerns life as it is and, within the setting it provides, existence itself achieves self-awareness. Rarely do we find a clear-cut distinction between the metaphysical negation of God and the existential objection. Indeed, more often than not, the philosophical positions adopted by atheists are based on a criticism of the divine attributes described by classical theodicy[1] which are seen as contradicting the theory of man advanced by modern thought. Thus atheism is often an offshoot of anthropology.

Proudhon perfectly expressed this anthropological root of atheism when he wrote 'man becomes an atheist when he feels himself to be better than his God'.

It is because present-day atheism is rooted in anthropology that it is the direct concern of psychology, which is the science of man in the concrete. It is the psychologist's business to examine the psychical processes at work in an atheistic anthropology, but this does not mean that he must necessarily juggle with ultimate truths and essential structures. He has to discover the basic tendencies which lead man to set his hope of human fulfilment outside the religious attitude and in opposition to it. Psychological atheism is defined in reference to the religious man.

But the psychologist does not have to take up a position on these lines. His observations do not rise to the heights of transcendental thought. He merely observes the psychological reasons which man has for committing himself to an atheistic attitude. The psychologist regards such an attitude as just one of the human possibilities; he tries to have some psychological understanding of it just as he does of the religious attitude. Here again his outlook is one of benevolent and critical neutrality.

We shall first give a few facts. Then we shall consider different psychological processes which may lead to the atheistic attitude. In this volume we shall not examine pathological atheism. There does indeed exist a form of atheism which originates in morbid motivations, just as do certain religious attitudes.

I. Atheism: Clear Position or Masked Religion?

Atheism is not so widespread a phenomenon as the controversial use of the word would lead one to believe. However, there is no doubt that the atheist movement is spreading in the countries of the free world as well as in those of the East. There is nothing to indicate just how far this phenomenon will go, but we may certainly expect that it will win over still greater masses of the population.

In a certain sense, atheism follows the line of history. Humanity, naturally religious in its origins, has very gradually come to discover that existence and society are both possible without God.

It is only in recent times that thinkers have taken up a position against theism in order to liberate man and build a future society in a humanist perspective. Barely four centuries ago declared atheism was still unthinkable. But today it has become much more than a simple hypothesis of life: even for the believer it is a very real point of reference and a permanent reason for self-questioning.

It is in the light of this history of religious thought that we must interpret statistics. The following table shows the facts observed in 1947.[2] In the absence of other enquiries it is not possible for the moment to evaluate either the meaning of these figures or the intensity of the atheist movement. But it is highly probable that the curve will continue to climb.

	Believe in God	Believe in the immortality of the soul
	%	%
BRAZIL	96	78
AUSTRALIA	95	63
CANADA	95	78
UNITED STATES	94	68
NORWAY	84	71
GREAT BRITAIN	84	49
HOLLAND	80	68
SWEDEN	80	49
DENMARK	80	55
CZECHOSLOVAKIA	77	52
FRANCE	66	58

Already in 1947 belief in God and in the immortality of the soul was seen to increase slightly with age:

	%	%
from 21–29 years	62	54
from 30–49 years	66	58
from 50–64 years	71	61

Statistics for atheism are always difficult to interpret. For, if the affirmation of God is a certitude of faith, the negation is also a judgement in the order of faith. When the believer has weighed all the arguments in favour of theism, he still has to leap from the visible to the invisible; and there are some very complicated psychological processes in the gap between reason and faith. Now, the negation of God is, of course, just as complex a phenomenon as is the affirmation of God. The atheist, in order to justify his position, is obliged to refute the signs which convince the believer. It is, then, not surprising that his position should often be very problematic and this is illustrated by the enquiry carried out in France in 1958:[3] 17% of the subjects said they were atheists; 13% claimed a strong conviction of atheism; 2% said their conviction was not strong; 6% doubted their conviction; 10% did not doubt it. Among the convinced atheists 24% acknowledged that they often discussed religion.

There is no fixed boundary between atheism and theism. We have already mentioned the deist civilizations of ancient times which acknowledged the existence of a supreme being who, though to a certain extent personal, was inactive (the *deus otiosus*). Some ethnologists, because of the absence of any cult in these civilizations, have even judged them to be atheistic. And they probably were so in practice. But their theism was revived in times of disaster, when it seemed that the only salvation for man lay in turning to the Author of life.

Since the eighteenth century a practical atheism of this kind has become very general and it now undermines the faith of believers. Through the desacralization of the modern world, God has been eliminated from the spheres which most closely concern man; that is to say, politics, economics, medicine, art, history, and even, in great part, philosophy and ethics. This means that the affirmation of God is often put on the same level as theorizing debates and has no influence in real life. May we, then, continue to speak of a real religious attitude? It would seem that only a dynamic point of view can help us to place this kind of deist attitude. When all religious questioning has ceased and the subject sees God only as a metaphysical cipher, detached from real existence, then we may speak of an atheist attitude, even if there is as yet no atheist philosophy behind it. This appears to us to be the fairly general position in certain working-class milieux. But in intellectual circles, the subjects are more inclined to reflective questioning; they try to give their philosophical faith some foundation. Even if they reduce religion to the dimensions of their human commitment, they still think they are doing the work of God; or at least doing a human work before God. In this perspective, God has not yet become an inactive God, nor a distant Creator reduced to nothing more than an all-seeing eye. Sometimes these subjects themselves wonder if they still believe: they do not see clearly in what they differ from atheists. But the drift of their reflection is unmistakable. For example, to what concept of God does their attitude refer? Perhaps they think that true faith should have a place in their life like that held by the ancient sacred.

With other believers, religious belief is stronger, but they are still not able to integrate it in their human life. They recognize that existence has both a vertical and a horizontal dimension and this distinction commands the rhythm of their life, lived as it is between two poles, God and humanity. For many believers, the family is the only setting in which these two dimensions coexist. Too easily we sometimes speak of Sunday Christians because we fail to realize how difficult it is to integrate an a-theistic world into faith. Those who succeed in so doing are few indeed. But faith is a goal, not an acquisition. As long as it remains a dynamic and heuristic vector, it is a living reality. But once there is a systematic partitioning, we may speak of practical atheism.

These considerations bring us to a position from which it is possible to deal with the question, so frequently raised, as to whether the atheist is seeking a substitute religion.

It has been pointed out by several writers, phenomenologists, sociologists and historians, that a number of humanitarian movements have certain characteristics which might be described as religious. They are therefore sometimes regarded as mystiques, or godless religions, and the phenomenon of Marxism is a typical example. It proposes the ideal of a perfect society to be set up at the close of history and interprets all previous civilizations in the light of certain so-called ultimate principles. Marxism treats these civilizations as merely pre-history because they prepare the way for the advance of man and for a completely humanized society. In view of this total fulfilment of man and society it demands from its adherents obedience and generous devotion. Other writers regard psychoanalysis as a complete humanism which will replace religion. Freud himself, moreover, spoke of psychoanalysis as a new scientific and enlightened religion destined to liberate man once and for all from guilt and set him up again as master of his life and ethical practice. The first disciples of Freud, it is well known, were inspired by a humanitarian mystique which gave them a kind of apostolic fellowship and spirit.

Yinger thinks that in movements of this type we can discern contemporary paths to salvation.[4] According to him, the religious inspiration of these movements can be seen in the close parallel which exists between their social forms and those of religious institutions: credo, idea of salvation, authority, worship, new brotherhood. Spengler even regarded atheism as a new mystical manifestation of the ancient religious spirit. This opinion is echoed, not without irony, by Sartre, 'an atheist was a queer one . . . a fanatic cluttered up with taboos . . . who had decided to prove the truth of his doctrine by the purity of his morals, who fought against himself and against his happiness to the point of depriving himself of the means of dying consoled; he was God's maniac who saw his absence everywhere and who could not open his mouth without naming his Name; briefly a gentleman with religious convictions. The believer had none: in two thousand years, Christian certainties have had time to prove themselves . . . it was the common heritage.'[5]

As we have already explained, we consider it false in principle, and unjust to both atheists and believers, to call these humanitarian movements religious. There is a confusion in this terminology which results from another much more serious one concerning the psychological interpretation of phenomena. To claim that we can discover the religious spirit in lay enthusiasm, or in Marxism, is to treat religion and the various humanisms as if they arose from the same tendencies. We might as well say that man's explicit intentions are of very little importance, and that all values are interchangeable. Only a very vague psychology of needs and tendencies could give rise to such aberrations.

We therefore disagree entirely with van der Leeuw when he writes that 'atheism is the religion of escape'; and 'they can pass from God to the devil, but the devil is also, in the language of phenomenology—a mode of "God". They can come back from God to man or to humanity, but this escape merely brings them back to the original potentiality.'[6] We also reject the theory of Jung who says that traces of repressed religion can be found in human mystiques. Jung would probably not have been able to put forward this theory had he not first reduced religion to man's simple self-possession. For Jung religion is no more than a means of acknowledging the archetypes which are present in the collective unconscious, and consequently a way of assuming what constitutes the human as such. Under these conditions, every non-religious mystique is a disguised manner of facing unconscious powers. Apologists and Christian psychologists who turn to Jung for proof of the profoundly religious nature of man unfortunately scarcely consider that such confusions empty religion of its substance.

The whole discussion can be finally reduced to one basic question: is the need for an absolute a naturally religious need? As we have already shown in Chapter 3, the origins of this need are to be found in affectivity. On the other hand, because it is rooted in narcissism, affectivity is essentially desire for totality. It is not surprising, then, that the humanitarian mystiques which fire their adepts with enthusiasm for the ideal of a perfectly harmonious society, project onto the human future a primitive memory of affective plenitude.

Hence, these mystiques are related to religion by many characteristics which have their source in a profound desire for plenitude found in harmonious union. Religion also is rooted in this desire. It is for this reason that Freud calls it an illusion. But the difference between religion and such mystiques is, after all, so radical that they obviously do not arise from the same psychological reality. We have insisted sufficiently on this in Chapter 3 and need only recall the fact here. The cleavage that the word, the law and the assent to the Other introduce into the subject has the effect of profoundly altering man in his relationship to God. These differences of structure are sometimes smoothed away by the use of such expressions as 'the atheists canalize their religious need towards a human object'. But here again the image gives a false idea of the asymmetry of the two situations. Humanitarian mystiques refer the desire for complete happiness to a human future which man himself has to realize by his own means. Are such mystiques either superior or inferior to religion? Are they truth or illusion? It is not for the psychologist to decide; all he has to do is to discover the similarities existing between religion and mystiques and to point out their very great differences.

Of course, not all atheism is a mystique. It is very possible that in fact the majority of men try to make up for their lack of religion by the substitute values[7] we have described. But, many of our contemporaries, while criticizing any religious desire, also seem to renounce every mystique on account of the illusory nature which they discover in such movements. Merleau-Ponty has given a good illustration of this new humanistic realism in his study *Le héros, l'homme*: '. . . is not faith, stripped of its illusions, the same thing as this movement by which, linking up with others and linking our present to our past, we find a meaning for everything, completing in one precise word the confused discourse of the world? The saints of Christianity, the heroes of past revolutions have never done anything else. They merely tried to believe that their fight was already won in heaven or in history. Men today no longer have this resource. Contemporary man's hero is not Lucifer, nor even Prometheus, but simply man.'[8]

Among our contemporaries the realism can be deceptively alluring. In an enquiry among young French people aged from 16 to 24, replies about the three essential values of life resulted in the following figures: 79%, health; 58%, money; 46%, love; and finally 12% for religious faith. 5 young people in 10 leave out love in their choice of the three major values, 8 neglect friendship and 9 religious faith.[9] In relation to this sceptical realism, the strength of the desire for passionate love, of artistic enthusiasm or of social dedication is such that these may take their place with religious mystiques.

It can happen that secondary phenomena accentuate the similarity between humanitarian movements and religion. Such is the case when there is mytical exaltation of a particular individual or group. Such deification, comparable with that of the Roman emperors, has been seen in modern times. We may recall the worship of the goddess Reason during the French Revolution and her liturgical enthronement in Notre Dame. More recently there has been the personality cult in Russia exemplified by Stalin who arrogated to himself among other divine titles, that of all-knowing and all-powerful father.[10] In the almost religious enthusiasm of these earthly mystiques we witness the rebirth among men of primitive aspirations to almightiness projected onto a symbolic figure in the hope that it will, in return, satisfy their desires for security and happiness. Spectacles of this kind make it easy to understand the disdain or distrust that certain atheists harbour against religion—does it not make use of the same illusory processes, thus alienating man from his true potentialities?

We have so far ignored the particular character of humanist atheism which, being essentially a project for human happiness, aims at achieving this through man. All humanistic atheism has something militant about it, but though it rejects religion, it leaves room for many different types of judgements ranging from simple negation to militant anti-theism. Atheism can intensify its character of closed humanism in different degrees. In humanist mystiques, the atheist commits himself to following his aim without choosing clearly and consciously between religion and humanism. He has only to give himself whole-heartedly to his ideal, throw himself into the future of the values to be realized and his atheism becomes a godless mystique. But if, on the contrary, he aims at formally realizing his project for man and by man, his atheism will take the form of a militant anti-theism. He then sees religious faith as nothing but an aberration which diminishes man and strips him of his human values.

It is possible that in atheism there is always a certain note of anti-theism. A declared humanist atheist feels in some way that religion reduces human values to dimensions which he cannot easily accept.

In order to understand atheism in the deliberately exclusive and militant form which it so often assumes we must now consider the psychological dynamisms which lie behind it.

II. Psychological Processes of Atheism

DEFENCE AGAINST THE DIVINE

We have seen how already in the ancient religions the sacred and the divine were considered to be a threat to man. The taboo was intended to protect him against the destruction he might encounter in the contact with a reality belonging to another ontological level. Man has always had a tendency to protect himself against God, or the gods.[11]

This fear of the sacred and of taboos was even capable of arousing in man a constant aggressiveness which could not show itself openly for fear of being destroyed. It therefore instinctively sought a compromise in reverence as can be seen in the rites to which priests, kings and seers were obliged to conform and which were so harassing that they lead us to suspect smothered hostility.[12]

In personalized religion this defensive action takes other forms. The believer can hide from God's sight by magically denying him. It can also happen that the gift of self in religious assent provokes a crisis of anguish. In order to protect himself against this, man sets up an opposition, sometimes openly, but more often by more or less consciously refusing to acknowledge the call.

In child psychology, as in clinical psychology, denial is a well-known psychological process. It cannot be identified with acting or with bad will. Denial is more spontaneous, has more of the nature of a drive. It is rarely sufficiently conscious to be really a sin against the spirit. It is a resistance arising from affective depths. This strongly affective nature of resistance to faith often astonishes us. We sometimes accuse such an attitude of being deliberately blind, but in so doing we only intensify the anxiety and resistance. We have no statistics to support our statement, but we nevertheless feel certain that this spontaneous resistance accounts for much in many cases of practical and even theoretical atheism.

The hint of anticlericalism which can be observed in many believers is probably also to be explained by this same more or less unconscious defence mechanism. The more we are anxiously on the defensive against faith, the more we shall expect of the priest and the more we shall notice his deficiencies.

SUPREMACY OF REASON

From its very first speculations on the world and man, philosophical reason has met with some temptation to practical atheism. In the view of the 'pastors' the divinity was so remote, so infinitely transcendent, that finally God was isolated from the world of men, and intellectual speculation was given full scope.

In the eighteenth and nineteenth centuries rationalism proudly claimed to submit reason to no other laws than those which she herself could construct and elucidate. Taine, converted to rationalism, very clearly expressed the sentiment of liberation which man can feel when he breaks with faith in order to profess complete autonomy for the intelligence: 'Reason appeared within me as a light . . . My religious faith was the first to fall before this spirit of examination . . . I had too much esteem for my reason to believe in another authority than its own: I wanted the ruling of my morals, the guidance of my thought to come from none but me. Pride and love of my liberty had set me free.'[13]

Religion has three characteristics which oppose this desire for autonomy, reason's creative force. In the first place, we cannot admit an Other without acknowledging unreservedly and as a first principle, that the ground of being is a mystery entirely beyond the complete understanding to which human intelligence aspires. From the outset, reason desires to clarify every mystery and to reduce it to the status of a problem, or, which amounts to the same thing, to something which will ultimately be explained, even if we have to wait until the end of time.

Secondly, reason cannot easily accept traditional religious truths, presented as they are, as eternal; scientific reason does not know what to do with such truths. Reason only masters relative truths which it can construct and assemble piece by piece.

Finally, Christian revelation has authority to impose inner truths beyond the grasp of reason. By its very nature the extrinsic character of dogmatic truth heightens the resistances of reason to religion.

Recent enquiries, however, lead us to think that the conflict between science and faith is waning, at least with believers. The enquiry conducted by Allport in 1948 shows that 70% of college students considered it possible for faith and science to be reconciled.[14] In the enquiry in France already quoted,[15] only 14% of the subjects between 18 and 30 years regarded modern science as incompatible with faith. Similarly, young people do not see faith as hostile to human happiness; only 7% said that it was in opposition to happiness here below. The point of view varies with the milieu. Unbelievers more frequently regard religion as opposed to science or social progress. In these milieux there is a picture of anti-humanistic religion which cannot easily be effaced. The lasting nature of stereotyped social categories is a general phenomenon often observed by social psychology. But this law is not enough to explain the present impact of the conflicts which, in the past, have often set up religion in opposition to the modern world. Many contemporaries are deeply influenced by past conflicts between faith, science, and social progress. Even if hostilities have ceased, the past misunderstandings have left the painful impression that religion has failed.[16] The past history of religion, more than science, bears witness against it.

Apart from this, the scientific climate has changed considerably. The myth of scientism has been shown up and it has been demonstrated that every scientific explanation presupposes a perceptual faith—Husserl calls it an inborn faith. Reason only becomes her own mistress if she submits to reality, whatever this may be. And reality is beyond us; it precedes, surrounds, envelops us. It leads us to think, but it somehow eludes the complete ascendancy of reason.

On the other hand, the renewal in theology has achieved a more judicious discernment of what is historic and what is eternal in religious truths. More especially, it has thrown light on their specific nature: these truths, theology tells us, belong to another reality, they cannot be identified with eternal abstractions. If the signs which manifest God are eternal, the ideas which express them are written in the history of civilizations and of thought. Man must not be satisfied with ready-made theories about these 'religious truths' any more than he is in any other sphere of human knowledge.

No one will dispute that conquering reason has enriched culture and purified religion. The early days of religious thought, like those of scientific thought, were marked by an indiscriminate mingling of theology and mythical science. This is something which gives full weight to the reproach made by atheism when it accuses religion of being a myth and 'projection' in which reason lives outside itself, in the objects to which it has transferred its own content. It therefore has to recover what it has given to the world of symbols. We may think for example, of the explanation of physical or biological evil by the influence of a diabolic power. We can see here a projection of inner psychological experiences on to the structures of the world. The development of physical sciences and human sciences inaugurated the study of the laws of nature and the criticism of mythical projections. It is understandable that in all religious thought atheists should suspect that there may be some remnant of such distortions of truth. The very fact of accepting revealed mysteries can give the impression that reason refuses to understand, and that it pursues the hope of a superior mode of understanding in symbolic thought.

In fact, the majority of scientists and believers know nowadays that the realities of faith in no way interfere with scientific laws. The conflict is now of another order and much deeper. The reappearance of the tension between the transcendence of faith and the autonomy of reason lies in the philosophical interpretation of the world and existence. The suspicion of mythical and projective thought has moved to this important sphere in which man has committed his whole being. Here the outlines of the problem are more hazy, and the opposition between reason and faith can always crop up again, under the ceaseless impetus of a powerful human desire for freedom and dominance.

DEMIURGE OR REBELLIOUS SON

Many early mythologies mention the demiurge or the rebellious son who kills a miserly and tyrannical father in order to become master of the world and its powers. On the other hand the myth of Prometheus symbolizes man the hero who snatches power from jealous gods. The resistance to an all-powerful God is no longer inspired by fear but by the desire to replace the father, evict him and become his peer. It is remarkable that Freud was able to interpret Christianity along these same lines, regarding it as the religion of the son who murders the father and then takes his place. Freud was able to project onto Christianity the ancient myth of the rebellious demiurge because it contains a very deep truth and expresses man's most secret desire; the desire to become his own father, to be self-existent, to depend on none but himself, in his powers and his happiness. This desire to substitute oneself for the father is such a powerful and original dynamism that it is to be found at the core of the conflict which man must suffer in order to humanize himself; that is to say, the Oedipus complex. Freud, fascinated by the universality of this conflict and unwilling to acknowledge that it had been overcome in Judaeo-Christianity, was rather of the opinion that this religion nurtured the conflict with a hidden violence.

Nietzsche said that man was rebellious by nature (*Aufständiger Mensch*). Heidegger thought technology was the result of a secret attitude of revolt.[17] There is something in this; the contemporary mystique of technology proves the truth of such statements. The ferment of atheism is contained in the exercising of technical power on the world rather than in the demands of scientific reason. Man thus exerts his will for autonomy, already mobilized by the Oedipus complex in opposition to the father.

18

This extraordinary desire for complete autonomy is expressed in a text by J. Rivière written a little before his conversion to Catholicism; it is the last resistance which he sets up against the call of the Christian faith: 'I have enough with myself. My life is enough for me, even if it gives me no end of suffering. I prefer to suffer rather than consent to domination, were it to last but an instant and give me eternal blessedness.' '. . . I only refuse to prefer God to myself, I do not think he asks anything else of us than the perfect and complete development of ourselves.'[18]

Recently, a German sociologist and psychoanalyst, A. Mitscherlich, has openly declared his wish to see the establishment of the 'brotherly society' and the elimination of the father symbol of which God is the highest and most demanding figure.[19] The Promethean myth has had its day, there is no doubt. Man no longer pretends to divinize himself in a defiant gesture towards the father. He aims at devoting himself to his simply human task. To Mitscherlich's mind there is nothing mythic about the promotion of the brotherly society. The ideal of this new fraternity, on the contrary, has a very humanist note about it; humanist, with all the resignation which this word suggests in our age of realism. Though not directly inspired by a desire for substitution, opposition to the father is none the less felt as being the essential condition for man's promotion.

LAWFUL PLEASURE

The conflict between the will for autonomy and divine authority is often accentuated by the question of pleasure and happiness. It may happen, in particular, that the desire for sexual pleasure disrupts the attitude of faith. Simone de Beauvoir in her autobiography acknowledges this with no mincing of words.[20]

Already, in the cosmo-vitalist outlook, religion was eclipsed by participation in the mystery of life. But the primitives were not aware of conflict because cosmo-vitalism brought the divine down into life and even into the celebration of pleasure. Here again, as in other tensions between the human and the religious, the Judaeo-Christian assertion of the absolute personal transcendence of God tends to set man in a definite perspective; the renunciation of life and pleasure as absolutes is now the condition of faith in God. Certainly, the antithesis between religion and pleasure must be overcome. We have noticed that in the Oedipus complex, pleasure and sexuality are regularized and become legitimate by identification with the father. Religious ethics furthers and completes this law of human growth. Nevertheless the illusory promise of unsurpassed happiness which the sexual stirring contains is felt to be more or less exclusive of religious faith.

It is scarcely necessary to emphasize the fact that the distrust which different dualist influences have long kept up in Christian circles, has often heightened the conflict to an extent which can become intolerable.

CONCLUSIONS AND REFLECTIONS

Even within religion, a certain anguish in face of God and the sacred drives man to defend himself against the divine presence or against the exactions of religion. This defence can take the form of denial, irony, or modesty which fights shy of religious things. The religious man often prefers to turn a deaf ear, keeping religion on the fringe of existence. This attitude often results in a certain practical atheism. Declared atheism, however, is based on other psychological motives.

We must not look for these motives in secret and exceptional events; they are written in the most elementary drives and desires. Every human power contains a germ of atheism. In the Judaeo-Christian religion, the natural tension between God and the man who sets himself up as master of his powers and pleasures is intensified because the heteronomy of religion in reference to the human is accentuated by the personal and transcendent nature of God. When God is no longer immersed in nature, there is no direct access to participation in the divine world by the simple exercise of human powers. God, being absolutely other, imposes demands for spiritualization and fidelity such as have never been made by other gods. It is for this very reason that declared and militant atheism necessarily originated in a Christian climate. It gives an answer to the absolute demands made by God, following on the separation between the divine and the earthly.

It will suffice for our critical reflection on atheism to take up again the basic ideas of the themes that we have already set out in our chapter on the divine fatherhood and human sonship. The believer does not consider that the act of faith in any way diminishes man. God's authority does not suppress man's autonomy; his truths do not darken reason; his demands do not destroy either happiness or pleasure. The believer knows this by the experience he has of religious assent. Really he only has to renounce an overdose of human sufficiency, give up the pretension of saving himself and fulfilling himself. But, seen from the outside, or in the actual moment of conflict, religious assent does seem to diminish man because his first and fundamental urge impels him to assert his own sufficiency increasingly and thus is naturally opposed to a God who presents himself as grace. In the act of faith man accepts his finitude, but without debasing it. We can say that religious assent brings into relief the reality principle which Freud recognized as an index of truth when confronted with the pleasure principle. But, as in every conflict, the true meaning of the opposed terms is only seen after the conflict has been settled. Hence the inevitable misunderstanding between atheists and believers. In reality, from the point of view of the demands of humanism, they both set store by the very same principles. But, atheists, unless they settle for agnosticism, have the impression that the humanism of believers is necessarily a reduced humanism since it is obliged to sacrifice to God the most legitimate of human powers.

This quarrel between atheism and theism is sometimes heightened by particular conditions. Thus the ambiguity of the motivations which quite often condition religious behaviour has led certain psychologists to adopt an attitude of disdainful atheism. In the preceding chapters we have had sufficient occasion for criticizing these religious forms; we need not return to them here. We have not thought it necessary in this analysis of atheism to do more than bring to light the fundamental and universal conflict which will always set theism and atheism in a confrontation which gives birth to true religion.

1 See A. Dondeyne, 'L'athéisme contemporain et le problème des attributs de Dieu', in *Foi et réflexion philosophiques, Mélanges Franz Grégoire*, Louvain 1961, 462–80.

2 See *Sondages*, Paris February 1948.

3 *Sondages* III 1959, 19.

4 *Religion, Society and the Individual*, New York 1957, 95.

5 *Les mots*, Paris 1964, 79.

6 *La religion dans son essence et ses manifestations*, 582.

7 See E. Erikson, 'Identity and the Life Cycle', *Psychological Issues*, New York 1959, 64–5; and G. W. Allport, *The Individual and his Religion*, 78–80.

8 *Sens et non-sens*, Paris 1948, 380.

9 *Les 16–24 ans*, Paris 1963.

10 See G. Gurvitch, 'L'effondrement d'un mythe politique: Joseph Staline', *Cahiers Internationaux de Sociologie*, 1963, 5–18.

11 See M. Eliade, *Traité d'histoire des religions*, 393–4.

12 See S. Freud *Totem and Taboo, Gesammelte Werke*, IX, Chapter 3.

13 In *De la destinée humaine*.

14 'The Religion of the Post-War College Student', *Journal of Psychology*, 1948, 3–33.

15 See *Sondages*, III, Paris 1959.

16 P. M. Kitay, *Radicalism and Conservatism toward Conventional Religion*, New York 1947.

17 See R. Boehm, 'Pensée et technique', *Revue Internationale de Philosophie*, Brussels 1960, 1–27.

18 J. Rivière and P. Claudel, *Correspondance*, Paris 1963, 65, 67.

19 *Auf dem Weg zur vaterlosen Gesellschaft. Ideen zur Sozialpsychologie*, Munich 1963.

20 *Mémoires d'une jeune fille rangée*, Paris 1958, 137–8.

Part Two

Part Two

OUTLINES OF A GENETIC RELIGIOUS PSYCHOLOGY

It would be presumptuous in these times to pretend to describe the complete genesis of the religious personality. In the first place it is not one of the constants of psychology. It is true to say that the child is essentially a being in becoming; nevertheless, his development does not follow a uniform curve as does an organism whose growth is determined only by the laws of internal development. If we compare the analyses made in different milieux and at different periods we shall see that the characteristic features of each educational milieu produce noticeable differences in the child's psychological growth. The child is an open, polymorphous being and it is precisely the task of education to develop one or other of the many possibilities his future holds.

The child's polymorphism makes the scientific study of his psychological growth very difficult. The different stages of a child's evolution may be scientifically observed and they must be interpreted according to child mentality and not according to adult norms as scientific psychology is only too often tempted to do. And how, indeed, can we avoid reference to the adult, once we have adopted the scientific patterns of thought which are borrowed from adult language and mentality? Educationalists, both religious and others, have remarked that psychology is in constant danger of rationalizing the child's world. It is this pedagogical intuition which accounts for their well-known distrust of theoretical psychology.[1] It sometimes happens that child educationalists, in reaction to this manner of reducing the child to the negative image of an adult in miniature, treat him as an adult, responsible for his vital choices, able to understand interpersonal relationships and even, to some extent, to achieve a living comprehension of religious mysteries. This accounts for the fact that in certain pastoral directives the Catholic Church treats of children as though they were spiritually adult.[2] But this seems to be only another way of centring the child on the adult. In the following outlines we shall be careful to avoid this double danger, taking pains to be attentive to the distance separating

271

the child from the adult and yet, since he is an adult in becoming, taking this fact into consideration too.

We shall indicate some of the lines followed by man's religious development in the western world. However limited they may be, the samplings to which we shall refer will allow us to define the characteristics of certain decisive moments of change in the religious attitude. No cross-section can adequately show the individual's religious evolution which goes far beyond the elements noted by psychology. Nor is it possible to fix the phases of religious growth. The different stages of affective, intellectual and social development overlap and intersect. We must therefore give up hope of tracing the curve of religious maturation. We can, however, determine the moments at which the child discovers a new dimension, enters into conflict with, or makes his own, one or other fact presented by his religious environment.

The child is a religious being of his own kind. He differs from the primitive because he already belongs to our cultural and religious universe and is trying to integrate himself with it. If he is related to some primitive cultures by certain traits it is because he is essentially polymorphous. In him are found, mixed up and inexplicit, all the potentialities which contribute to the common fund of humanity. We shall have occasion to show that the child really thinks out God, but in his own way. The child's way is that of naïve and open anthropomorphism. We shall never discover the same thing in an adult mind. The moments in development which we can fix are just those in which a religious content, as yet undifferentiated, begins to take more definite shape. These periods of change are always times of option in favour of a determined specific form.

This evolution is not pre-destined. At every new cross-roads the child has the possibility of coming to a stand-still. But if he does, he is no longer the child he was. Having rejected a certain possibility of evolution he settles himself in an attitude, fixes on an image or a concept which was part of his acquired equipment but to which he now clings, thereby hardening it. The child is now closed to certain potentialities of his former polymorphism and is therefore modified.

All the points we shall consider concerning the child, his anthropomorphism, his imaginative conduct, his self-centredness, will have to be judged by this criterion which resets phenomena in their dynamic becoming. It is at the moment when the child leaves behind a certain anthropomorphism that the preceding religious concepts will begin to have a clear anthropomorphic significance for him. They probably had this meaning before, but being then more pliable and more open, they were suitable means by which he could represent God, on infantile lines of course, but without denaturing the image of God as such. There is only real and formal disfiguration of the divine image if the child continues to have an anthropological image beyond the stage of development at which this is normal. It is then in contradiction with his affective and intellectual evolution in other spheres. Once he begins to criticize religion he must be able to replace his first representations of God with more suitable ones; otherwise he will identify God with concepts which, formerly valid, are henceforth marked with the negative sign of infantilism.

Nothing is more difficult for the adult than to understand the child. He runs the risk either of treating him as his equal or as his inferior. In both instances he transfers onto the child forms of thought and behaviour which are so foreign to his psychology that any affective relationship between child and adult is destroyed.

1 In connection with this we may quote the opinion of the famous religious educationalist, H. Lubienska de Lenval, who says that she expects nothing of 'learned psychology'. See *L'éducation du sens religieux*, Paris 1946, 92–3.

2 See *À l'écoute du Seigneur. Guide I, Part A*, edited by the Office diocesain de l'enseignement religieux, Tournai 1962, 19.

CHAPTER I

RELIGION DURING CHILDHOOD

The Child's 'Natural' Religiosity

Strictly speaking nothing is 'natural' in a child because the cultural universe to which he comes helps to form and define his behaviour. Nor is the child simply a void. The idea of God does not grow up in his mind by spontaneous generation. Certain psychological characteristics can favour the child's taking early possession of the religious heritage. Rousseau was not inclined to accept that the child has a true religious sense. More recently the psychiatrist Rumke[1] has shown great wariness with regard to the child's natural religiosity. But practical enquiries[2] and pedagogical experience have both indicated that he is very much disposed towards religion. Thun, on the evidence of his own enquiries, even stated that the absence of scepticism is, up to the age of 9 years, the essential characteristic of religion in children. In an enquiry conducted among Danish students for the purpose of making a comparative study of the formation of religious attitudes and political attitudes, Iisager[3] observed that religious attitudes appear very early on; the first stirring of religious sentiments takes place between 7 and 14 years, whereas political attitudes only take shape between 15 and 18 years of age.

The early awakening of religious sentiments depends on strictly psychological factors which we shall examine later. But the child's disposition to religion can only develop if given early education.

Family Influence on the Religious Attitude

It has been confirmed by observation that parental influence is the most decisive factor in the formation of religious attitudes. According to the enquiry made by Iisager, the factors which play a part in religious formation are first family education, then personal reflection, and finally, schooling. For the political attitudes the factors are reflection, discussion, reading, influence of family and friends. The sociologist Wach[4] states that in any culture the religious attitude of adults depends very largely on the religious experience that they have had in their early environment, and especially the family.

Family influence is not restricted to a form of early training. Several authors emphasize the close connection existing between family and religion. Murphy[5] says that the family structure is virtually religious and, similarly, that religion is deeply marked by family psychology. Such symbiosis of sentiments, structures and membership is found in no other pair of institutions. Thus sociologists have discovered in their analysis of institutions, the same relationship between religious psychology and family psychology as we have discussed in Chapter 3 of Part One. Without any doubt it is this relationship which accounts for the greater importance of family influence in the formation of religious attitudes. If family religious education has such great influence on the children, it is because the family is the model for both religious relationships and values. The religious gestures and the language of the parents fit into an affective experience by which they are immediately symbolized. And, on the other hand, the family, as the source of well-being and authority, naturally calls for its continuation in the religious world upon which it is founded. Thus another sociologist[6] has observed that religious gestures are given greater value by family participation, and at the same time, religious gestures and the celebration of religious festivals create a special family bond. This makes a lasting impression on the childhood memories of many adults, and is a determining factor in their sentiments of religious membership.

In this symbiosis between religion and the family, the child's 'natural' religiosity finds scope for development. A child has a vital need to live in a well-made, happy, reassuring and stable world. For him, the sacred is part of a perspective of vital growth. The family and religion together offer him the whole universe of his desires. A child with no faith in the religious world of his family could not help but be a very disturbed child. But later on, when the child has become adult, this same connaturality between childhood and religion will give place to anxious questioning. He will wonder whether perhaps, after all, religion is only the highest illusion of human desire, sprung from childhood days.

Many enquiries have shown the extraordinarily lasting nature of religious attitudes.[7] This is certainly to be explained by the very great influence of family education.

There are adults who wonder whether it would not be better to deprive a child of any religious education before puberty in order to leave him entirely free to choose at this age his own theory of life, either religious or atheist. They consider that under such conditions the adult's religious attitude would no longer result from social pressure or educational conditioning, but from a truly personal commitment. This point of view surely arises from the best of intentions and, moreover, it expresses a longing which these adults themselves feel for a genuine religious experience free from social pressure. But for all that, it is really an excess of rationalist naïvety. When human liberty has to be exercised in a world of cultural values it can only be acquired if the human possibilities it has to assume have been developed by a corresponding cultural education. The free religious commitment must be based on an acquired experience of religious values.

The Child's Conception of God

At the beginning, aged about 4, a child has no difficulty in imagining God. It is the golden age of his interest in the religious world.[8] The universe of the divine is of the same marvellous order as the world of fairy stories and it arouses sentiments of fascination. But the ambivalence of the sacred, pointed out by Otto, can be seen from the beginning of religious interest; already in his third year the child shows towards the sacred a characteristically religious respect and fear.[9] This ambivalence becomes stronger as the deity image is profiled behind the parental image, especially that of the father. It would even appear that the deity image is confused with the parental image.[10] Like the parents, God seems to the child's eyes all-powerful and all-knowing and is regarded as a protector at the child's service. This representation of God is both imaginary and affective. The sentiments of family piety are transferred from the parents to God; sentiments of dependence, trust, security, respect. With Bovet we may use the expression of paternalization of the divine, rather than divinization of the father. The intuition of a sacred world becomes more exact by being based on the sentiments which develop towards the father.

Between the ages of 5 and 7 years, the child begins to be aware of the distinction between God and parents.[11] The child's disappointments as he comes to discover his parents' limitations have something to do with this dissociation.[12] The parents do not know everything, nor are they able to do everything. Furthermore the child gradually notices their contradictions and their faults. But we should be wrong to think that these first conscious conflicts direct the child immediately to a Father who really is all-powerful and perfect. However important a role these negative moments may play in the formation of the image of God, the passage to a Father-in-Heaven can only be effected if it has been prepared by the parents. Nothing leaves a deeper mark on the child's religious attitude than the way in which the parents associate themselves with him in a common human recognition of the transcendent God. To measure the effect of this witness of human equality before God we have only to watch the astonishment of the child of 4 or 5 years old when his father or his mother speaks of their own parents, using the same terms as he does himself: 'Father' or 'Mother'. The myth of an absolute parent collapses in the face of such a revelation and sometimes this is a cause of scandal to the child.

The dissociation of the father from God results in a more univeral image of God. At the age of 6 the child thinks of him essentially as being the maker of all that is in the world. Furthermore the world takes on a universal dramatic meaning; the child thinks of God as the power for good fighting against his enemy the devil.

It has often been remarked that the child's idea of God is anthropomorphic. The child obviously sees God as a human being just as he thinks of his action on the world as human action. But progressively from 6 to 11 years his idea of God becomes more spiritual. Clavier[13] has given some of the facts of this evolution. At 6 or 7 years old the anthropomorphism is simple and material: God lives in a house with a garden; he picks flowers; from 8 to 11 years the anthropomorphism becomes less marked and the child thinks of God as a man who is different from other men; he sits up with the angels; we cannot touch him; at the age of 12, 60–70% of girls and 40–50% of boys have a spiritualized idea of God; he is everywhere, invisible, and we cannot make a drawing of him. Clavier forces his results, as was normal for the rationalist spirit which prevailed in the psychology of his times. If we compare these data with others we see at once that the young child's anthropomorphic image does not have the realistic meaning which Clavier gives it. Even in children of 6 years old Gesell was able to remark a first difficulty: the child is mystified by the fact that God is invisible and this difficulty is even greater at the age of 7. On the other hand, the enquiries carried out by Harms show that at 7 years human realism in the representation of God does seem to show a development, and is not, as one might think, a continuation of a previous stage. At this age God is no longer a fairy-story person as he is for the 3–6 year-olds. He is in close relationship with human life and especially moral life; he 'supervises the ways of men on earth'.

This anthropomorphism is also seen in the way in which the child imagines God's action in the world. Bovet,[14] following Piaget, speaks of the child's artificialism which is one with his animism. Between 6 and 11 years, every child explains nature and the world by animist or artificialist theories. By 'artificialist'

Piaget means the child's tendency to see the world as made by man, or as making itself after the fashion of human technology. According to Bovet, the artificialist attitude allows the child, at the period when he begins to doubt the all-powerfulness of his parents, to transpose to a divine being the qualities and actions which, before the crisis, he attributed to adults. But we point out that Piaget's theory of the child's general artificialism has recently been queried. We think that the expression continues to have some value as long as one is careful not to interpret it in adult technical terms.

The child's religious anthropomorphism indicates, then, his attempt to represent the reality of God. But at the same time, because he is influenced by sentiments of piety, trust, admiration and fear, this anthropomorphic concept for God goes beyond the human and so takes on a symbolic value. The child imagines God on the lines of some human model and he thinks that God is as real as man. From time to time, however, he dissociates God from man to set him in a world beyond this one. Thus anthropomorphism must be considered as a first rudimentary form of analogical thinking.

The child is not yet able to represent God to himself in a truly symbolic way because before arriving at a specifically symbolic perception he must first have some idea of God. Research work which we have carried out in Louvain[15] shows that it is only at the age of 11–12 years that the majority of normal children learn to have a clear perception of the symbolic function of signs. The importance given to the material nature of signs gradually becomes less with age.

B. Mailhot[16] has some remarkable facts showing the curious influence which Christian catechesis has on the child's idea of God from 4 to 6 years old. For 71 % of children Jesus is a generic word; they speak just as much of daddy Jesus, mummy Jesus, as of baby Jesus. For 92 % of the children who were asked to draw God and Jesus, they are one and the same person. They see God as a child like themselves but to whom they attribute magical powers. It is he who protects their parents. The child Jesus is also the centre of the adult world. He is the perfect child, admired, adored and served by his parents. And once the children have learnt about Jesus as an adolescent or an adult, they no longer think of him in religious terms.

Is not this a process analogous to that by which the child passes from his parents to God? He transfers to the divine child the all-powerfulness which he would like to have for himself. But he also transfers his affective narcissism because he sees the child Jesus as an equal who, because he is perfect, draws all the affective attention of grown-ups.

We are not yet in possession of enough data to allow us to judge from a religious point of view the benefit which children draw from the worship of the divine child. But one is inclined to feel that it can be a real danger for religious development. It accentuates the child's affective ego-centrism without turning him away from himself towards a truly Other God.[17]

Sentiment of the Sacred

Though the child of 3 begins to have a certain fear of the marvellous, he nevertheless continues to have a naïve confidence in it up to the age of 8 or 9 years. Research work carried out on this theme allowed us to observe the gradual awakening of the sense of the ambivalence of the sacred. A semi-projective test put the subjects in an imaginary situation where they identified themselves with Moses and assisted at the theophany of the burning bush. The children showed progressively more fear with age. The figures were as follows: kindergarten and grade 1: 8%; grade 2: 21%; grade 3: 44%; grade 4: 47%; grade 5: 70%; grade 6: 69%. It was noticed in addition that the sense of the reverence due to God, the sentiment of his transcendence, and the notion of the *tremendum* increase with age. From this we can draw the conclusion that the subjects have a growing sentiment of religious fear which is normal and not incompatible with trust. The older children realize more clearly the ambivalence of the sacred, and may even feel it more strongly. They gradually come to understand that God is not only nice and kind, but that he is also the Almighty who is to be feared. At 10–12 years the children grasp the symbolism of fire. It is no longer something materially dangerous, and Moses would not have been burnt had he drawn near to it, but he would have offended God and merited a moral punishment rather than a corporal one.

Other studies have confirmed this progression from naïve trust to the understanding of a majestic, remote divine transcendence which is only to be approached with fear and reverence.[18] There is, then, a natural link between the sense of the Other and a feeling of awe. The religious man holds both poles of the sacred; he manages to reconcile the two contrasts in his life. Trust would appear to come after fear, as a victory over fear. The passage which we have quoted (Part One, Chapter 1) from St Augustine is an admirable expression of the religious dynamic which is awareness of the Other whom man discovers with awe, but in whom he dares to trust.

The fact that some psychologists regard religious fear as bad, shows us how misleading can be an inadequate idea of mental balance and of the ideal of the religious adult. One psychologist,[19] for example, concludes that children of denominational schools are religiously inferior to other school-children because they give a higher percentage of positive answers to questions about the fear of God. But, it is surprising to notice that these answers are not compared with those about God's goodness. The same children show higher percentages of positive replies here also. There is another study which may be mentioned as being a typical result of the lack of understanding which some psychologists show. Mathias[20] made a study of the religiosity of adolescents in an average American town. Any reference to the mystery of God or religious fear is scored negatively because he considers such sentiments to be incompatible with an emancipated religion inspired by the healthy principles of a scientific age. Evaluations of this kind cannot be in any way justified by the analysis of either religious traditions or psychological investigations. They are far from a true sense of the religious because they dismember the experience of the sacred, and isolate each of the moments which make of this experience a profound unity. Doubtless there are very different types of religious fear: reverence, primitive awe, fright, sense of sin, pathological anxiety.

Those authors who are acquainted with the facts of religious psychology should take care to distinguish between these different kinds of fear, which should all be recognized as variations, possibly significant, of the same fundamental religious sentiment.

Affective Self-centredness, Magical Beliefs and Conduct

At 3 years old, the child sees all the objects and people of his surroundings as thinking as he does and sharing his feelings. The moon shines for him, and follows him wherever he goes. He can hurt the table by hitting it. Piaget has shown that the child is not subjective in the first instance. He does not go through subjective states which he then transfers to the world around him. On the contrary, he is completely turned to the outer world; even his ego is considered to be an objective reality. For want of self-awareness, the ego and the outer world remain undifferentiated and the child endows the outer world with his own sentiments. Here again we must be careful not to describe the infantile mentality in terms which give a distorted impression. A child has no real notion of the physical world any more than he has of the psychical. Self-centred transferences onto the outer world do not have the realistic meaning they have for adults who are more influenced by reason.

Social language, jealousy and the processes of the Oedipus complex introduce reality principles into the child's psychology. He is thus gradually turned away from himself as centre and comes to recognize objects and other people. This conversion of the child's psyche is very gradual and God long remains more or less a prisoner in affective self-centredness. The affective relationships with the parents continue to be stronger than the relationship with God. It is possible for dependence on God to be lived and felt by the child as an invitation to passive obedience and he may think of God as the providence who gives everything good and assures every security.

We have already seen (Part One, Chapters 3 and 4) how this initial self-centredness of the affective and religious life may have a lasting effect on the relationship with God and give rise to future atheistic criticisms. What the child saw as religious truth often appears to adult eyes looking back on the past as mere religious infantilism; and this adult view leads man to shake himself free from a religion which he now feels to be unworthy of him.

The same self-centredness, or affective narcissism is also the source of all the traces of magic which can be seen in infantile religiosity. Three kinds of studies have helped to separate the magical elements from the truly religious elements in child religion and have shown how the religious attitude is the result of a gradual purification. The first of these studies, inspired by research carried out by Piaget and Miss Rambert[21] was concerned with the sentiment of immanent justice in the world. The authors noticed that a child of 6 years is convinced that a fault is automatically punished by an unhappy event—for example, a bridge collapses just as an escaping robber is crossing it. Piaget explains this belief in an immanent justice by the child's animism which attributes intention to the universe. The world, so the child believes, is animated by ends which can be used by either adults or children. This intentionalism is not directly religious, but it has been noticed that children who have received religious education readily connect this immanent justice with the will of God. Here, as with belief in God and in providence, the child mentality, independently of any religious instruction, is affectively disposed towards belief in God. This means, of course, that such belief is to some extent denatured. The magical representation of automatic punishment becomes less marked with age. It is found in 13% of children aged 6; 73% of 7–8 year-olds; 54% of 9–10 year-olds; 34% of 11–12 year-olds.

These findings of Piaget and Rambert have been confirmed by other research workers.[22] Two[23] have observed the same regression of the belief in the immanent justice of things among little Africans aged between 6 and 12 years. But these same peoples show, between the ages of 11 and 18 years, an increased belief in immanent justice by divine intervention; there is also increased belief in the magic effect of spells. We may hope that a parallel enquiry will soon throw light on the reactions of western populations to the belief that faults are automatically punished by God.

Belief in the immanent justice of the universe disappears in western consciousness at the age of puberty, but clinical psychology has shown that with many subjects it persists in the unconscious. It revives under the stress of great anxiety or intense unconscious guilt and greatly influences the idea of God among believers. But this is a phenomenon which, in adults, is already pathological. Among children these religious attitudes merely represent a mixture of religion and belief in magic. Though this is a rudimentary form of religion, it must not be regarded as false. It is open to gradual purification and should be acknowledged as a religious attitude which seeks God by means proper to affectivity and imagination at this age.

Fr Godin and Miss van Roey[24] have studied the belief which Catholic children have in an animist type of protection. They have observed that between the ages of 6 and 8 years the idea of protective intention in God's dealings is much less pronounced than that of a punitive intention. The curve rises to the age of 12 and descends rapidly after the age of 14 years. It must, however, be pointed out that this belief varies according to the object of the protection under consideration. Between 12 and 14 years it seems to be restricted to actions in favour of another person. The authors attribute this trait to the influence of Christian education. Fr Godin concludes that the 9–12 year-olds see divine almightiness and protection from a self-centred angle; prayer is all-powerful because God is at the child's service.

Similarly, in an enquiry into the causal efficacity of prayers of petition, Thouless and Brown[25] have noticed that such prayers gradually become less frequent during adolescence: at 12–13 years, 35% of children believe in the efficacity of such prayers; at 14–15, 29%; at 16–17, 19%. Nevertheless the older subjects continue to believe that such prayers should be said. It may be remembered that we ourselves observed this same phenomenon in the enquiry among 16–19 year-old adolescents. Thus an inconsistency can be remarked between the subject's genuine belief in the efficacity of prayers of petition and his expectations.

He expects his prayers to be answered, but he has ceased really to believe in their efficacity, because experience has taught him that they remain unanswered. This contradiction tests his faith and, as we have seen, leads to a drop in religiosity. But if the believer overcomes this religious crisis his faith will be purified and his prayer become more truly religious.

Symbolic signs and Christian sacraments are, of course, special targets as illustrating the magic mentality. There is many an analogy to be found between sacramental practice and magic: magic gestures are ritual; the chantings are carried out in a special language supposedly that of the gods or the spirits; the sorcerer and the gathering believe in the efficacity of the rites and the magical formulas.[26] But there is also a great difference between magic belief and religious faith. In magic it is believed that divine force can be taken hold of automatically without any real act of submission to God.[27] Between these two distinct extremes, that is to say, the hardy conquest of the immanent force of things, and the humble plea for divine grace, there is room for a whole series of intermediate attitudes. As long as God is not acknowledged as being absolutely transcendent in relation to natural forces, religious faith will always be marked with magical belief. Rather than harden the opposition between religion and magic, this should be considered as a pre-religious mentality which can give place to religious symbolism and sacramental practice. The magic mentality is also part of the pattern of affectivity and imagination which helps the child to acquire the habit of true religious worship.

Fr Godin and Sister Marthe[28] have studied the magical elements in the belief which children and pre-adolescents have about the efficacity of the sacraments—in particular, the sacraments of holy eucharist and penance. Their findings show that at 8 years the majority of children think sacraments automatically have some effect which is produced independently of the subject's consciousness and attitude. From 11 years onwards sacramental practice starts to be purified but there still remains some magic belief even at the age of 14. Since there is no established correlation between belief and intelligence the magic mentality must be attributed to the affective state of this age group though educational factors can also account for its persistence.

The belief in magical signs and rites may also be taken to signify a beginning of the socialization of the child's religion, since both rite and efficacious sign are social elements. Thus the magic-religious belief is the outcome of a double psychological movement. The child recognizes the religious signs in society and he enters the religious institution bringing with him a fund of affectivity which can be described as ritualist. Even outside a religious context many 6–9 year-olds have all kinds of symbolical practices which are supposed to produce some good effect automatically. They avoid, for example walking on cracks in the pavement or on certain stairs: they repeat certain numbers, count certain groups of things as they come across them. Thus when they bring a ritualist behaviour to symbolic and institutionalized religious practices, they come to practise a magico-religious ritualism. Our centre for research in religious psychology has studied some of these modes of religious conduct and has given special attention to their origin and evolution. Our collaborators[29] have examined the meaning which children attach to two particular symbolic signs: the red lamp, institutional sign of the presence of the Blessed Sacrament, and the sign of the cross made with holy water as a ritual for approach to the sacred.

Our aim in this enquiry was twofold: to determine when and how the child comes to understand the religious significance of an object and the meaning of an entrance rite; and secondly to discover exactly how the child connects God with these symbolic signs. The results we obtained led to a very clear distinction between the attitude of boys and that of girls. A boy is definitely more open to the institutional realities. He regards the religious object as having a very specific role, and the rite quickly comes to be treated as an instrument which is to be used. The boy's attention is taken up by what has to be done and directed to the reason for which certain objects are found in a church. The little boy's formalism is evident already at the age of 7; he wants to find out exactly what the religious object signifies and how to use it. At 8–9 years he insists that the red lamp must be kept in its place and that we must show we belong to God's people by taking holy water on entering a church. The awakening of the moral conscience at this age accounts for the note of obligation which the child gives to his ritualism. He feels that if he does not carefully observe institutional rules, he will have committed sin or sacrilege. Around 10–11 years the boy becomes conscious that he is a sinner and feels that a rite of purification must precede his approach to the sacred.

The girl does not pay so much attention to the gestures and ritual objects. She has a marked preference for the symbolic meaning rather than the actual practice. The church for her is the place of the divine presence. Objects and rites only hold her attention in so far as they express her personal encounter with God. Between 8 and 10 years the divine presence becomes the more personal presence of Jesus. The red lamp reminds us of him and the holy water ritual is a way of greeting him. Between the ages of 10 and 12 years the institutional meaning of objects and rites is well grasped; the replies which speak of memorial, adoration, respect, signify the interiorization of the religious attitude. The ritual gesture signifies the girl's adoration and God's blessing.

The big difference which can be noticed between girls and boys is due to their conception of God. The boy's God is markedly connected with the law. A boy pays more attention to what God wants him to do than to what he is for him. A boy wants to do what the grown-ups ask, and then what God asks him to do. Thus the sign, the red lamp, has an absolute and unvarying significance: it expresses the will of God. The water ritual is an instrument which the boy can use. 'The boy's God is, then, transcendent by his strength, power, moral perfection.'[30]

The girl's God is a God of love who gives himself to her in a loving encounter. The red lamp says that he himself is there, nearby. More than in what God wants her to do, the girl is interested in what he is for her. His presence draws her. From the age of 8 she begins to distinguish the two divine persons, God and Jesus. The holy water rite is not connected with a sense of guilt for the girl; it is not the condition of a meeting with God, but it symbolizes it.

There is no doubt that these two distinct religious attitudes depend upon very different psychological structurings; we discover the effects of the particular way in which girls and boys have lived the Oedipus complex. The boy, more strongly marked by the Oedipean conflict, is more guilty; identifying himself with the father, he is also more sensitive to the exactions of the law and more orientated to action. He will more easily grasp God's transcendence and power but will find it difficult to recognize the symbolism of signs and religious rites and to assume them in a personal attitude before God. The socialization of religion is brought about by the acceptance of rules and institutional signs. But this acceptance is conditioned by a legalist psychology. Hence sign and signified are much the same thing. The sign becomes an almost autonomous reality. It itself produces the religious effects and its reference to God and the community is almost absorbed in its material presence.

The girl is more affected by the fascinating marvellous being which the father represents. In religious practice she will be more mystical and less likely to be caught up by the magic of symbols and religious rites. But she will have a tendency to ignore the transcendence of God. The absence of psychological legalism will not help her to take part in socialized and institutionalized religion. Certain psychologists, distrustful of the institutional-ization of religion, may prefer the girl's type of religion which is more directed towards a personal relationship. But that is a theological opinion with which not everyone agrees.

1 *Karakter en aanleg in verband met het ongeloof*, Amsterdam 1949, 48. E. tr. *The Psychology of Unbelief*, London 1952.
2 See T. Thun, *Die Religion des Kindes*, Stuttgart, 249.
3 'Factors influencing the Formation and Change of Political and Religious Attitudes', *Journal of Social Psychology*, 1949, 253–65.
4 *Sociologie de la religion*, 28 ff.
5 G. Murphy, 'Social Motivation' in *Handbook of Social Psychology* edited by G. Lindzey, Cambridge Mass., 1956, 615–6; see also A. T. Boisen, *Religion in Crisis and Custom: A Social and Psychological Study*, New York, 35.

6 J. H. Bossard and E. S. Boll, 'Ritual in Family Living', *American Sociological Review* 1949, 463–9.

7 See for example: 'Les attitudes religieuses de la jeunesse', *Sondages*, III, 1959, 7–10; G. Allport, *The Individual and his Religion*, 39–40; J. van Houtte, *De mispraktijk in de Gentse agglomeratie*, 334–37.

8 See E. Harms, 'The Development of Religious Experiences in Children', *American Journal of Sociology*, 1944, 112–22.

9 See A. Gesell 'The Child from five to ten', London 1946; and P. Bovet, *Le sentiment religieux et la psychologie de l'enfant*, Neuchâtel 1951, 12–13.

10 See A. Gesell, *op. cit.*

11 P. Bovet, *op. cit.*, 38. See also the pertinent remarks made by A. Godin *Le Dieu des parents et le Dieu des enfants*, Tournai 1964, 104.

12 See A. Gesell, *op. cit.*

13 *L'idée de Dieu chez l'enfant*, Paris 1962.

14 *Op. cit.*, 51–64.

15 C. van Bunnen, *Le buisson ardent: ses implications symboliques chez des enfants de 5 à 12 ans*, Lumen Vitae, Brussels 1964, 349–52.

16 *Et Dieu se fit enfant. Réactions d'enfants et de groupes d'enfants à l'âge préscolaire*, Lumen Vitae, Brussels 1961, 115–27.

17 We have recently carried out in Louvain some more advanced research work on the relation between the parental images and the child image, and their connection with the deity image. The finely graded results which we have obtained do not confirm those put forward by Mailhot. We hope soon to be able to publish the whole of our research.

18 C. van Bunnen, *op. cit.*, 341–54.

19 L. Patino, *L'attitude religieuse chez l'enfant*, Lumen Vitae, Brussels 1960, 85–104.

20 *Ideas of God and Conduct*, New York 1943.

21 *Le Jugement moral chez l'enfant*, Paris 1956, 157–260.

22. I. Caruso, *La notion de responsabilité et de justice immanente chez l'enfant*, Neuchâtel 1943; R. J. Havighurst and B. L. Neugarten, *American Indian and White Children*, Chicago 1955, 143–59.

23 G. Jahoda, 'Immanent Justice among West African Children', *Journal of Social Psychology*, 1958, 241–8; and H. Loves, *Croyances ancestrales et catéchèse chrétienne*, Lumen Vitae, 1957, 365–89.

24 *Justice immanente et protection divine chez des enfants de 6 à 14 ans*, Lumen Vitae, 1959, 133–52.

25 *Les prières pour demander des faveurs. Recherches sur leur opportunité et leur efficacité causale dans l'opinion de jeunes filles de 12 à 17 ans*, Lumen Vitae, 1964, 129–46.

26 See M. Mauss, *Sociologie et anthropologie*, Paris 1950, 37 ff; and C. Lévi-Strauss, *Anthropologie structurale*, Paris 1958, 184–5.

27 H. Aubin, *L'homme et la magie*, Paris 1952, 227.
28 *Mentalité magique et vie sacramentelle chez les enfants de 8 à 14 ans*, Lumen Vitae, 1960, 269–88.
29 A. Dumoulin and J. M. Jaspard, *Perception symbolique et sacralisation de l'attitude religieuse dans le rite*, Louvain 1965 (thesis for the Licentiate in Educational Psychology).
30 *Op. cit.*, 189.

CHAPTER 2

RELIGION DURING ADOLESCENCE

During adolescence religion is deeply affected by maturing intelligence, the developing need for friendship, the sentiment of guilt which accompanies sexual growth, the crisis of independence and the awakening of the ego. These are elements which greatly favour the religious attitude, but they also have an unsettling influence; particularly the feelings of guilt and the doubts about faith.

The Concept of God

Deconchy[1] has undertaken some very thorough research among children and adolescents with the purpose of discovering the different ideas which the word 'God' brings to their minds. Carrying out his research on boys and using the method of free association he was able to distinguish three important stages in the development of the idea of God. The first phase, reaching a peak at 9-10 years, is what we may call an 'attributional phase'. During this period the child tends to think of God in terms that he has picked up during catechism classes. The descriptive terms fall into three main groups: objective attributes connected with greatness, omniscience, omnipresence, spirituality; subjective attributes centred round the moral qualities of God, such as kindness and justice; and affective attributes, for example strength and beauty. This last group seems to be the dynamic factor which leads the child to the second phase of development. Around the age of 12–13 we notice that the affective attributes are no longer sufficient for establishing divine transcendence and the pre-adolescent enters the phase of the personalization of God, God-Saviour, God-Father. These three distinct themes tend to lose their specificity and to become one. This phase leads to that of interiorization which is at its height at about 15–16 years. At this stage the idea of God is fully contained in subjective attitudes: love, prayer, obedience, trust-dialogue, doubt, solitude, fear. The most active of these are trust-dialogue and fear, but it is only the first which seems to integrate the subjective development of the concept of God with the religious development taken as a whole. Fear and doubt tend to be disturbing elements.

We believe that, to a certain extent, these three phases coexist in all subjects and that the mounting curve with age is to be accounted for by the affective development which is natural in adolescents. The sequence of these phases appears to us to be highly significant. We shall come back to this later. As Deconchy has remarked, we notice that the adolescent rarely presents attributional themes and subjective themes at the same time. 'But attributional themes are closely connected with personalist themes which, in turn, are equally connected with themes of interiorization.'[2] Is this way, the personalist themes which serve as the chronological link between the attributive and the interior phase also serve to connect the interior God with the objective God as he is reflected in objective attributes. This brings home to us the great religious problem to which we have so often referred: the believer has real difficulty in identifying God as he is in himself with the God of his conception. The believer hesitates to choose between a religion made up of metaphysical concepts and an interior religion which he finally comes to distrust. The personalist themes should be the gauge of a religion which is both objective and personal. Deconchy points out that these themes risk being assimilated into abstract thought processes or else falling into purely subjective experience. We can recall here what we have already said about the father symbol of God: during adolescence, the themes of God-Father, God-Saviour are still so laden with the subject's affective needs that their religious content is very relative.

It would be rash to try to draw up a table showing the adolescent's religious development; the research work on this subject is still insufficient. We shall have to be content with indicating some of the psychological factors which underlie the adolescent's religious attitude and give it a specific orientation, stimulating his development as also does the succession of crises which he must undergo in order to become fully adult.

Friendship and Interiorization of Religion

The crisis of adolescent years brings man to self-awareness. An adolescent is acquainted with loneliness. He suffers from this, but he also in some way loves his solitude because in it he discovers his own self. In day-dreaming and retirement into himself he becomes present to his own inner world. And yet there is aroused in him at the same time a longing for participation with the outside world and others.

The experience of loneliness is accompanied by the discovery of friendship and awakens a desire for affective and symbolic participation with the world. These psychological elements are stronger in girls than in boys; among boys it seems that a classical education accentuates these elements more than does technical training.

The sensitivity aroused at adolescence affects religion. It will be remembered that the concept of God becomes more personalized at this age. In the first and second chapters of Part One we pointed out that the personal God of the adolescent is a providential father who watches over him in all his difficulties, both material and moral. The adolescent is especially sensitive to God's friendship and this counterbalances affective solitude. Even the 15–16 year-old regards God as primarily the friend who listens to his inner soliloquy. The enquiries which we carried out among hundreds of Belgian adolescent boys and girls show that the first quality which they appreciate in God and Christ is that of understanding. That is also the first quality they expect to find in a friend. Often, too, the adolescent seeks affective participation

with the universe. In the classical humanities group we noticed
(Part One, Chapter 1) that the subjects long for affective fusion,
a longing which is accompanied by a sense of the sacred. This
often favours the development of a pantheist religiosity.[3] God is
felt to be an extension of nature and this leads them to surround
natural symbols with a sacred halo.

The adolescent has a second characteristic: he idealizes his
friends and also the adults whom he imitates. But the sublime
perfection which he sees in them is really only the reflection of
the ideal image which he unconsciously has of himself. Psychoanalysis has shown that idealization springs from affective
narcissism: the subject transfers to the other the perfection he
would like to have, and he thus receives it indirectly from a model
with whom he can identify himself, or from an ideal partner
whom he can engage in exalted dialogue. Idealization is a powerful
factor in psychological development. It also carries the germ of
disappointment which may even sometimes degenerate into hate.

The adolescent's religion is influenced by this affective process.
For boys religious idealization takes the form of setting up an
ideal model. God is seen as the pure and perfect being. This
vision often leads to the exclusion of his historical and personal
reality;[4] he becomes the ego's absolute. The girl's idealization
takes the form rather of a loving relationship. God is the ideal
person in whom to confide, he understands everything and gives
himself entirely to her. These two modes of idealization correspond with the particular characteristics of the boy and the girl.
The boy tends to realize his personality through an ideal image.
The girl seeks to satisfy her affective lack by a total presence.
The fact that the religious life wanes after adolescence is to be
explained, among other things, by the regression of affective
idealization, and by its orientation towards men once the subjects
have become fully integrated in their environment.

The figure of Christ is particularly suitable for furthering
idealization. We should learn much if we knew which qualities
in Christ are most attractive to adolescents. At the present time
we have the results of only one not very detailed enquiry carried
out by our research centre.[5] It appears that from 13–17 years,

adolescent preference generally goes to the Christ who risks his life for a friend, who has a firm and assured personality, who is heroic, merciful and compassionate towards sinners. On the other hand, adolescents do not seem to think that Christ should have special friends, or ask us to love our enemies, that he should ever feel afraid, that he should be tempted by the devil, or even that he should overthrow the customs of his times.

These are all typical of adolescent affective tendencies. Christ is expected to be a super-human model, the perfect friend to all, understanding even sinners.

Guilt and Religious Moralism

Let us first recall briefly what we have already said about the psychology of guilt. Sexual development with its problems concerning masturbation causes a really psychological guilt which is characterized by feelings of unworthiness and social isolation (See Part One, Chapter 3).

Boys suffer from this more than girls. This is due partly to the fact that they are more sensitive to the exactions of the law and partly to the fact that they feel sexual desire in a more marked way, in the search for erotic satisfaction and in aggression. And we have already seen that these moral worries lead to intensified religious practice (Part One, Chapters 2 and 3). However, since this is directed to the solution of moral problems, it is disorientated and its strictly religious intention very much reduced. This phase of moralism favours the sense of sin; but this is such a heavy burden for the affectivity that at the close of adolescence there is often complete abandonment of sacramental confession. It may even happen that, by a healthy defence reaction, a boy shakes off the religion which is the cause of his guilt when this becomes too great a burden for him. Some adolescents hesitate between moral laxity and rigid moralism.

The moral worries of adolescents are not, of course, restricted to those connected with guilt. It is even characteristic of adolescence that a particular moral attitude develops, marked by the desire to realize the ideal of the moral ego. This ethical orientation is also one of the poles around which religion crystallizes.

20

Thus we can say that the adolescent's religious universe has several centres of radiation: friendship, the desire for a more or less pantheist participation in the sacred, guilt, the moral ideal.

Adolescence is, as it were, a second phase in the Oedipean structuring. Every one of the phenomena proper to the Oedipus complex is reproduced at the level of affective experience and cognitive consciousness, both of which are now explicitly formed and aware of themselves. It is, then, normal that the adolescent moral attitude should be definitely centred on the subject's own perfection, or, to use technical terms, that it should still be very much tainted with narcissism. Adolescent religion has some part in this ethical orientation which, in its turn, has something to give religion in the way of support. For the adolescent, religion is real and important because it helps him to become morally perfect. But the functional character which it receives from its ethical orientation reduces part of adolescent religion to human purposes. To some extent we can say that the adolescent uses God to serve the ends of his ideal ego. This religious development is normal and is certainly not to be condemned; but we must bear in mind its obvious limitations. After adolescence, many believers discover that human ethical practice is a purely human enterprise which does not necessarily need to be supported by religion. We have already seen that at this point some give up the faith which they had identified too closely with a human ethic. From generation to generation man will always have to relive the religious crises undergone by humanity at the beginning of the modern era when it began to separate ethics from religion, and discovered that man was able to set up his humanity by himself.

There is then nothing pejorative in the word moralism; it merely underlines the doubly insufficient nature of the adolescent's ethico-religious attitude: the narcissism of an ethic based on the desire to set up an ideal ego, and the partial polarization of religion towards an ethical accomplishment.

The pursuit of the ethical ideal varies in different environments according to the way in which the role of law and obligation is emphasized. In France, for instance, Fr Babin has observed that the conscience of Catholic adolescent pupils is strongly marked by the binding nature of religious ethics, whereas for children of non-denominational schools this is a much less important feature. For the Catholics God is someone who is to be served, adored and loved. God is the beginning and the end of all life and those who want to return to him are bound to observe his commandments. The other adolescents, though they may be very desirous of fulfilling their moral ideal, give much more importance to the reasons dictated by the heart. 'The explicit motive which will be called upon as a basis for moral conduct is the need for a subjective, even sympathetic, pact between God and man. Often too there is a need for success and happiness. The heart seems to impose a desire to live which will be fulfilled by means of a pact with a God whose essential quality is goodness rather than almightiness.'[6]

We may presume that in all the more homogeneous and closed religious circles we shall find this same predominance of the law over the personal relationship, though this interpretation must be modified in view of other aspects of religion. Thus we have seen that even among adolescents in Catholic schools God and Christ are considered primarily as being friends with whom intimate dialogue is possible. Any emphasis on the law has only negative effects. The law has a necessary structuring force for the humanization of life as well as for religious development: it is part of the truth of the father symbol. But if the law is exaggerated it will overshadow the other elements of the father symbol and tend to subordinate man to God as to a foreign and hostile will.

Religious Doubts

It has been shown by a number of enquiries[7] that adolescence is the age of doubts about faith—75% of boys aged 13–16 years and 50% of girls aged 12–15 years go through this crisis. Desabie made a sociological study[8] of 350 subjects who had left the Church and given up the faith. He observed that the great majority had lost their faith between 15 and 19 years of age—at this age 46% lost faith in the Church and 35·2% lost faith in God.

Among adolescents religious doubts are profoundly affective as is seen by their comprehensiveness. According to an enquiry carried out by W. Smet[9] in Belgium, out of a large population of Catholic adolescents, 44% expressed doubts about the existence of God; 27%, about Catholicism in general; 15%, about certain dogmas.

There seem to be three principal sources of the adolescent's religious doubts. He discovers his interior world during a period of crisis and wants his autonomy. Since his early years have been lived in family dependence he often feels that he can only become truly autonomous by setting himself free from every guardian. But religion can appear precisely as the supreme sign and the final foundation of dependence simply from the fact that all authority and all ethics refer to it. The adolescent's tendency to assert his autonomy may then take the rebellious form of a rejection of authority. But it may also occur in a less violent form and merely question authority. The adolescent no longer has the same confidence in adults that he has had during childhood, and this has an inevitably disturbing effect on his religion which, to a great extent, was founded upon that very confidence. For the first time the adolescent can, and even must, make his own critical synthesis of life. This leads him to reconsider his religious convictions. He can no longer freely accept them without moments of doubt. The awakening of his free faculty of criticism necessarily leads him to become aware that religious truth is no longer a self-evident thing. The doubt which he now feels about his faith is part of the passage which he is making from childhood fideism to personal assent. The comprehensiveness of his doubt is to be accounted for both by its absolute nature and the nature of the link which connects it to the deeply affective discovery of his own interior world.

The violence of erotic emotions is a second factor responsible for doubt. For, if they often cause a painful feeling of doubt, they also contain the promise of fully satisfying pleasure, complete self-possession and affective union with another.

These emotions cannot be simply assimilated with the question of moral purity. The adolescent knows even less than many still very puritan educators about how to cope with the affective side of his awakening eroticism. He is therefore sometimes tempted to reject the moral and religious code simply because it seems to impede the normal development of his affective nature. The text which we have already quoted from Simone de Beauvoir (Part One, Chapter 5) is a moving testimony to a religious crisis brought about by the first awakening of sexuality. Let us not forget, either, the doubts of faith which an overwhelming feeling of guilt can arouse in the adolescent who is so often brought up against the impossibility he feels of being able to conform to the norms of purity.

These doubts can be traced also to the crisis through which the general confidence of many adolescents passes in the course of the affective storms of puberty.[10] The adolescent's interior peace is often shaken, and he comes to doubt the love of his parents, teachers, school companions and friends. This leads him to feel that life is absurd. And, as we have already seen (Part One, Chapter 3) religious confidence can only be established on the basis of a certain feeling of well-being though sometimes the experience of the absurdity of the world and anxiety in face of its apparent senselessness can also lead to a movement of hope in God. It has however been observed that man rarely comes to religious life from a generalized lack in his affectivity. He needs to feel that he is loved in some way or other and he must be able to feel some human affection. Here again we refer the reader to the conclusions of our analysis of religious experience. Furthermore, our enquiries among university students have shown that often the religious crisis originates in a conflict between parents and children. This conflict leads to a revolt against religious authority, but above all it causes a general feeling of unhappiness which is harmful to the movement of confidence implied in the religious attitude. It must be insisted, however, that doubts about faith constitute a trial which purifies religion unless they are caused by a rather general and pathological sense of the absurd. An enquiry carried out by Delooz[11] has even revealed a slightly positive correlation between religious doubts and the finer and more spiritual motivation of religion.

Doubts tend to lessen towards the age of 15 when adolescents, Gesell tells us, begin rather to search in uncertainty than to completely reject ideas: they are half-believing, half-disbelieving.[12] Generally, at about 16-17 years, doubts are appeased—the adolescent has made his choice. If doubts re-appear later they tend to be more intellectual—which does not mean that they are any less intense. But after adolescence the young believer thinks more freely about the meaning of existence. He must make his mental synthesis of the world. He has come to be less centred on himself and is more deliberately committed to human society. This leads him to query the different theories of life with which he meets; he also reflects on the human necessity of having some religious belief and on the significance of institutionalized religion. This new questioning is more objective than earlier doubts had been, and is part of the effort which the adolescent makes to assume personally the religion he has inherited. Man does not acquire true religious faith, that is, a really personal faith recognized in its transcendent finality, before the age of thirty years. Experience has shown that after adolescence the whole religious formation apparently has to undergo revision—not because the child or the adolescent has not hitherto been authentically religious, but because man does not acquire sufficient maturity to make a real personal choice and to recognize reality, before he has become adult.

We do not intend to complete this outline of genetic psychology by a survey of the adult religious attitude. What we have said concerning the religious attitude (Part One, Chapter 4) has established the essentials: creative liberty, access to the Other recognized in his alterity, reconciliation and sonship, human solidarity, integration of the exchange with God and the temporal commitment. It would be a mistake to think that the adult religious attitude develops in a spontaneous growth according to circumstances—such, for example, as the establishment of the sexual bond, experience of parenthood, professional commitments. These events are only the setting for the full development of the adult's religion.

But, in reality, what we call adult religion is something transcending the level of truly psychological norms. In the first place these are no more adequate to describe the adult man than they are to describe the normal man. Two elements, in particular, characterize the adult: creative liberty, and the recognition of reality and of others. This implies that the adult is precisely the man who is able to free himself in some measure from his psychological determinisms and to transcend his interior world of drives and affective demands. We may say that the adult has leapt over the wall of psychologism. And, as we have shown in Part One, the religious attitude transcends psychological motivations once it is lived as presence to the Other. It is exchange and recognition. It establishes a new relationship which comes into being beyond needs and anxieties. Adult religion completes the rupture between God and man's psychical movements. It introduces a new value into psychological religiosity.

We must be constantly on our guard not to be misled by the mirage conjured up by psychological myths. They always minimize the adult and his religion.

Once psychology has traced the curve of man's religious becoming from childhood to adulthood it has finished its task. It must now withdraw and leave man free to enter into communion with his God.

1 *L'idée de Dieu entre 7 et 16 ans*: *base sémantique et résonance psychologique*, Lumen Vitae, 1964, 277–90.
2 *Op. cit.*, 286.
3 Babin, *Dieu et l'adolescent*, 224–5.
4 *Ibid.*, 229.
5 X. Viejo, *L'attitude des adolescents devant le Christ*, Louvain 1965 (thesis for the Licentiate in Psychology).
6 *Op. cit.*, 249 ff.
7 See Starbuck *The Psychology of Religion*, 232 ff; W. H. Clark, *The Psychology of Religion*, 1958, 137 ff; G. Allport, *The Individual and his Religion*, 99 ff; P. De Looz, *Une enquête sur la foi des Collégiens*, Brussels 1951, and *La foi des jeunes filles de l'enseignement secondaire catholique en Belgique*, Brussels 1957; A. Gesell, *The adolescent from ten to sixteen*, London 1948.
8 *Le recensement de pratique religieuse dans la Seine*, Paris 1958.
9 *Godsgeloof in de Jeugd*, Louvain 1949, 223 ff. (thesis for doctorate in Educational Psychology).
10 F. Mitzka (*Die Glaubenskrise in Seelenleben*, Innsbruck 1928, 20) believes that affective motives are the most frequent in religious doubts.

11 See *La foi des jeunes filles de l'enseignement secondaire catholique en Belgique.*

12 A. Gesell, *The Adolescent from ten to sixteen.*

EPILOGUE

We have submitted the psychological structure of the religious act and its evolution throughout life to a double enquiry and we have thus been led to discover a single perspective: religion results from comprehensive experience of the world and others; and this experience, in its turn, is a constant challenge to religion. We have remarked that any univocal formula is incomplete. God does not impose himself on man as being the goal of his desires; he is not part of the world's cohesion. The world is in a state of constant change. Man's desires lead him towards changing and contradictory ends. God polarizes human desires but he none the less confutes them. He gives the world its consistence but he is also the essential mystery.

There is no natural religious development which springs from itself. Religious experience opens up the presence of the Other, but can never name him without reference to the religious discourse. Man has only to effectively realize his human aspirations at the point where his own life meets the world and others, and he will turn as easily to religion as to atheistic humanism.

Indeed, the God who, for many men, is profiled at the term of their natural tendencies, needs and desires, is the ambiguous figure of a God who is too human to be truly Other and yet too absolute to be no more than the mere image of man.

God is there when man has his first real experience of the world, and he withdraws leaving man to grapple with the question of his being. God is the object of man's motives and demands and he remains silent, leaving man to wonder about the reality or the illusion of his religious experience. God is salvation offered to human hope and he introduces into religious desire the remoteness of his otherness. But that is not all. God gives man the good news of divine paternity, inviting him to accept a covenant of sonship. The recognition of the fatherhood of God is free from neither doubt nor conflict. It might well appear as the point at which all illusions converge. It questions man's most powerful and most secret desire and thus may sometimes appear to be the most absolute negation of humanity. In order to discover the inner meaning of divine paternity man must undergo a profound conversion which transforms him at the roots of his being and at the heart of his religious aspirations.

Thus, God reveals himself to the man who travels along the roads of his humanity in the process of becoming, to the man who knows how to listen to the Other, hearing him above every aspiration and every desire which points the way to him.

The psychological study of man and his religion reveals the psychological dynamisms at work in the gradual building up of the religious relationship, and helps us to realize how far beyond merely psychological man such a relationship is.

SELECT BIBLIOGRAPHY

The following list covers a variety of approaches to the study of religious psychology, analytical, phenomenological, behaviourist, developmental and pastoral, Catholic and non-Catholic. It is confined to works published in English.

ALLPORT, G. W. *The Individual and his Religion*, Constable, London, 1951.

ARGYLE, M. *Religious Behaviour*, Routledge and Kegan Paul, London, 1958.

BABIN, P. *Crisis of Faith*, Gill, Dublin, 1964.

BERRIDGE, M. M. NORBERT. *The Religious Development of Children*, Cavendish Square College, London, 1966.

CARRIER, H. *The Sociology of Religious Belonging*, Darton, Longman & Todd, London, 1965.

CLARK, W. H. *The Psychology of Religion. An Introduction to Religious Experience and Behaviour*, Macmillan, New York, 1958.

CURRAN, C. A. *Counselling in Catholic Life and Education*, Macmillan, New York, 1962.

GODIN, A. (ed.) *Lumen Vitae, International Review of Religious Education*, Special issues on religious psychology: 1957 (XII, 2); 1961 (XVI, 2); 1964 (XIX, 2).

GOLDMAN, R. *Readiness for Religion*, Routledge and Kegan Paul, London, 1965.

HOSTIE, R. *Religion and the Psychology of Jung*, Sheed and Ward, London, 1957.

JAMES, W. *Varieties of Religious Experience*, Collins, London, 1902, reprint 1964.

LINDWORSKY, J. *The Psychology of Asceticism*, Edwards, London, 1936.

NUTTIN, J. *Psychoanalysis and Personality*, Sheed and Ward, London, 1956.

O'DOHERTY, E. F. *Religion and Personality Problems*, Clonmore and Reynolds, Dublin, 1965.

ORAISON, M. *Love or Constraint: the Psychological Basis of Religious Education*, Burns and Oates, London, 1959.

OTTO, R. *The Idea of the Holy*, Oxford University Press, 1950.

RÜMKE, H. *The Psychology of Unbelief*, Barrie and Rockliff, London, 1952.

STARBUCK, E. D. *The Psychology of Religion*, Walter Scott, London, 1899.

THOULESS, R. H. *An Introduction to the Psychology of Religion*, Cambridge University Press, 1946, reprint 1961.

WHITE, V. *God and the Unconscious*, Harvill Press, London, 1952.

ZILBOORG, G. *Freud and Religion*, Chapman, London, 1958.